WARNER MEMORIAL LIBRARY
EASTERN COLLEGE
ST. DAVIDS, PA. 19087

SAY'S LAW

Say's Law

AN HISTORICAL ANALYSIS

THOMAS SOWELL

PRINCETON UNIVERSITY PRESS

7/12/83

HB 105 .S25 S68
Sowell, Thomas, 1930--
Say's law :

Copyright © 1972 by Princeton University Press
ALL RIGHTS RESERVED
LC: 78-38515
ISBN: 0-691-04166-0

This book has been set in Linotype Times Roman

Publication of this book has been aided by a grant
from the Whitney Darrow Publication Reserve Fund of
Princeton University Press

Some passages in this book have been incorporated
by permission of Oxford University Press and the
University of Toronto Press from *Oxford Economic Papers*
(November 1963, July 1967) and the *Canadian Journal of
Economics and Political Science* (February 1967).

Printed in the United States of America by
Princeton University Press, Princeton, New Jersey

CONTENTS

ACKNOWLEDGMENTS

I AM INDEBTED to Professor George J. Stigler of the University of Chicago, whose interest in (including opposition to) many of the ideas developed in this work has led me to redefine and reformulate my concepts over the years. This book developed out of a doctoral dissertation at the University of Chicago, though the bulk of it was written since receiving the degree. I have also benefited from comments and suggestions by the other members of the dissertation committee, Professors Milton Friedman and Larry A. Sjaastad, as well as comments and suggestions on the present version by Professor Abba P. Lerner of Queens College, City University of New York. The general interest of Professor Joseph S. Berliner of Brandeis University in forwarding this project is also appreciated, as are grants from Cornell University, Brandeis University, and the University of California (Los Angeles), which enabled me to complete the work earlier than otherwise. No one mentioned above shares any responsibility for any errors or conclusions in this work.

Los Angeles   THOMAS SOWELL
November 22, 1971

SAY'S LAW

CHAPTER 1

The Early Development of Say's Law

THE IDEA THAT supply creates its own demand—Say's Law—appears on the surface to be one of the simplest propositions in economics, and one which should be readily proved or disproved. Yet this doctrine has produced two of the most sweeping, bitter, and long-lasting controversies in the history of economics—first in the early nineteenth century and then erupting again a hundred years later in the Keynesian revolution of the 1930's. Each of these outbursts of controversy lasted more than twenty years, involved almost every noted economist of the time, and had repercussions on basic economic theory, methodology, and sociopolitical policy. The shock waves from these controversies were felt well beyond the confines of economics, and evoked powerful emotions among people unacquainted with the technical issues involved or even with economics in general. In retrospect it is clear that the history of Say's Law is an important part of intellectual history generally, and has important implications for the dynamics of controversy, the nature of intellectual orthodoxy and insurgency, and the complex relationships among ideology, concepts, and policies.

While the two great controversies over Say's Law which shook the foundations of economics were similar in many ways, they were different in one crucial respect: the supporters of Say's Law won a resounding victory in the nineteenth century, while its opponents triumphed in the twentieth century. In each case the victory was followed by intellectual guerrilla warfare. The most prominent of the later nineteenth century opponents of Say's Law was Karl Marx. The Keynesian ascendancy, after dethroning Say's Law in the 1930's and 1940's, has been challenged even more effectively—to a point approaching a counterrevolution, in which the most prominent name has been Milton Friedman. Say's Law has been debated for more than a hundred years, and its origins go back more than two hundred years.

The basic idea behind Say's Law is both simple and important. The production of goods (including services) causes incomes to be paid to suppliers of the factors (labor, capital, land, etc.) used in producing the goods. The total price of the goods is the sum of these payments for wages, profits, rent, etc.—which is to say that the income generated during the production of a given output is equal to the value of that output. An increased supply of output means an increase in the income necessary to create a demand for that output. Supply creates its own demand. Can a nation then have *excessive* production: a "general glut" as it was called in the nineteenth century? The serious implications of this issue range from mass unemployment to imperalism and the wars which it could entail. The basic logic of the process by which supply is able to create its own demand is relatively simple, but the amplifications, implications, and applications of Say's Law have been complex and changing over time. Moreover, the historical development of an idea seldom follows its *logical* development, that is, it does not begin with the simplest premise and then build on that. Often, as in the case of Say's Law, it begins with a relatively complex conclusion whose

4

basic logic has to be distilled over time, in the course of analysis and controversy.

Say's Law has both lost and acquired meanings in the long process of theoretical refinement since its beginnings in the classical period. This modernization of Say's Law has, on the one hand, produced greater clarity and precision by revealing the essential logic running through the often loose, ambiguous, or even contradictory statements of the classical economists. On the other hand, it has led to grotesque distortions of history where the general glut controversy that reached its peak in the 1820's is treated as a debate over Say's Law in its modern sense, or where Marx or Hobson are peremptorily labeled predecessors of Keynes.

There was, for example, no "great debate on the internal consistency of an ever-expending capitalist economy," no "dire predictions of permanent overproduction," or of "secular stagnation" in the classical period, despite interpretations of this sort in the modern literature.[1] Those economists who opposed Say's Law in the early or classical period (principally Malthus, Sismondi, and Marx) had no such conclusions in mind. Malthus stated unequivocally that "the question of a glut is exclusively whether it may be general as well as particular and not whether it may be permanent as well as temporary."[2] Except for short-run frictional problems,

---

[1] Don Patinkin, *Money, Interest and Prices,* 2nd edn. (New York: Harper and Row, 1965), p. 364; M. Blaug, *Economic Theory in Retrospect* (Homewood: Richard D. Irwin, 1962), p. 140, see also pp. 149, 150, 158; Mark Blaug, *Ricardian Economics* (New Haven: Yale University Press, 1958), p. 93.

[2] Thomas Robert Malthus, *Definitions in Political Economy* (London: John Murray, 1827), p. 62.

5

economic development "is absolutely unlimited."[3] Sismondi likewise saw the "natural path of nations" as being "the progressive increase of their prosperity, the increase, in consequence, of their demand for new products and of the means of paying for them."[4] There would, of course, be "violent crises"[5] from time to time, which his theory attempted to explain. Similarly, Karl Marx saw economic crises as "momentary"[6] and "transient"[7] phenomena, and declared, in the midst of an unsparing criticism of Say's Law: "There are no permanent crises."[8]

Many of the misinterpretations of the nineteenth century controversies which abound in the literature must be blamed on the tendency to seize upon features that are striking to the modern eye, either because of their apparent similarity to, or sharp contrast with, present-day analysis. For example, Malthus' reference to "propensity to spend,"[9] various neo-Physiocratic notions

[3] Malthus to Ricardo in *The Works and Correspondence of David Ricardo,* ed. Piero Sraffa (Cambridge: Cambridge University Press, 1952), Vol. VI, 318.

[4] J. C. L. Simonde de Sismondi, *Nouveaux Principes d'économie politique,* troisième edn. (Geneva-Paris: Edition Jeheber, 1953), Vol. II, 303.

[5] *Ibid.,* p. 247.

[6] Karl Marx, *Capital,* Vol. III, ed. Frederick Engels, trans. Ernest Untermann (Chicago: Charles H. Kerr & Co., 1909), p. 292.

[7] *Ibid.,* p. 568.

[8] Karl Marx, *Theories of Surplus Value-Selections,* ed. and trans. G. A. Bonner and Emile Burns (New York: International Publishing Co., Inc., 1952), p. 373n.

[9] James J. O'Leary, "Malthus and Keynes," *Journal of Political Economy,* L, No. 6 (December 1942), 905; Paul Lambert, "Malthus et Keynes: Nouvel Examen de la Parenté Profonde des Deux Oeuvres," *Revue d'économie politique,* 72, No. 6 (Novembre-Decembre, 1962), 791.

in the writings of such glut theorists as Lauderdale, Spence, Malthus, and Chalmers,[10] and the classical use of barter examples and depreciation of the role of money[11] have erroneously been treated as analytically important distinguishing features of the two sides in the general glut controversy. Yet in the context in which Malthus used the three words which now seem so significant (in the light of modern Keynesian monetary economics), he did so while arguing the *irrelevance* of this propensity for the issue at hand.[12] Physiocratic notions were indeed present in the early British dissenters, but they were also present in such pillars of orthodoxy as J. B. Say and James Mill.[13] The classical tendency to reason in terms of a barter economy rather than a money economy was equally prevalent among the general glut theorists.

Sismondi "deliberately" developed his basic model "without speaking of money" because money "was not necessary" to it, and only made the process difficult to

[10] Joseph J. Spengler, "The Physiocrats and Say's Law of Markets," *Essays in Economic Thought*, eds. J. J. Spengler and W. R. Allen, pp. 161–214; Ronald L. Meek, *The Economics of Physiocracy* (Cambridge: Harvard University Press, 1963).

[11] John Maynard Keynes, *Essays in Biography,* ed. Geoffrey Keynes (New York: Horizon Press, Inc., 1951), p. 116; Paul Lambert, *L'Oeuvre de John Maynard Keynes* (The Hague: Martinus Nijhoff, 1963), Vol. I, 78.

[12] Thomas Robert Malthus, *Principles of Political Economy,* 2nd edn. (London: John Murray, 1836), pp. 402, 403.

[13] For example, the doctrine that agricultural output had the peculiarity that any extension of it, whther initially demanded or not, would lead (via the population principle) to an increased number of consumers who would then cause it to be in demand. Jean-Baptiste, *A Treatise on Political Economy,* trans. C. R. Prinsep (Philadelphia: Grigg & Elliot, 1834), p. 326; James Mill, *An Essay on the Impolicy of a Bounty on the Exportation of Grain* (London: C. & R. Baldwin, 1804), p. 24.

7

grasp.[14] For Chalmers also, money served merely to "obscure the character of the proceeding, without essentially changing it."[15] The idea that anyone would wish to hoard was dismissed out of hand by Malthus, Chalmers, and Spence.[16] Whatever income was not consumed would be saved and invested, and "equally spent in either way,"[17] according to Chalmers. Spence argued repeatedly in his rejoinder to Mill's *Commerce Defended* that the latter's "errors" were due to thinking in money terms, when in fact exchange was essentially barter.[18] The classical argument that purchasing power was necessarily equal to the value of output[19] was wasted on Sismondi and Malthus, both of whom repeatedly affirmed the same thing.[20] Sismondi had in fact said so before Say, Mill,

[14] Sismondi, *Nouveaux Principes*, Vol. I, 118. See also pp. 120, 121.

[15] Thomas Chalmers, *On Political Economy*, (Glasgow: William Collins, 1832), p. 158.

[16] *Ibid.*, p. 96; T. R. Malthus, *Definitions in Political Economy*, p. 238; T. R. Malthus, *Principles of Political Economy*, 2nd edn., p. 38; William Spence, *Tracts on Political Economy* (New York: privately printed, 1933), pp. 30–31.

[17] Thomas Chalmers, *On Political Economy*, p. 96.

[18] William Spence, *Agriculture: The Source of the Wealth of Britain*, reprinted in *Tracts on Political Economy*, pp. 126, 149, 157, 164.

[19] James Mill, *Commerce Defended* (London: C. & R. Baldwin, 1808), pp. 81, 83; J. B. Say, *A Treatise on Political Economy*, p. 170; John Stuart Mill, *Principles of Political Economy*, ed. W. J. Ashley (London: Longmans, Green and Co., 1909), pp. 557–558; *ibid.*, variorum edn. (Toronto: University of Toronto Press, 1965), pp. 571–72.

[20] "A nation must certainly have the power of purchasing all that it produces." Malthus to Ricardo, *The Works and Correspondence of David Ricardo*, Vol. VI, 132; see also *ibid.*, Vol. IX, 10; T. R. Malthus, *Principles of Political Economy*, p. 359; [T. R. Malthus] "Tooke—On High and Low Prices," *Quarterly Review*, XXIX, No. LVII (April 1823), 226. The primary authority for identifying this and other anonymous articles

or Ricardo.[21] The point here is not to represent the glut theorists and their classical contemporaries as being equally obtuse about monetary phenomena. On the contrary, each side was considerably more sophisticated on the subject than might be suspected from a survey of their dogmatic-sounding assertions taken out of context, without regard to their long-run or short-run, *ex ante* or *ex post* meanings. The point is that the kind of evidence which has been used to put the classical economists on one side of a real-analysis-versus-monetary-analysis debate would put their opponents on the same side. The general glut controversy was simply not that kind of debate. As a definitional note, by "general glut" economists will be meant those economists who challenged Say's Law in the first two decades of the nineteenth century, as distinguished from the later dissenters—notably Marx and Hobson—who argued beyond the pale after the general glut controversy had ended in the victory of the orthodox.

It should be noted that there were not merely opposite sides in the general glut controversy; there were different levels as well. Among noneconomists there were the ever-popular underconsumptionist arguments that markets were limited because the maldistribution of income left the workers too poor to buy what they had produced. Robert Owen and Karl Rodbertus, for ex-

---

cited herein is the series of articles on anonymous authorship by Professor Frank W. Fetter in the *Journal of Political Economy* (June 1953), (February 1958), (April 1958), and (December 1962). ". . . the national revenue and the annual production mutually balance each other and appear as equal quantities." Sismondi, *Nouveaux Principes,* I, 103; see also J. C. L. Simonde [de Sismondi] *De la Richesse Commerciale* (Geneva: J. J. Paschoud, 1803), I, 84–85, 105n.

[21] Sismondi, *Richesse Commerciale,* I, 84–85, 105n.

ample, argued this way, urging that commodities be made to sell according to the labor time which went into their production, as part of a scheme to insure that the total purchasing power would equal the total value of output.[22] But these were not the arguments of the economists involved in the general glut controversy, or of Marx in the later period. Sismondi and Malthus repudiated Owen's arguments, just as Marx and Engels repudiated those of Rodbertus.[23] Nevertheless such popular arguments were historically important, if only because the proponents of Say's Law felt so strongly the need to counter them. John Stuart Mill depicted Say's Law as an exposé of "the shallowness of the political reasonings of the last two centuries,"[24] rather than simply an argument against contemporary economists, and was worried as to how the debate over general gluts would look to the "enemies" of economics.[25] This crusade against popular fallacies affected the general glut controversy because of the tendency of orthodox economists to read these fallacies into the arguments of the dissenters and to attack their own creations rather than the argu-

[22] Robert Owen, *A New View of Society and Other Writings,* Everyman edn. (London: J. M. Dent and Sons, Ltd., 1963), pp. 247–53; Karl Rodbertus, "Overproduction and Crises," *History of Economic Thought,* eds. K. William and Lore L. Kapp (New York: Barnes and Noble, 1963), pp. 248–67.

[23] Sismondi, *Nouveaux Principes,* II, 251 (see also pp. 243, 289); T. R. Malthus, *Principles of Political Economy,* p. 325n; Karl Marx, *Capital* (Chicago: Charles H. Kerr & Co., 1906), II, 475–76; Frederick Engels, "Preface," Karl Marx, *The Poverty of Philosophy* (New York: International Publishers, 1963), pp. 7–24.

[24] John Stuart Mill, *Essays on Some Unsettled Questions of Political Economy* (London: John W. Parker, 1844), p. 48.

[25] John Stuart Mill, *The Earlier Letters of John Stuart Mill, 1812–1848,* ed. Francis E. Mineka (Toronto: University of Toronto Press, 1963), p. 236.

ments actually advanced. It is significant that Torrens included a refutation of Sismondi as a digression in a review of the writings of Robert Owen.[26]

[26] [Robert Torrens], "Mr. Owen's Plans for Relieving the National Distress," *Edinburgh Review* (October 1819), 453–77; the digression on Sismondi occurs pp. 470–75. While the authorship of this anonymous article has been disputed, the evidence that it was written by Torrens, rather than by McCulloch as sometimes claimed, seems overwhelming: (1) many passages repeated verbatim statements made in an earlier speech by Robert Torrens as reported in the newspaper *The Scotsman*, August 21, 1819, pp. 265–66; (2) Malthus's criticisms of the anonymous article were answered at considerable length in Robert Torrens, *An Essay on the Distribution of Wealth* (London: Longmans, Hurst, Rees, Orme, and Brown, 1821), pp. 384–97; (3) Ricardo was sufficiently confident that the author was Torrens that he both corrected Malthus' contrary view and informed McCulloch with amusement that Malthus had thought that he—McCulloch—was the author (Works, VIII, 159); (4) Malthus was sufficiently convinced that he in turn repeated to Sismondi that Torrens was the author (*ibid.,* p. 376). See also *ibid.,* pp. 82, 159, 163–164, 227. The basis of the view that McCulloch wrote this article can be readily understood without accepting its validity. In a rejoinder to the review in 1820, Sismondi admitted not knowing the name of the critic to whom he was replying, but in reprinting this rejoinder in the appendix to the second edition of *Nouveaux Principes* in 1827, he identified the critic as McCulloch (II, 252n)—certainly a "curious" opinion, as Mr. Sraffa characterized it (*op. cit.,* p. 376n), in view of Malthus' letter in 1821, but an opinion which is explicable in the light of other events. McCulloch did write an anonymous article in the *Edinburgh Review* which criticized Sismondi, but in March 1821. Sismondi met McCulloch in 1826, and at that time could easily have learned that McCulloch had written *an* article against him some years earlier in the *Edinburgh Review,* and mistaken it for the one to which he had replied, which in fact contained many of the same kinds of arguments. Sismondi said in 1827 that his identification of McCulloch as the author of the 1819 review was based on what he had learned since his 1820 article. It was undoubtedly also after Malthus' positive statement in 1821 that Torrens had written the review, a view which only a statement of authorship

11

There was no definitive statement of Say's Law in classical economics. Even its origin has not been unequivocally established. Aside from the conflicting claims of Say and James Mill, there is the fact that important elements of it had appeared earlier in Adam Smith, and particular fragments of it can be traced even further back.[27] During the age of classical economics—from Adam Smith to Karl Marx—there were differences among its three leading exponents, J. B. Say, James Mill, and David Ricardo. Say criticized the Ricardian application of the principle, and Ricardo in turn criticized Say's exposition and questioned whether James Mill had really met their critics head-on.[28] Even the familiar assertion that "supply creates its own demand" is not a direct quotation from any of them. Nevertheless there was a solid core of propositions on which the whole orthodox tradition was agreed and a penumbra of corollaries and related ideas to which some subscribed and some did not. Probably no individual economist inside or outside the classical tradition ever wholly agreed or wholly disagreed with everything that was included in the omnibus phrase, "Say's Law."

---

by McCulloch himself seems likely to have overturned. Arguments that McCulloch wrote the review may be found in John S. Chipman, "A Survey of the Theory of International Trade: Part 2, the Neo-Classical Theory," *Econometrica,* 33, No. 4 (October 1965), 710n–711n; see also Jacob Viner, *Studies in the Theory of International Trade* (New York: Harper and Brothers, 1937), p. 194n. I am indebted to Professor Viner for generously pointing out to me some of the evidence which was opposed to his opinion.

[27] Paul Lambert, "The Law of Markets Prior to J. B. Say and the Say-Malthus Debate," *International Economic Papers,* No. 6 (1956), pp. 7–22; J. J. Spengler, "The Physiocrats and Says Law of Markets," *Essays in Economic Thought,* ed. J. J. Spengler and W. R. Allen, pp. 161–214.

[28] Ricardo, *Works,* IX, 131.

The basic practical meaning of Say's Law was implied in J. B. Say's rhetorical question: "how could it be possible that there should now be bought and sold in France five or six times as many commodities as in the miserable reign of Charles VI?"[29] The proposition that there was no secular limit to the expansion of aggregate output was one on which there was complete agreement between the Say-Ricardo school and the Sismondi-Malthus general glut school. Sismondi, like Say, illustrated his belief on this point by comparing the increase of output from a past era—a purported quadrupling of production since Louis XIV—and Malthus, Lauderdale, and Chalmers took similar positions.[30] The only suggestion of a long-run limit to output during this period was in fact the Ricardian "stationary state."

The term "glut" was widely used but seldom defined. It usually referred to a situation in which goods were either unsold or were saleable only below cost-covering prices.[31] Both the Say-Ricardo school and the Sismondi-Malthus school were agreed that there could be "partial" gluts in which this condition existed for some sectors of the economy. They differed on whether this could be true for all sectors simultaneously, whether aggregate output would be sold at less than cost-covering prices, that is, whether there could be a *general* glut.

Implicit in this issue is the more basic question, whether there is such a thing as an equilibrium level

[29] J. B. Say, *A Treatise on Political Economy,* p. 137; Jean-Baptiste Say, *Cours Complet d'économie politique,* 3rd edn. (Paris: Guillaumin et cie, 1852), I, 339.

[30] Sismondi, *Nouveaux Principles,* II, 308; Ricardo, *Works,* VI, 318; Lauderdale, *Nature and Origin of Public Wealth,* (New York: Augustus M. Kelley, 1962), pp. 215, 227–28; Chalmers, *On Political Economy,* pp. 136, 476, 140.

[31] T. R. Malthus, *Definitions in Political Economy,* pp. 246, 247; John Stuart Mill, *Principles of Political Economy,* p. 557.

of aggregate real income. In their affirmative position on this question, the general glut theorists did stand in the tradition of the Physiocrats and John Maynard Keynes, but not in the substance of their theory. While the concept of an equilibrium national income does not contradict the essential logic of Say's Law, it was perceived as a threat by the defenders of Say's Law as it had developed historically when Sismondi introduced his theory of equilibrium income in 1819. Their attacks on Sismondi's theory, and then on Malthus' extensions of it, initiated the controversies that continued for decades in British and French journals, books, and correspondence. Earlier controversies, revolving around the writings of Lauderdale (1804) and Spence (1808), had played a role in the development of Say's Law, but these were relatively brief exchanges involving only a very few individuals. In a later period, Karl Marx was to make the last attack on Say's Law within the classical framework, but by then he stood alone. Neither the earlier nor the later period was comparable to the massive outpourings which constituted the general glut controversy of the 1820's and 1830's, and whose termination may be dated by the appearance of John Stuart Mill's *Principles* in 1848. Only the similarly massive outpourings set off much later by the Keynesian revolution could rival that of the general glut controversy. During the classical period there were also important developments in monetary theory, notably by Henry Thornton in 1802, and important beginnings in business cycle theory, notably by Clement Juglar in 1860, but these were not part of the controversies revolving around Say's Law, however important they might be in a general history of the developments which led up to Keynes' *General Theory* and post-Keynesian macroeconomics.

14

Before proceeding to the general glut theories and the controversies to which they led, some closer consideration will be given to the set of propositions known collectively as Say's Law, at the stage of development that they had reached when the controversy began. The modern meanings of Say's Law will also be briefly sketched. The development of Say's Law during the controversy will be discussed in Chapter 4. In attempting to clarify opposing positions on various propositions, it will not be assumed that each side was always clear as to what its opponent was asserting or denying, or as to the full implications of its own position, or that it remained consistent over time. The scope and duration of the controversy would in fact suggest the opposite. The sketch below will simply focus on various key propositions in the classical version of Say's Law and attempt to indicate the role of particular individuals in its development.

ADAM SMITH

The Wealth of Nations presented three important features of Say's Law:

1. The doctrine that money merely facilitated the barter of goods,[32] without itself changing real results. Although this doctrine was not peculiar to the supporters of Say's Law, it is important for understanding how the monetary problems emphasized by modern Keynesian analysis were consistently overlooked in both classical and early heretical discussions of Say's Law. Both sides regarded themselves as disciples of

[32] "The sole use of money is to circulate consumable goods." Adam Smith, *The Wealth of Nations* (New York: Random House, 1937), p. 323.

15

Adam Smith. The pertinent question for income determination theory is whether Smith's monetary neutrality was a long-run generalization or something which was expected to apply continuously through all short-run periods as well. Smith argued that just as money constitutes the demand for goods, goods constitute the demand for money. He repeatedly referred to goods purchasing money,[33] and said of gold and silver that "as they are the price of all other commodities, so all other commodities are the price of these metals."[34] However, although money is something "for which every thing is readily given in exchange," it "is not always with equal readiness to be got in exchange for everything."[35] But despite the fact that "goods do not always draw money so readily as money draws goods," still "in the long run" goods draw money even "more necessarily" than vice-versa.[36] The intriguing reference to the possibility of short-run excess demand for money was not explored or elaborated. In the long run, the only demand for money to consider was the transactions demand. It should be noted that much of Smith's discussion of money took place in a chapter dealing with the mercantilists, where the salient question was whether a larger quantity of money in a country added either to its wealth or to its ability to clear its own markets. Smith was disputing with the mercantilists over permanent institutionalized practices, not short-run cyclical policies, so that his views on the short-run demand for money were of tangential importance, and so only sketchily indicated. In this context, Smith expressed what might be considered an early version of Say's Law: "But though a particular merchant, with abundance of

[33] *Ibid.*, pp. 323, 324, 404, 405, 406, 407.   [34] *Ibid.*, p. 404.
[35] *Ibid.*, p. 407.   [36] *Ibid.*

goods in his warehouse, may sometimes be ruined by not being able to sell them in time, a nation or country is not liable to the same accident."[37] Although this assertion was made in a generally long-run context, it is in itself a timeless statement, and the observation that a partial glut "sometimes" ruins a particular producer or merchant suggests in this context that a general glut cannot exist for the economy as a whole even "sometimes."

2. The doctrine that savings are always invested and spent. "The consumption is the same, but the consumers are different."[38] Again this was a belief common to both sides, and both sides usually proceeded as if this saving and investment took the form of wage goods rather than fixed capital.

3. Saving rather than consumption promotes growth.[39] This might mean (a) that a higher savings function (as a function of income and/or the rate of return) would lead to higher levels of output in subsequent time periods, or (b) that an increased quantity saved—without considering whether it is on the savings function receiving its supply price or not—would lead to higher levels of output in subsequent time periods. The first was the meaning more probably intended by Smith and later supporters of this doctrine, but they were never explicit, and the second meaning was the principal object of attack by the dissenters.

J. B. SAY AND JAMES MILL

The question whether Say or Mill originated Say's Law is one which has often been debated, and although Adam Smith developed parts of it before either of them,

[37] *Ibid.*   [38] *Ibid.*, p. 322.   [39] *Ibid.*

there is still a question as to their relative contributions to the remainder.

The chapter on markets (*"Des Débouchés"*) in Say's *Traité d'économie politique* underwent considerable development in the five editions that appeared in Say's lifetime. From a few sketchy pages in the first edition of 1803, it grew into a substantial chapter in its classic form in the fourth edition of 1819—the edition available in English translation—and then added major modifications in the fifth edition of 1826, as a result of the controversies of the period, particularly Say's polemical exchanges with Sismondi.[40] Say's later letters and his textbook, *Cours Complet d'économie politique* (1828–1829), also reflected these modifications. James Mill's early formulations of his ideas were more complete and remained relatively fixed over time, so that even though Say took up the subject before him this does not automatically preclude Mill from having priority on particular propositions, and it is a matter of judgment which of these propositions are the key ones that can be regarded as the essence of Say's Law. Mill's analysis first appeared in his review of Lauderdale's theory of overinvestment in *The Literary Journal* in 1804,[41] his

[40] J. C. L. [Simonde] de Sismondi, "Sur la balance des consommations avec les productions," *Revue encyclopedique,* XXII (May 1824), 264–98; Jean-Baptiste Say, "Sur la balance des consommations avec les productions," *Revue encyclopedique,* XXIII (July 1824), 18–31; J. C. L. Simonde de Sismondi, "Notes sure l'article de M. Say, intitulé 'Balance des consommations avec les productions,'" *Nouveaux Principes,* II, 306–09. See also J. C. L. Simonde de Sismondi, *Political Economy and the Philosophy of Government* (London: John Chapman, 1847), p. 449. This last-named work should be distinguished from *Political Economy,* a reprint of Sismondi's encyclopedia article of the same name.

[41] [James Mill], "Lord Lauderdale on Public Wealth," *The Literary Journal,* IV, No. 1 (July 1804), 1–18.

first major discussion in *Commerce Defended* in 1808, and his final formulations in the three editions of his *Elements of Political Economy* which appeared in 1821, 1824, and 1844.

From the first edition of his *Traité d'économie politique,* Say repeated Adam Smith's doctrines that savings are always spent as investment,[42] that money's only role was to facilitate barter, and that the volume of money had no effect on the volume of real transactions.[43] On the contrary, the volume of transactions determined the demand for money.[44] Say took this conception a step further: "This shows, I hope, that it is certainly not so much the abundance of money which makes outlets easy, but the abundance of other products in general. This is one of the most important truths in political economy."[45] The idea that "products are paid for with products"[46] was not new, having appeared even before Adam Smith.[47] But from this simple statement, two important corollaries were drawn:

1. A country offers *increased* markets in proportion to its increased output. Supply creates its own demand. Here purchasing power was conceived of in essentially barter terms—people "can pay for more

[42] Jean-Baptiste Say, *Traité d'économie politique* (Paris: Deterville, 1803), II, 177n.

[43] Jean-Baptiste Say, *Traité d'économie politique,* 1803, I, 152–53.

[44] Adam Smith, *The Wealth of Nations,* p. 322; J. B. Say, *A Treatise of Political Economy,* p. 138; J. B. Say, *Traité d'économie politique,* 2nd edn. (Paris: Deterville, 1814), p. 146.

[45] J. B. Say, *Traité,* 1803, I, p. 153.

[46] *Ibid.,* p. 154.

[47] Paul Lambert, "The Law of Markets Prior to J. B. Say and the Say-Malthus Debate," *International Economic Papers,* No. 6 (1956), pp. 8–9.

things in proportion to what they produce more"[48]—rather than in the sense that factor payments to individuals jointly producing commodities add up to the value of national output. Products "can never be too abundant, since some provide the means of purchasing the others."[49]

2. ". . . when a nation has too many products of one kind, the means of disposing of them is to create another kind."[50] For every case of excess production in the economy, there was simultaneously a corresponding deficiency elsewhere in the economy—and therefore no *aggregate* overproduction, even temporarily. Say recognized the existence of disequilibrium situations, but "a glut can take place only when there are too many means of production applied to one kind of product and not enough to another."[51] There was no general overproduction or overinvestment, for "means of production are lacking" for one commodity "insofar as they are superabundant" for another. While there may be a "lack of sales" during the disequilibrium, this comes "not from superabundance, but from a defective employment of the means of production."[52] The arguments of the first edition of Say's *Traité* suggested that equilibrium could be restored by applying a given volume of inputs to producing a different output mix, but his later editions and the writings of the Ricardians went further, arguing that a net increase of inputs, directed toward the relatively deficient good(s), could restore the required proportions of output at a higher level of aggregate production. This clearly implied that there was no such thing as an equilibrium aggregate income or output, an implication which brought the supporters

[48] J. B. Say, *Traité*, 1803, I, 154.   [49] *Ibid.*, II, 179.
[50] *Ibid.*, I, 154.   [51] *Ibid.*, II, 178.   [52] *Ibid.*

of Say's Law into contention with Sismondi and Malthus.

Just as Adam Smith's doctrine on the neutrality of money served as Say's point of departure, Smith's argument that "parsimony" promotes the growth of wealth was James Mill's starting point.[53] In his review of Lauderdale in 1804, James Mill referred to "accumulation" (investment) and "parsimony" (saving) as equivalents, as the source of growth, and argued that the two are always equal (*ex ante*) because savings are made only because of, and to the extent of, the desire to invest.[54] If a man "cannot employ what he saves with any advantage, he will not save it."[55] Investment is "the sole motive" for saving.[56] The possibility of miscalculation of prospective returns was not considered. Later, in *Commerce Defended,* Mill brought together Adam Smith's doctrine that savings are always spent as investment,[57] thereby promoting growth,[58] and Say's arguments that increased production creates correspondingly increased demand[59] and that there can be disequilibrium in national output only in the sense of internal disproportionality, not excess aggregate production:

> . . . a nation may easily have more than enough of any one commodity, though she can never have more than enough of commodities in general. The quantity

[53] [James Mill], "Lord Lauderdale on Public Wealth," *The Literary Journal* (July 1804), 12.

[54] *Ibid.,* p. 13.   [55] *Ibid.*   [56] *Ibid.*

[57] James Mill, *Commerce Defended,* pp. 76, 84. Where Adam Smith had said that such savings were probably spent in almost as short a time as direct consumption expenditures, James Mill claimed that it was probably spent in a shorter time. Adam Smith, *The Wealth of Nations,* p. 321; James Mill, *Commerce Defended,* p. 76.

[58] James Mill, *Commerce Defended,* pp. 70, 71, 74, 78.

[59] *Ibid.,* pp. 81–82.

of any one commodity may easily be carried beyond its due proportion; but by that very circumstance is implied that some other commodity is not provided in sufficient proportion. What indeed is meant by a commodity's exceeding the market? Is it not that there is a portion of it for which there is nothing that can be had in exchange. But of those other things then the proportion is too small. A part of the means of production which had been applied to the preparation of this superabundant commodity, should have been applied to the preparation of those other commodities till the balance between them had been established. Whenever this balance is properly preserved, there can be no superfluity of commodities, none for which a market will not be ready.[60]

It is clear that Say's Law, as implied in this passage, did not preclude disequilibrium, and that the "balance" referred to was not an accounting identity persisting through all conditions of the market, but an equilibrium condition that could be reached in a "properly" functioning economy. However, this equilibrium was defined in terms of internal proportions, not aggregate quantity, of output, and the fact that a substantive theory was involved did not preclude the use of identities under polemical stress. Later, in his *Elements of Political Economy,* Mill argued more explicitly that overproduced goods had to be made with capital withdrawn from the production of other goods, which were then necessarily underproduced.[61] This assumed full employment of a given quantity of capital, thereby dispensing with a sub-

[60] *Ibid.,* pp. 84–85.
[61] James Mill, *Elements of Political Economy* (London: Henry G. Bohn, 1844), pp. 234–35.

stantial part of the issue that arose in the general glut controversy.

In addition to elaborating the ideas of Smith and Say (Mill had already read Say when he wrote *Commerce Defended*)[62] he added his own arguments to Say's Law:

1. The idea that output necessarily equals purchasing power was made plainer and more insistent in *Commerce Defended* than in Say's *Traité*. A country's purchasing power was explicitly identified as "the annual revenue of its inhabitants,"[63] and the further proviso added that all income—"every farthing's worth"[64] was spent on either consumption or investment, "which will always wholly exhaust" output.[65] Hoarding was rejected.[66]

2. The *Elements of Political Economy* argued that increased quantities of goods supplied by an individual were in direct proportion to that individual's quantity demanded of other goods which he expected to receive in return.[67] That these expectations might be disappointed, as unfulfillable simultaneously, was not considered. Given the *ex ante* equality of quantity supplied and quantity demanded for each individual, it followed that aggregate supply and demand were also equal.[68] Mill's truistic *ex post* identity of purchases

---

[62] James Mill, *Commerce Defended*, p. 76n.
[63] *Ibid.*, p. 81.   [64] *Ibid.*, p. 83.
[65] *Ibid.*, p. 75.   [66] *Ibid.*, pp. 75, 77.
[67] James Mill, *Elements of Political Economy*, pp. 228, 231, 237, 241.
[68] "But if the demand and supply of every individual are always equal, to one another, the demand and supply of all the individuals in the nation, taken aggregately, must be equal." *Ibid.*, p. 232.

and sales were part of the attempt to prove this *ex ante* equality based on this behavioral theory.[69]

Both Say and Mill used their doctrines explicitly in opposition to the Physiocratic emphasis on consumption embodied in the work of Mercier de la Rivière in 1767.[70] Since the meaning of a theory can sometimes be clarified by referring to what it opposed, here is the passage in Mercier de la Rivière which they cited:

> CONSUMPTION IS THE PROPORTIONAL MEASURE OF REPRODUCTION. Indeed, expenses and labor will not be borne in order to procure production from which no enjoyment can be derived. That reflection, by showing us the truth of that axiom, will lead us to derive other truths. When we say that consumption is the proportional measure of reproduction, it must be understood to mean a consumption which returns a profit to those whose labor and expense will reproduce the output; a consumption which will leave absolutely no utility will certainly not cause them to work and to spend in order to renew the things which it would absorb.[71]

Although Mercier de la Rivière went further than his argument required in suggesting a zero utility of output above the equilibrium level (rather than simply a marginal utility less than the marginal disutility of producing it), he nevertheless made an important distinction which

[69] *Ibid.*, pp. 237–38; James Mill, *Commerce Defended*, p. 82.

[70] J. B. Say, *Traité d'économie politique*, 1803 edn., II, 358–59; James Mill, *Commerce Defended*, p. 76n. Mill misquoted Mercier de la Rivière, attributing Say's paraphrase to him, which suggests that he had not in fact read the original.

[71] [Pierre Francois Joachim Henri Le Mercier de la Rivière], *L'Ordre Naturel et Essentiel des Sociétés Politiques* (London: Jean Nourse, 1767), II, 138–39.

Say and James Mill did not make: between the market's being cleared and its being cleared at such prices as to cause "reproduction" of the same level of output in subsequent time periods. But despite the possibility of "unconsumed" output or "superfluity," which would cause people to "cease to make advances" of resources for their future production,[72] Mercier de la Rivière did not argue for secular stagnation and was at pains to say that equilibrium would "be maintained always and *necessarily,* provided that we do nothing to disturb it."[73]

By contrast, the supporters of Say's Law argued that (1) the disequilibrium implied by an uncleared market cannot *persist,*[74] and that (2) adjustments to equilibrium take place not in aggregate production (or employment of resources) but in its internal composition.[75] The Say-Mill argument that the "consumption"—both "productive" (investment) and "unproductive" (consumption proper)—of a given period (t) always equals the output of that period may be summed up as:

$$Y_t = C_t + I_t$$

Y_t = aggregate output (income) of a given time period, t

C_t = consumption during time period t

I_t = net investment during time period t

---

[72] *Ibid.,* p. 250.   [73] *Ibid.,* p. 140.

[74] James Mill, *Elements of Political Economy,* p. 242; [Robert Torrens], "Mr. Owen's Plants for Relieving the National Distress," *Edinburgh Review* (October 1819), 473; Robert Torrens, *An Essay on the Production of Wealth,* p. 425; John R. McCulloch, *Principles of Political Economy* (Edinburgh: Adam and Charles Black, 1864), pp. 144, 145.

[75] [Robert Torrens], "Mr. Owen's Plans for Relieving the National Distress," *Edinburgh Review* (October 1819), 471–72; J. R. McCulloch, *Principles of Political Economy,* p. 145; James Mill, *Elements of Political Economy,* pp. 234–35.

These are *ex ante* magnitudes, conditionally equal (not an identity) but *invariably* equal, as a necessary consequence of rational behavior.

The Physiocratic argument may be summed up as:

$$Y_{t+1} = C_t + I_t$$

C_t and I_t are defined as above

Y_{t+1} = aggregate output (income) of the *subsequent* time period

This assumed rational response by producers to the aggregate demand of the preceding period, without requiring correct forecasts or immediate adjustments during the initial period. There is no logical contradiction between the two equations, or between the explicit arguments of the Physiocrats and the classical economists on this point. The differences between them center on the implied proposition:

$$Y_t = Y_{t+1}$$

Mercier de la Rivière explicitly allowed for a difference between "production" (Y_t) and "reproduction" (Y_{t+1}), while Say and Mill postulated a constancy of aggregate output (with given production functions, tastes, etc.), even though its internal proportions may vary through miscalculation. While logically the issue reduces to the constancy (not stability in a more rigorous sense[76]) of output, it is not clear that the arguments of Say and Mill against Mercier de la Rivière were always directed to this point. On the contrary, they charged

[76] In Say and Mill, there is no endogenous tendency of aggregate output to change, but also no tendency of it to return to its initial level if displaced from it. On the contrary, as will be clear from the succeeding text, any level of output, once attained, tends to be self-perpetuating.

26

him with claiming that consumption in the narrow sense (C_t) promotes more growth than does investment spending.[77] This was purely a straw man as regards any recognized economists among their contemporaries or predecessors.

The whole notion of an output which remains constant in the aggregate while varying in its internal proportions runs into the difficulty of meaningfully aggregating varying product mixes (the index number problem), which may be met by measuring output in units of inputs (the Keynesian labor unit, Ricardian-Marxian "value," Malthus' "labor command," etc.). Although this approach gets around the index number problem, when it is combined with the proposition that output so measured remains constant in the aggregate, it implies that either (1) factor suppliers substitute leisure (in the case of laborers) or current consumption (in the case of capital suppliers) for future output at the same rate with one product mix as another, which would make the concept of disproportionality meaningless, or that (2) there is an infinitely inelastic supply of labor and capital at a level determined exogenously, that is, a zero elasticity of substitution of leisure for goods (and of current for future consumption). Given any (nonzero) elasticity of substitution of leisure or current consumption for future goods, and any preferences among various product mixes, miscalculations which affect internal proportions can also affect aggregate output.

The whole question of the elasticity of substitution of leisure for goods was ignored by the supporters of Say's Law and emphasized by the general glut theorists, particularly Sismondi, who also emphasized the substitu-

[77] J. B. Say, *Traité d'économie politique*, 1803 edn., II, 358–59; James Mill, *Commerce Defended*, p. 76n.

tion of present for future consumption.[78] This was in keeping with the fact that Sismondi was dealing with a theory of equilibrium output while Say and Mill argued the sustainability of any level of output, with no endogenous tendency to change, which amounted to treating the aggregate demand function as coincident with the familiar 45-degree line (aggregate supply function) of neo-Keynesian diagrams. A more charitable interpretation might be that the aggregate demand function of Say and Mill did not coincide with the 45-degree line but that the only observed levels of output would be those at which aggregate demand equaled aggregate output, but this would be in contradiction to the oft-repeated proposition of the classical supporters of Say's Law that disproportionality can be cured by *increasing* aggregate production.[79] There was no unique equilibrium of aggregate income in the classical version of Say's Law until it was modified during the general glut controversy of the 1820's. Say's Law originally involved a positive denial that there was such a thing as an equilibrium aggregate income.

[78] ". . . the present is exchanged against the future, things that one has against those that one will have, food and clothing which are furnished to the worker against the subsequent product of his labor." Sismondi, *Richesse Commerciale*, I, 53; see also *ibid.*, pp. 35, 37, 52, 54, 87. The substitution of leisure for goods was emphasized in the later writings: Sismondi, *Nouveaux Principes*, I, 76, 84, 88, 110, 250, 251; *ibid.*, II, 259, 260, 261, 265, 292.

[79] "It is not a consequence of production being too much increased, but of its being too little increased. Increase it more." J. R. McCulloch, "The Opinions of Messrs SAY, SISMONDI, and MALTHUS . . ." *Edinburgh Review* (March 1821), 102–03. See also [Robert Torrens], "Mr. Owen's Plans . . ." *ibid.*, (October 1819), 47; Robert Torrens, *An Essay on the Production of Wealth*, pp. 391, 392, 396; J. B. Say, *A Treatise of Political Economy*, pp. 139, 140n.

DAVID RICARDO

The first systematic attempt to reconcile the facts of depression and unemployment with Say's Law was the chapter in Ricardo's *Principles of Political Economy* entitled, "On Sudden Changes in the Channels of Trade." Internal disproportionality of output and the consequent "change of employments"[80] of capital and labor explain depressions. The cause of such disproportionalities were variously (1) changes in "the tastes and caprice" of consumers,[81] (2) transition to or from wartime production,[82] and bad economic legislation.[83] Depression phenomena were described in the light of this theory: ". . . during the interval while they are settling in the situations which new circumstances have made the most beneficial, much fixed capital is unemployed, perhaps wholly lost, and labourers are without full employment."[84]

Ricardo's correspondence during the post-Napoleonic war depression shows him initially confident that such transitions would be short-lived,[85] but eventually he confessed that "I can scarcely account for the length of time" that capital and labor "perservered in their old employments" through the "delusion" of an impending change for the better.[86]

The important point throughout the Ricardian writings was to distinguish the temporary depression due to disproportionality from the permanent Ricardian stationary state,[87] and from the argument that production may be excessive in the aggregate: ". . . it is at all times the bad adaptation of the commodities produced to the

[80] Ricardo, *Works*, I, 264.   [81] *Ibid.*, p. 263.
[82] *Ibid.*, p. 265.   [83] *Ibid.*, p. 265; Vol. VIII, 275.
[84] *Ibid.*, I, 265.   [85] *Ibid.*, VII, 49; VIII, 257.
[86] *Ibid.*, VIII, 277.   [87] *Ibid.*, I, 265.

wants of mankind which is the specific evil, and not the abundance of commodities."[88]

Ricardo did not minimize depressions—they were "disastrous"[89]—but lack of "adaptation" to "the wants and tastes of society" was "the only cause of the stagnation which commerce at different times experiences."[90] Like Say and Mill, he seemed to assume that laissez-faire would reduce or eliminate the recurrence of disproportionality.[91]

In another chapter of his *Principles,* Ricardo discussed investment in the light of Say's Law. Adam Smith's theory that secular increases of capital caused secular declines of profits (or interest) due to increased competition among the capitals, was rejected: "M. Say has, however, most satisfactorily shewn, that there is no amount of capital which may not be employed in a country, because demand is only limited by production."[92] Competition among increased quantities of capital was competition in producing an increased quantity of output,[93] so that there was no basis here for declining rates of return. There was no question of increased competition to hire labor, since the supply curve of labor was considered infinitely elastic in the long run.[94] Ricardo's theory of secular decline of profit rates depended on increasing marginal costs of wage goods—as did Adam Smith's, despite Ricardo's denials.[95] This amounted to saying that although the long-run supply curve of labor

[88] *Ibid.,* II, 306.   [59] *Ibid.,* III, 94.   [90] *Ibid.,* II, 415.

[91] *Ibid.,* VIII, 275; J. B. Say, *Traité d'économie politique,* 1814, p. 150; *ibid.,* 1817, p. 147; *ibid.,* 1826, p. 185; James Mill, *Commerce Defended,* p. 85.

[92] *Ricardo, Works,* I, 290.

[93]*Ibid.,* pp. 289–90.   [94] *Ibid.,* p. 289.

[95] Adam Smith, *The Wealth of Nations,* pp. 92–93; Cf. Ricardo, *Works,* I, 289, 290, 296.

was infinitely elastic with respect to real income, it was rising with respect to the labor cost of that given real income.

Sismondi and Malthus were later to transpose the elements of this Smithian (and Ricardian) model from the long run to the short run—with rising supply curves of labor being due to the inability to increase the adult labor force in the short run—thereby moving the Ricardian stationary state from the long run to the short run. However, the conclusion which Ricardo drew (ignoring the rising supply curves implied by Smith) was that "there is no limit to demand—no limit to the employment of capital while it yields any profit . . . however abundant capital may become."[96] Elsewhere, Ricardo saw that it was not a question of "any" return on capital, but of a sufficient return to cause a continuance of the same level of investment.[97]

In discussing short-run phenomena, Ricardo unequivocally (and ungrudgingly) acknowledged the vital role of money. He quoted David Hume on the long-run quantity theory of money *and* on the fact that the proportionality of money to the value of output "varies, on some occasions," depending as it does on the "rapidity of circulation."[98] Despite the tendency of post-Keynesian literature to depict supporters of the quantity theory of money as believing in a constant velocity of circulation (through all phases of the business cycle), this was certainly not true of the classical economists (including Hume). Neither did they assume infinite price flexibility in the short run, so as to nullify the effect of monetary changes on real variables. Ricardo recognized that a sharp contraction of money or credit would have "the

[96] Ricardo, *Works,* I, 296.
[97] *Ibid.,* IV, 178.   [98] *Ibid.,* III, 90.

31

most disastrous consequences to the trade and commerce of the country," causing "much ruin and distress" in the economy.[99] This did not prevent his denying, in the same writing, the possibility of a general glut[100]—which was a different phenomenon, both in his eyes and in the eyes of the general glut theorists.

An important feature of the Ricardian system that greatly complicated the general glut controversy, though not logically part of Say's Law, was its comparative statics approach. Ricardo himself finally noted this after years of fruitless controversy with Malthus:

> It appears to me that one great cause of our difference in opinion, on the subjects which we have so often discussed, is that you have always in your mind the immediate and temporary effects of particular changes—whereas I put these immediate and temporary effects quite aside, and fix my whole attention on the permanent state of things which will result from them.[101]

The same comparative statics approach was implicit in the other defenders of Say's Law, just as the dynamic approach was implicit in the general glut school, it was not only their differences in this regard, but the fact that these differences were usually implicit, which made it difficult for the two sides to understand and come to grips with each others' arguments.

SUMMARY AND CONCLUSION

Say's Law as it appeared in classical economics involved seven major propositions:

1. Production necessarily generates purchasing power of equal value, in the form of factor payments,

[99] *Ibid.,* p. 94.   [100] *Ibid.,* p. 103.   [101] *Ibid.,* VII, 120.

so that it is always objectively possible to sell any given level of output at cost-covering prices. (James Mill)

2. People's behavior patterns are such that they will not desire to save more than they desire to invest, nor do they generally desire to hold money balances beyond that needed for transactions in the immediate period. (Adam Smith)

3. Investment does not reduce aggregate demand, but merely transfers it from one group of potential consumers (capitalists) to another (workers in the investment goods sector). (Adam Smith)

4. As output increases, increased quantities of some goods exchange against increased quantities of other goods; increased supply creates correspondingly increased demand. (J. B. Say)

5. Each individual works only in anticipation of consumption equal to his own output, so that the aggregate quantity supplied equals the aggregate quantity demanded *ex ante* as well as *ex post*. (James Mill)

6. Increased savings (quantity or function not distinguished) increase the rate of growth. (Adam Smith)

7. Periods of unsold goods are due to internally disproportionate production, which can be eliminated by increasing the output of some other goods which will be traded for the goods currently in excess. (J. B. Say)

Although the first four propositions are related to (though not identical with) the central meanings of Say's Law as it has been refined in modern times, the last two are more central to the contemporary preoccupation with growth and the classical denial of the emerging

33

theory of equilibrium income, both of which were key issues in the general glut controversy. Say's Law as outlined above does not include the modifications—not all improvements—which came as that controversy proceeded. It should also be noted that the classical arguments cut across the modern post-Keynesian versions of Say's Law as Walras' Law, Say's Identity, and Say's Equality:

1. *Walras' Law* states that the sum of the respective values (quantities times money prices) of goods supplied plus money supplied equals the sum of the respective values (quantities times money prices) of goods demanded plus money demanded. It implies that an excess quantity of goods supplied is the same as an excess demand for money. This latter proposition was clearly stated by George Poulett Scrope and by John Stuart Mill, and was suggested by various classical economists.[102] In the dissenting tradition it was also suggested by the leading figures (Sismondi, Lauderdale, Malthus, and Chalmers) and explicitly stated by Marx: "At a given moment the supply of all commodities may be greater than the demand for all commodities, because the demand for the general commodity, money, exchange value, is greater than the demand for all particular commodities."[103] Walras'

[102] "General Glut of Goods—Supposes a General Want of Money": page title, George Poulett Scrope, *Principles of Political Economy* (London: Longman, Rees, Orme, Brown, Green & Longman, 1833), pp. 214–15; John Stuart Mill, *Essays on Some Unsettled Questions of Political Economy*, pp. 70, 72; John Stuart Mill, *Principles of Political Economy*, Ashley edn., p. 561; *ibid.*, Toronto edn., pp. 514–75; James Mill, *Elements of Political Economy*, pp. 233–34; J. B. Say, *Letters to Malthus*, pp. 45n–46n; Robert Torrens, *An Essay on the Production of Wealth*, pp. 421–22.

[103] Karl Marx, *Theories of Surplus Value*, p. 392.

Law involves essentially the same logic as James Mill's proposition that goods are supplied only because of, and to the extent of, one's desire for other goods, though Mill's goods did not include money balances or leisure.[104]

2. *Say's Identity* states that the sum of the respective values (quantities times money prices) of goods supplied are *identical* with the sum of the respective values (quantities times money prices) of goods demanded—because there is no excess demand for money. This proposition, or the implication that there was no demand for money beyond the transactions demand, was subscribed to by some of the same classical economists who subscribed to Walras' Law.[105] The apparent inconsistency was due to an implicit shift from a short-run perspective, in which monetary demand could be temporarily deficient, to a long-run perspective, in which the price level adjusted in accordance with the quantity theory of money.

3. *Say's Equality* states, as an equilibrium condition, that the sum of the respective values (quantities times money prices) of goods supplied equals the sum

---

[104] Mill did say that "money is itself goods," but it was followed immediately by the statement that "no man wants money but in order to lay it out, either in articles of productive or articles of unproductive consumption." James Mill, *Elements of Political Economy*, pp. 233–34. The notion that money is a commodity appeared also in J. B. Say and in James Mill's earlier *Commerce Defended*, but in both cases as rejections of mercantilism rather than as implications for demand for cash balances. J. B. Say, *A Treatise of Political Economy*, p. 153n; James Mill, *Commerce Defended*, p. 43.

[105] J. B. Say, *A Treatise of Political Economy*, p. 137; John Stuart Mill, *Essays on Some Unsettled Questions of Political Economy*, p. 69. See also Adam Smith, *The Wealth of Nations*, p. 407; David Ricardo, *Works*, I, 290, II, 305.

of the respective values (quantities times money prices) of the goods demanded. The classical economists referred to the restoration of equilibrium in terms of internal proportions, not aggregate quality (or value) of output.[106] The very idea of an aggregate value of output was ridiculed in the classical period,[107] and Ricardo argued that there could be no theory of aggregate quantity.[108] Sismondi and Marx might be said to have subscribed to Say's Equality, in an oblique sort of way, since they treated its necessary conditions as reasons for disequilibrium when such conditions were not met.[109]

Say's Law, in both its classical and its modern versions, is based on the premise that the production of a given output necessarily generates incomes sufficient to purchase that output. No economist of either period ever denied this, though some popular writers of both periods developed theories which argued that it will not necessarily be *spent*. For this, it is necessary to add that

[106] James Mill, *Elements of Political Economy,* pp. 235, 242–43; Robert Torrens, *An Essay on the Production of Wealth,* pp. 417, 425.

[107] [John Stuart Mill], "Political Economy," *Westminster Review,* III, No. V (January 1825), 224; Samuel Bailey, *A Critical Dissertation on the Nature, Measure, and Causes of Value* (London: R. Hunter, 1825), p. 154; Anonymous, *Observations on Certain Verbal Disputes in Political Economy* (London: R. Hunter, 1821), pp. 10, 18, 20, 22, 36, 57, 59.

[108] Ricardo, *Works,* VIII, 278.

[109] The prerequisties of intersectoral equilibrium in Marx's celebrated reproduction schemes in Vol. II of *Capital* were treated by Marx as conditions which imply "the possibility of crises, since a balance is an accident under the crude conditions of this [capitalist] production." Karl Marx, *Capital,* II, 578. The prerequisites of aggregate equilibrium were also sketched by Sismondi, *Nouveaux Principes,* I, 103. In his *Theories of Surplus Value,* Marx said that disequilibrium occurs "because all these pious wishes are not fulfilled." (p. 411)

people's behavior patterns are such that they do not hold, or attempt to hold, the money they receive but instead spend it directly for consumer goods or indirectly for investment goods (by turning their savings over to intermediary financial institutions which invest it). During the classical period, both the proponents and opponents of Say's Law largely accepted this assumption. In modern economics it has been challenged. However, modern economics recognizes the basic logic of the classical Say's Law which is incorporated into Walras' Law, that aggregate supply (including money flow as well as other goods) necessarily equals aggregate demand (including demand for money balances).

From the standpoint of Walras' Law, an "overproduction" of goods relative to money is simply a special case of internal disproportionality, not essentially different from an excess of any goods x accompanied by a corresponding deficiency of any other goods y. It should also be noted that leisure may be included among the goods, and can therefore be overproduced or underproduced, due to lack of perfect foresight, without violating the logic of Walras' Law. This was in fact a central element in the theories of Sismondi and Malthus.

The classical economists (and their "general glut" opponents as well) went beyond Walras' Law to assert Say's Identity, that there is in general no excess demand for money holdings—and/or that such excess demand for money as may develop in unusual circumstances is a consequence rather than a cause of disequilibrium. Say's Identity was of course flatly denied by Keynes and the Keynesians. No economist of the classical or modern period ever denied Say's Equality—that it is always *possible* for a given output to be purchased by the income generated in its production, whether or not the appropriate path can or will be found to that equilibrium position. But Say's Equality is not an insignificant statement, for it contradicts recurring popular fears that ever-growing output cannot continue to be absorbed indefinitely by the market.

Say's Equality, as an equilibrium condition, says nothing about the actual path required to reach that equilibrium, how long it will take, and how much suffering will be required in the process—or whether there are less painful alternative routes. Sismondi, Malthus, Marx, and Keynes each had his own alternative, which did not require him to deny that the market path of adjustment existed in theory or in practice, but only to assert that it was intolerable. In the Ricardians' comparative statics model, the path of adjustment never appeared, and in their ad hoc comments they clearly assumed it to be relatively rapid and relatively painless—certainly as compared to any interventionist alternative.

The division of Say's Law into three distinct propositions (Walras' Law, Say's Identity, and Say's Equality) is itself a product of more than a century of analysis and controversy. The participants in the controversies did not begin with such distinctions, and grasped the logic of these distinctions only to varying degrees and applied this logic only inconsistently in the heat of polemics.

CHAPTER 2

Sismondi and Equilibrium Income

J. C. L. SIMONDE DE SISMONDI (1773–1842) was in many ways the most important of the general glut theorists. He has also been the most neglected, with many of his ideas being attributed to Malthus, and others being forgotten entirely. The concept of equilibrium appeared in Sismondi's earliest economic writing, *Richesse Commerciale* in 1803, and reappeared with increased frequency and importance in his later works. He used both the modern word, "equilibrium" ("l'equilibre")[1] and the modern concept. Occasionally he used the word in a sense which was so vague that it might have implied mere equality,[2] as some of his contemporaries sometimes used the term, but far more often it referred to a situation with no endogenous tendency to change,[3] or to a situation which would tend to be reestablished after a disturbance,[4] although his later works repeatedly stressed the difficulties retarding the reestablishment of equilibrium.[5]

The characteristically Sismondian economic analysis first appeared in an encyclopedia article, "Political Econ-

[1] Sismondi, *Richesse Commerciale,* I, 63, 139, 145; Sismondi, *Political Economy,* pp. 60, 86; Sismondi, *Nouveaux Principes,* I, 25, 234, 235; *ibid.,* II, 148, 253, 269, 284, 303.
[2] Sismondi, *Nouveaux Principes,* I, 25, 235; *ibid.,* II, 149, 294; Sismondi, *Richesse Commerciale,* I, 145.
[3] Sismondi, *Richesse Commerciale,* I, 139.
[4] *Ibid.,* I, 150n; *Nouveaux Principes,* II, 148, 253, 303.
[5] *Nouveaux Principes,* I, 235, 247, 254–55, 260; II, 166.

omy," written in 1815, later expanded into his best known work in economics, *Nouveaux Principes d'économie politique* (1819) and repeated in his later *Études sur l'économie politique* (1837–1838). The earlier *Richesse Commerciale* was intended only as a popular exposition of Adam Smith's doctrines,[6] but even here Sismondi's own ideas and approaches were very much in evidence at particular points, and serve as useful guides to this later thinking.

The First Sismondian System

In *Richesse Commerciale,* after apologies for the use of mathematics in the social sciences, Sismondi proceeded to develop a simple algebraic model of national income determination, first in a closed economy and then in an economy with international trade. His symbols were:[7]

N = "necessary" wages, or the subsistence component of the aggregate wages of "productive" workers (workers producing goods rather than services) during the immediately preceding period, during which the output currently on the market was being produced

D = expenditure ("*dépense*") for goods other than the "necessary" wage goods of "productive" workers

P = production, or annual output minus services

X = ΔN, "the difference between the former necessary wages and those advanced during the current year, a difference which can be zero, positive, or negative"

[6] *Ibid.,* I, 28.
[7] *Richesse Commerciale,* I, 105n.

40

C = annual deficit (*"créance"*) incurred in the international trade of material goods (a surplus would be $-C$).

These are all annual flows net of services. The deliberate omission of services was in keeping with the general economic thinking of the time, which was concerned with the *growth* of output, and which therefore made a distinction between "productive" labor, consumption and, expenditure, whose objects were accumulable, and their "unproductive" counterparts, whose objects were not. In trying to distinguish production which was accumulable as wealth from that which was not,[8] Sismondi shared the common confusion between accumulability and materiality.[9] In his later writings, Sismondi was to point out that education was "a kind of fixed capital"[10] and that it had been "accumulated"[11]—but without changing his general position on the exclusion of services from the analysis of national income and wealth.

Sismondi used a lagged model, with 1799, 1800, and 1801 being $t-1$, t, and $t+1$, and with incremental output in the current year being a linear function of investment in the preceding year.[12] He apparently thought in terms of agricultural production which, he was to claim repeatedly in his later writings, provided particularly good examples for illustrating general economic principles.[13] In a completely agricultural economy,

[8] *Ibid.,* I, 20, 28–29, 31n.

[9] *Ibid.,* I, 10, 29; *Nouveaux Principes,* I, 129, 131; *Political Economy,* pp. 32, 33.

[10] *Nouveaux Principes,* I, 131; see also *Richesse Commerciale,* I, 38, 47n.

[11] *Political Economy,* p. 32; *Nouveaux Principes,* I, 130.

[12] *Richesse Commerciale,* I, 100–04, especially p. 101n.

[13] *Nouveaux Principes,* pp. 96–98, 114; *Études sur l'économie politique,* I, 147; *ibid.,* II, 223; *Political Economy and the Philosophy of Government,* p. 240.

P would be last year's harvest currently on sale, N the past consumption of food by the agricultural laborers (living at subsistence) who produced it, $N + X$ their current consumption, D the current expenditures of land-owners (both directly and through support of service producers) and C current food imports.

Revenue and savings were also defined, but without explicit symbols for them. In this first Sismondian system, *"P-N will be the revenue."*[14] Revenue thus indicates the current profitability, as discovered *ex post,* of goods produced in the preceding period. It was a disposable surplus, like the Physiocrats' *produit net,* and consisted of "rent, profit, and superfluous wages"[15] above the minimum supply price of labor. Adding the symbol R for revenue:

$$(1) \quad R = P\text{-}N$$

The simple definition of revenue gave way to a variety of shifting definitions in Sismondi's later writings, its original meaning continuing as one among several.

Current consumption, according to Sismondi, "is $D + (N + X)$,"[16] that is, current spending on wage and nonwage goods combined. "When a country has no foreign trade at all, its consumption is equal to its production," Sismondi said. This was clearly meant as an equilibrium condition rather than a necessary identity. The two would be equal "because if it produced more than it could consume, not making any exports at all," part of the national output "would be useless"—presumably become excess inventory—"and would arrest production for the following year."[17] Sismondi argued, in passing, that wealthier nations were able to absorb excess

[14] *Richesse Commerciale,* I, 105n.   [15] *Ibid.,* p. 345.
[16] *Ibid.,* p. 105n.   [17] *Ibid.,* p. 96.

inventory before precipitating price reductions that discourage future output:[18] the idea that he was thinking in terms of unintended inventory investment is thus not simply a projection of modern concepts into older economists. Implicitly assuming equilibrium, Sismondi proceeded with his equations:[19]

$$(2) \quad D + (N + X) = P, \text{ or}$$
$$D = P - (N + X)$$

Sismondi argued that economic growth (or retrogression) "depends on the evaluation of X, or the difference between the necessary wages of one year and that of the following year."[20] Another way of saying the same thing was that growth depended upon the difference between "revenue" and "expenditure"[21] as defined. Sismondi did not explain why these expressions were equivalent, but this can be readily derived from his equation (2) above and his definition of revenue which has been rendered as equation (1):

$$(3) \quad D = P - (N + X) = (P\text{-}N)$$
$$- X = R - X$$

$$(4) \quad X = R\text{-}D$$

In this model, X equals net investment, since wage goods are the only form of investment considered. In parallel numerical examples, Sismondi called Revenue minus Expenditure "savings" when positive and "deficit" or dissavings when negative,[22] corresponding to $+X$ and $-X$ in the algebraic model. This interchangeable use of saving and investment in a closed economy context

---

[18] *Ibid.*, pp. 111n–12n.   [19] *Ibid.*, p. 105n.
[20] *Ibid.*, p. 106n.   [21] *Ibid.*, p. 82.   [22] *Ibid.*, pp. 103, 104.

was not merely loose usage, for Sismondi used other examples in which savings differed from investment when there was an import surplus or an export surplus.[23]

With international trade, aggregate demand equals output plus imports in equilibrium. In Sismondi's equation:[24]

$$(5) \quad D + (N + X) = P + C$$

If, instead of having a net import surplus, a nation has a net export surplus (or is lending), then the sign of C becomes negative.[25] In more modern terms, "production" is Y_t; "reproduction" is Y_{t+1}; "revenue" is current income minus past wages $(Y_t - W_{t-1})$; and "expenditures" by the propertied class are (in equilibrium) simply total output minus current wage payments $(Y_t - W_t)$. In a closed economy, the difference between "revenue" and "expenditure" of a given period equaled the "savings" of the same period in Sismondi:[26]

$$(1) \quad R_t - D_t = (Y_t - W_{t-1}) - (Y_t - W_t)$$
$$= Y_t - W_{t-1} - Y_t + W_t = W_t - W_{t-1} = S_t$$

These savings could be either positive or negative, according to Sismondi.[27]

Since wage payments were the only form of investment, incremental wage payments were equal to net investment during a given period:

$$(2) \quad W_t - W_{t-1} \neq I_t$$

Since this is also S_t by equation (1),

$$(3) \quad S_t \neq I_t$$

[23] Ibid., I, 103; see also pp. 105n–107n, 215n–216n.
[24] Ibid., I, 106n. [25] Ibid.
[26] Ibid., I, 103–04. [27] Ibid., I, 103, 104.

44

Sismondi assumed that the income of one period was a simple multiple (2.5) of the wages of the previous period:[28]

(4) $Y_t \neq kW_{t-1}$

Incremental output was therefore the same multiple of net investment:

(5) $Y_{t+1} - Y_t = k(W_t) - k(W_{t-1})$
$$= k(W_t - W_{t-1}) = kI_t$$

(6) $Y_{t+1} = Y_t + kI_t$

The Sismondian argument can now be compared with the classical argument (also in a closed economy with no government) that current aggregate demand—"consumption" in classical terms, both "productive" (investment) and "unproductive" (consumption proper)—equaled current aggregate output or income:

(7) $Y_t \neq C_t + I_t$

This classical argument was no refutation of the Sismondian view that future growth was a function of current net investment (equation 6). In fact, the two equations can be combined:

(8) $Y_{t+1} = Y_t + kI_t = C_t + I_t + kI_t$
$Y_{t+1} = C_t + (1 + k)I_t$

Since Sismondi's k was 2.5, the basic Sismondian growth model becomes:

(9) $Y_{t+1} = C_t + (1 + 2.5)I_t = C_t + 3.5I_t$

Various complications were introduced into this model to illustrate various propositions,[29] but these are unessential for the present purpose.

[28] *Ibid.*, I, 101n; 100–02.
[29] *Ibid.*, I, 105n–107n, 215n–216n.

From the foregoing sketch of the early Sismondian system, several things are clear:

1. Sismondi had a conception of equilibrium aggregate output as of 1803, and developed an "absolutely new" way of "presenting the national balance"[30] at that time. This balance was not an *ex post* accounting identity because Sismondi recognized the possibility of imbalance at several points.[31] Despite his own later statements that *Richesse Commerciale* merely popularized Adam Smith[32]—a view accepted and repeated by most later commentators[33]—it developed a conceptual apparatus which could readily be used for non-Smithian purposes and conclusions, though it was not so used in this early work.

2. Sismondi used period analysis in contrast to Ricardian comparative statics. Although in doing so he followed in the footsteps of the Physiocrat Mercier de la Rivière, he opposed Physiocracy in this work as later.[34]

3. The concept of "reproduction" (Y_{t+1})—as distinguished from "production" (Y_t)—appeared in *Richesse Commerciale,* and was to be repeated in Sismondi's later writing.[35] This was not only in keeping with his period analysis, but suggested his position on the related distinction between the question of clearing the market currently and the question of

---

[30] *Ibid.,* I, 99.   [31] *Ibid.,* I, 96, 97, 111.

[32] *Nouveaux Principes,* I, 28.

[33] An important exception being J. A. Schumpeter, *History of Economic Analysis* (New York: Oxford University Press, 1954), p. 493.

[34] *Richesse Commerciale,* I, 60n, 100; *Nouveaux Principes,* I, Book I, Chapter VI.

[35] *Richesse Commerciale,* I, 100; *Nouveaux Principes,* I, 98, 110, 114, 345; *Political Economy,* p. 21.

sustaining the existing level of output in subsequent time periods. The concept of "revenue" as a return during the current period reflecting the *ex post* profitability of past production and thereby governing "reproduction" fits into this same general framework.

None of this implied an attack on Say's Law, though it provided the elements of a later theory which the supporters of Say's Law chose to attack. In fact, *Richesse Commerciale* closed with a dismissal of "all the solicitude of the legislators of Europe" who "fear that buyers are lacking for national factories."[36] Sismondi said:

> . . . they do not perceive that the national factories are not sufficient to provide for the buyers. They fear that capitals cannot find profitable employment by animating manufactures, and they do not perceive that manufactures are paralyzed only by the lack of capital. They fear that consumers do not spend enough for their wants to call to work all the artisans who must satisfy them, and they do not perceive that they spend too much to enable new productive labor to be set in motion with their savings. Incessantly they take precautions against abundance, and it is scarcity which pursues them. Finally, they simply cannot see that consoling truth, namely, that whatever check which some of our manufactures may experience, the national capital will never remain idle, in the hands of its owners, and that it will never be employed by them in any other way than in maintaining productive labor, directly or indirectly, spreading the comforts of life among the workers, and opening up new manufactures, making up for the closing of those which unfavorable circumstances may have destroyed.[37]

[36] *Richesse Commerciale*, II, 446.   [37] *Ibid.*, II, 446–47.

At this point, Sismondi was still clearly a supporter of Say's Law.

EQUILIBRIUM OUTPUT AND GENERAL GLUTS

Although Sismondi made passing references in *Richesse Commerciale* to automatic readjustments of aggregate output when it surpassed a sustainable level,[38] his explicit theory of equilibrium income originated in his encyclopedia article, "Political Economy," which was elaborated in his major work, *Nouveaux Principes,* and later restated in his *Études sur l'économie politique.* In contrast to his earlier algebraic model and his glossary of carefully defined terms,[39] the later writings proceeded by analogy, plausibility, and vague appeals to the "facts" of history or of the contemporary scene. In all three of the later works, the analysis began with a solitary individual, stranded like Robinson Crusoe on a desert island. The principles involved in the economic behavior of this individual were considered directly transferable to the economy as a whole: "Society is exactly like that man; in dividing its roles it does not at all change the motives which guide it."[40]

In the simple Crusoe model, "the only productive labors, or those which create wealth, are those which leave after them a profit at least equal in value, in the eyes of the solitary man, to the pain which they have cost him."[41] The individual must not only weigh goods against each other, he must weigh goods as a whole against leisure, deciding "if he prefers frugal sustenance

[38] *Ibid.,* I, 96, 111.
[39] *Ibid.,* I, 104n–108n, 215n–216n, 342–48.
[40] *Nouveaux Principes,* I, 110; *Political Economy,* p. 16; *Études,* I, 69.
[41] *Nouveaux Principes,* I, 75.

with time reserved for the exercise of his mind, like the Greeks of old, or for repose and pleasure like the savages; or if he chooses a constant labor with a more substantial sustenance."[42] While Sismondi's analysis was seldom rigorous, his meanings were usually clear. The respective marginal utilities of goods costing a given disutility must not only be equated to each other in equilibrium, but must also be equal to that disutility. It was "useless" to push production beyond the point where the additional utility balanced the disutility of the additional labor that produced it, or—in terms of earnings in society—without being assured that from such production will come "a new revenue fully proportioned to the efforts which are required for it."[43] At some level of output "it will be necessary to say: that is too much."[44]

When "man labored for himself alone" the proper balancing of labor and output took care of itself.[45] After the division of labor in a commercial society, "each no longer worked for himself, but for an unknown person" who would consume his output, so that "diverse proportions" arose "between the desire and that which could satisfy it," that is, between the utility of output and the disutility of labor.[46] Producers had to proceed "by divination" in an area where "even the most able had only conjectural information."[47] Yet in a free market they could guide themselves by price movements, so that annual output, investment, and consumption automatically adjust and can grow over time "at an equal pace" with-

---

[42] *Ibid.,* II, 259–60.   [43] *Études,* I, 134.
[44] *Ibid.,* I, 62; see also *Nouveaux Principes,* I, 82.
[45] *Nouveaux Principes,* I, 251; *Études,* I, 95, 119.
[46] *Nouveaux Principes,* I, 251.
[47] *Ibid.;* see also *Études,* I, 120; II, 249.

out needing to be "held by the hand" by the government.[48] However, Sismondi feared that governmental growth schemes were "indiscriminately pushing production"[49] and trying to grow industries "in hot houses."[50] This was his central practical concern.

Unlike private capitalists, who are directed by self-interest in the Smithian manner to "do what suits the country best,"[51] government economic activities "have not followed the indications of the market at all."[52] The government may "suddenly given a great development to a manufacture which, after its initial debut, cannot be sustained"; it leads investment into channels "which personal interests had designedly overlooked."[53] While Sismondi sometimes argued that government-supported overinvestment and overproduction in particular sectors were simply an inefficient transfer from alternative investment opportunities elsewhere,[54] his more usual assumption was that this was a net increase of aggregate investment and output above the equilibrium level, leading—via temporarily higher wages—to an above equilibrium level of population which must later be reduced in size through poverty and starvation.[55]

Although there was nothing here that was logically inconsistent with classical analysis, or even classical ideology, there were polemical attacks on Sismondi by

[48] *Nouveaux Principes,* I, 114; *Political Economy,* p. 28; *Études,* I, 108.

[49] *Nouveaux Principes,* I, 260.

[50] *Ibid.,* II, 304; *Études,* I, 112; II, 364.

[51] *Political Economy,* p. 74; *Études,* I, p. 106.

[52] *Nouveaux Principes,* II, 305; *Études,* I, 113.

[53] *Political Economy,* p. 70.

[54] *Ibid.*

[55] *Nouveaux Principes,* I, 330–31; II, 203; lagged population growth in response to temporary prosperity is also mentioned *ibid.,* pp. 207, 242, 302; *Études,* I, 108.

supporters of Say's Law,[56] who initiated the general glut controversy of the 1820's. The main proposition to which they objected was Sismondi's implication that it was possible to have an "above-equilibrium" level of output, even as a temporary phenomenon. Based on the writings of Say and Mill, who had declared that supply always equals demand, whatever the level of output,[57] they denied Sismondi's argument that at some level of output supply would exceed demand. The classical economists were never guilty of the absurdity sometimes attributed to them of denying the *existence* of depressions, unsold goods, and unemployment, but their *explanation* was not the modern one of deficient aggregate demand, even in the short run. These phenomena were a result of internally disproportionate production (relative to the consumers' preferred mix), not excessive aggregate output, even temporarily. The first attack on Sismondi in the Ricardian *Edingurgh Review* defined a "glut" as an *undersupply* of the goods needed to fill out the proper equilibrium proportions of aggregate output: "A glut is an increase in the supply of a particular class of commodities, unaccompanied by a corresponding increase of those other commodities which should serve as their equivalents."[58] According to McCulloch, a glut "is not a consequence of production being too much increased,

[56] [Robert Torrens], "Mr. Owen's Plans for Relieving the National Distress," *Edinburgh Review* (October 1819), 470–75; [John R. McCulloch], "The Opinions of Messrs. SAY, SISMONDI, and MALTHUS, On the Effects of Machinery and Accumulation, Stated and Examined," *Edinburgh Review* XXV, No. LXIX (March 1821), 102–23; Jean-Baptiste Say, "Sur la balances des consommations avec les productions," *Revue encyclopedique,* XXIII (July 1824, 18–31.

[57] [Robert Torrens], *op. cit.,* p. 473; J. R. McCulloch, *Principles of Political Economy,* p. 156n.

[58] [Robert Torrens], *op. cit.,* p. 471.

but of its being too little increased. Increase it more."[59] Similar statements abound in the literature of the period.[60] They said in effect that the only kind of glut possible was a partial glut. Although disproportionality was the operative factor, it was still consistent to argue that too little had been produced in the sense that more output—creating the proper proportions at a higher level of aggregate output—would restore equilibrium. This argument appeared repeatedly in the writings of Say, James Mill, McCulloch, and Torrens, and Ricardo's only reservations about it were practical rather than theoretical.[61] For Ricardo, short-run depressions represented only a "bad adaptation," "faulty distribution," or "bad selection" of goods, which was "the only cause" of the problem.[62] There was no general glut or aggregate overabundance: "Men err in their productions, there is no deficiency of demand."[63]

Sismondi's first reply to this argument showed that he saw the crucial point in dispute—"fundamental in political economy"[64] as a science and of the highest im-

[59] [John R. McCulloch], op. cit., pp. 106–07.
[60] Robert Torrens, An Essay on the Production of Wealth, pp. 391, 392, 396; John R. McCulloch, Principles of Political Economy, p. 145; "M. Say tells us, that if there is a glut of commodities, the way to cure it is to produce more." [Samuel Bailey], Observations on Certain Verbal Disputes in Political Economy (London: R. Hunter, 1821), p. 84; J. B. Say, A Treatise of Political Economy, pp. 139, 140n; J. B. Say, Letters to Malthus, pp. 8, 49; James Mill, Commerce Defended, p. 85; James Mill, Elements of Political Economy. pp. 234–35, 240, 241.
[61] Ricardo, Works, VIII, 227; see note 60. These views were also found on the popular level of Harriet Martineau, The Moral of Many Fables (London: Charles Fox, 1834), p. 128.
[62] Ricardo, Works, II, 306, 366, 413, 415.
[63] Ibid., VIII, 277.
[64] Nouveaux Principes, II, 252; Études, I, 96–97.

portance practically—to be the existence of an equilibrium level of aggregate output. This was not a mere verbal dispute but a confrontation of principles with diametrically opposite implications:

> Two opposing explanations are given for that public distress which causes so much turmoil. You have made too much, say some; you have not made enough, say the others. Equilibrium will be reestablished, say the first, peace and prosperity will be created again only when you have consumed all this surplus of merchandise which remains unsold on the market, and when you have regulated your production hereafter by the demand of the buyers; equilibrium will be re-created, say the others, provided that you redouble the efforts to accumulate as well as to produce. You are mistaken when you believe that our markets are glutted; only half our stores are filled; let us similarly fill the other half, and these new riches, exchanged against the others, will revive commerce.[65]

It should be noted that the problem discussed by Sismondi does not exist in a long-run comparative statics model, such as that used by Ricardo and his disciples. The attack on Sismondi in the *Edinburgh Review* referred to what would happen "after the readjustment had been effected."[66] It was a common argument against the general glut theorists that "the state of things here described could not be permanent," that it "would infallibly produce its own remedy,"[67] that it could not

[65] *Nouveaux Principes,* II, 253.
[66] [Robert Torrens], *op. cit.,* p. 473.
[67] Robert Torrens, *An Essay on the Production of Wealth,* p. 425; see also James Mill, *Elements of Political Economy,* p. 242.

"continue,"[68] etc. Numerous contemporary reactions to this kind of reasoning failed to shake the Ricardians. A letter from Ricardo's friend Trower insisted on the practical importance of the "intervals" which were being ignored, but they remained for Ricardo "only intervals."[69] An anonymous pamphlet of the period, probably by Samuel Bailey, declared it "quite useless to repeat like a parrot, that things have a tendency to find their level," that economists were "dismissing from their minds the very long temporary *interval* during which the process is going on," ignoring considerations which were like "friction in mechanics" which would "falsify the conclusions of too general theory."[70] Malthus argued that the tendency to recuperation was no proof that the malady did not exist, and that the periods of time involved were "serious spaces" in human life.[71] Sismondi also denounced Ricardo's "synthetic manner of reasoning,"[72] his assumption that "a perfect equilibrium is always maintained,"[73] and said that Ricardo's results were arrived at "by making abstraction of time and space, as the German metaphysicians do."[74]

In considering short-run situations, the Ricardians emphasized that whatever was produced could always be sold, since aggregate income or purchasing power

[68] [John Stuart Mill], "War Expenditure," *Westminster Review*, II (July 1824), 42.

[69] Ricardo, *Works*, VIII, 270, 302.

[70] [Samuel Bailey], *An Inquiry into those Principles respecting the Nature of Demand and the Necesssity of Consumption lately advocated by Mr. Malthus* (London: R. Hunter, 1821), pp. 72, 75.

[71] T. R. Malthus, *Principles of Political Economy*, 2nd edn., p. 437.

[72] Sismondi, *Nouveaux Principes*, I, 69.

[73] *Ibid.*, I, 234.

[74] *Ibid.*, II, 283; *Études*, I, 85n–86n.

necessarily equaled the value, or cost of production, of aggregate output. If some goods were sold below their cost of production because of a partial glut or disproportionality, then other goods were necessarily sold above their cost of production, and there was therefore no general glut.[75] Since both sides in the controversy shared the assumption that savings were all invested,[76] there were no leakages from the circular flow of income and output. The market could always be cleared—and at cost-covering prices, where "costs" were implicitly *ex post* costs actually incurred, rather than *ex ante* supply prices of the given output. The crucial difference between the two schools on this point was that the glut theorists were concerned with *ex ante* costs or supply prices, which in turn meant that they were not concerned with whether the market could always be *cleared* but with whether every level of output could be *sustained*.

[75] "It is therefore universally true, that, as the aggregate demand and aggregate supply of a nation can never be unequal to one another, so there can never be a superabundant supply in particular instances, and hence a fall in exchangeable value below the cost of production, without a corresponding deficiency of supply, and hence a rise in exchangeable value, beyond cost of production in other instances." James Mill, *Elements of Political Economy*, p. 240. ". . . precisely at the same time that one commodity makes a loss, another is making excessive profit." J. B. Say, *Treatise on Political Economy*, p. 130. J. R. McCulloch, *Principles of Political Economy*, p. 156; [John Stuart Mill], "Political Economy," *Westminster Review*, III, No. v (January 1825), 231.

[76] James Mill, *Commerce Defended*, pp. 77, 92; J. B. Say, *Letters to Malthus*, p. 36n; [John Stuart Mill] "War Expenditure," *Westminster Review*, II (July 1824), 38–39; Ricardo, *Works*, II, 89, 309, 424, 449; *ibid.*, VI, 133; Sismondi, *Nouveaux Principes*, II, 82; T. R. Malthus, *Definitions in Political Economy*, p. 238; T. R. Malthus, *Principles of Political Economy*, p. 38; Thomas Chalmers, *On Political Economy*, p. 96; William Spence, *Tracts on Political Economy*, pp. 30–31.

The question which Sismondi asked in *Nouveaux Principles* was whether the producer could "recommence his operation,"[77] whether the seller's price would enable him to "profitably reproduce the thing that was sold, under the same conditions,"[78] whether he could "recommence and accomplish the same work."[79] Sismondi was concerned with production for "the following year,"[80] with "reproduction."[81] He was concerned with whether expectations *ex ante* were realized *ex post*. The producer may have "imagined" that he had a larger market than he did;[82] he based his output on the "presumed disposition of the buyer";[83] he may have "believed" while producing his output that he was "proportioning it to the needs of the market" but he may have ordered a given quantity of work to be done "without sufficient reason,"[84] paying "a wage which cannot continue," and in turn showing the worker "in prospect" a demand for labor which cannot continue.[85]

In this model, current output is a function of past anticipations of returns, future output a function of current realized returns, in the manner of the cobweb theorem. There are, in effect, two cobwebs—one for capital and one for labor. When the workers receive above-equilibrium wages as a result of the capitalists' overinvestment, population increase follows because of more marriages, more births per marriage, and higher survival rates among new and existing children—all leading to a lagged growth of the labor force as the additional children reach working age, and as a result

[77] *Nouveaux Principes,* I, 111, 113.   [78] *Ibid.,* I, 257.
[79] *Ibid.,* II, 108.   [80] *Ibid.,* I, 253.
[81] *Ibid.,* I, 98, 110, 345; *Political Economy,* p. 21; *Richesse Commerciale,* I, 100.
[82] *Political Economy,* p. 83.   [83] *Études,* II, 245.
[84] *Nouveaux Principes,* I, 105.   [85] *Ibid.,* I, 247.

"the wages of each worker diminish."[86] However, the essential reasoning can be illustrated in one diagram:

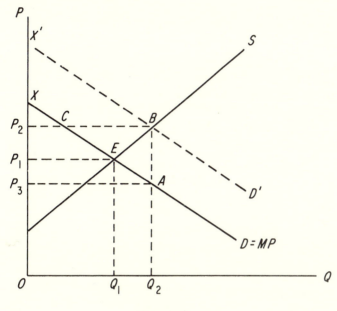

Figure 1

If S and D represent the supply and demand (marginal product) of "capital"—nonlabor factors, assumed for simplicity to be supplied in fixed proportions by the same decision-making units—then an anticipated rate of return P_2 would lead to Q_2 being supplied in period t, leading in turn to a total output OQ_2AX in period $t + 1$. The normal return to labor, the equilibrium wages fund P_1EX, expands to P_3AX as the *ex post* rate of return to this quantity of capital turns out to be P_3. Sismondi, like his contemporaries, assumed the short-run supply curve of labor to be rising and relative inelastic,

[86] *Ibid.*, I, 247–48.

with the long-run supply curve horizontal as the sub-sistence level, so that a larger wages fund meant higher wages per capita in period $t + 1$ and lagged growth of the labor forces in $(t + 2)$ and subsequent periods—just when the quantity of capital being supplied begins to contract now that it is earning less than its supply price, declining in quantity period for period as the labor force continues to grow period for period, until the generations reduced by poverty reach labor force age.

Essentially the same argument reappeared in Malthus, who was likewise concerned with "continued produc-tion,"[87] "subsequent production,"[88] the "continued sup-ply" of output,[89] etc. The "conversion of revenue into capital pushed beyond a certain point," or equivalently (since savings equal investment), "the adoption of parsimonious habits in too great a degree," tends to be "accompanied by the most distressing effects at first, and by a marked depression of wealth and population after-wards."[90] Dynamic analysis, though not so explicitly pe-riod analysis, was again implied by references to "at first" and "afterwards." The "distressing effects" were made more explicit in Malthus' analytical appendix: "saving, pushed beyond a certain point, will destroy profits."[91] Malthus repeatedly argued that an "abundance

[87] T. R. Malthus, *Principles of Political Economy*, p. 361; [T. R. Malthus], "Tooke—On High and Low Prices," *Quarterly Review*, XXIX, No. LVII (April 1823), 229.

[88] *Quarterly Review* (April 1829), 229.

[89] [T. R. Malthus], "Political Economy," *Quarterly Review* (January 1824), 318; T. R. Malthus, *Principles of Political Economy*, p. 71.

[90] T. R. Malthus, *Principles of Political Economy*, p. 326. "Afterwards" in the 2nd edn. replaced "permanently" in the 1st edn.; *ibid.*, 1st edn. (London: John Murray, 1820), p. 369.

[91] *Ibid.*, 1st edn., p. 572. All other references are to the 2nd edn. unless otherwise noted.

and competition of capital . . . would necessarily occasion a different division of what was produced, and award a larger proportion of it to the labourer, and a smaller proportion to the capitalist."[92] As in Sismondi, "a great temporary saving, commencing when profits were sufficient to encourage it"—Q_2 and P_2 in Figure 1—would not leave "an adequate share" to the investor—P_3 being less than P_2—so that there is "first an unnatural demand for labour, and then a necessary and sudden diminution of such demand," which will "throw the rising generation out of employment."[93]

The same argument, complete with emphasis on lags, appeared still later in Malthus' disciple, Thomas Chalmers,[94] with the same suggestions of the cobweb theorem found in Sismondi and Malthus,[95] the same temporary rise in per capita wages,[96] the same reduction of investment when the capitalists "come to find" that the anticipated profits cannot be "realized."[97] Dynamic analysis was clearly implied, as in Sismondi and Malthus.

Unlike the Keynesian analysis, in which "excess" savings refer to savings greater than investment, in Sismondi and Malthus savings always equal investment,[98] but each is "excess" in relation to the rate of return which will be discovered *ex post*—that is, they are savings made off the savings schedule. An "insufficient demand" also takes on a non-Keynesian meaning in the context of this analysis, in which nothing has been lost from the circular

[92] *Quarterly Review* (January 1824), 323.
[93] Malthus to Ricardo, *Works*, IX, 20.
[94] Thomas Chalmers, *On Political Economy,* pp. 81–82, 89–90.
[95] *Ibid.,* pp. 113–14.   [96] *Ibid.,* pp. 82, 143.
[97] *Ibid.,* pp. 145–46.
[98] T. R. Malthus, *Definitions in Political Economy,* p. 238; T. R. Malthus, *Principles of Political Economy,* p. 38; Sismondi, *Nouveaux Principes,* I, 98, 247–48, 269; *ibid.,* II, 81.

flow of income and output. A "sufficient" demand would be D', which would permit capital to earn its expected rate of return while labor continues to receive a sum (P_2BX') equal to its expanded wage fund (P_3AX). Both Sismondi and Malthus seemed to assume that the basic problem was one of distribution between capital and labor, that capital did not continue to receive its supply price simply because labor received more than its supply price, when in fact the incremental product of capital (EQ_1Q_2A) would be less than its supply price (EQ_1Q_2B) even if labor continued to work for its equilibrium wages fund (P_1EX).

In this lagged model, in contrast to the Ricardian comparative statics system, the value of aggregate output can be less than its cost of production *ex ante* or its supply price.[99] *There can be a general glut.* Profits specifically are below the supply price of "capital." Sismondi argued that one should not "push" additional production unless the revenue from it will be "fully proportioned to the efforts which that production requires." Increased output as such is not "a sign of prosperity" unless the increment proves to be "profitable."[100] Malthus likewise defined a glut in terms of inadequate profit. A condition which would "lower profits almost to nothing, is precisely what is meant by a general glut."[101] A general

[99] Aggregate output $= OXAQ_2$
ex ante "capital" cost $= OP_2BQ_2$
ex ante labor cost $= P_1XE$
$OP_2BQ_2 > OP_1EAQ_2$, by construction
Therefore:
$OP_2BQ_2 + P_1XE > OP_1EAQ_2 + P_1XE$
$OP_2BQ_2 + P_1XE > OXAQ_2$
Therefore aggregate output $(OXAQ_2)$ is less than its cost of production *ex ante* $(OP_2BQ_2 + P_1XE)$.

[100] *Études,* I, 125.

[101] T. R. Malthus, *Principles of Political Economy,* 1st edn.,

glut exists when output in general sells "below the elementary costs of production,"[102] which are elsewhere defined as supply prices—"the conditions of the supply"[103]—rather than as whatever costs happen to have been paid (including unexpectedly low returns to capital). Sismondi also defined costs of production as supply prices—"not what it has actually cost, but what it would cost hereafter"[104]—necessary for "reproduction." The concept of "reproduction," which had appeared in the earlier analysis in Sismondi's *Richesse Commerciale* (and in the Physiocrats) reappeared prominently in his later work, as well as in the writings of Lauderdale and lesser known glut theorists, with substantially the same arguments being made without this specific term in Malthus and Chalmers.[105]

Sismondi and Malthus both emphasized the importance of being able to rehire the same quantity of labor for future production as employed in producing the current output.[106] The quantity of labor which could be employed by a given quantity of goods varied greatly

---

pp. 354, 570; in the 2nd edn., all that was required was "lower profits," which would "check for a time further production"; *ibid.*, 2nd edn., p. 316.

[102] T. R. Malthus, *Definitions in Political Economy*, p. 247.

[103] *Ibid.*, p. 242.   [104] *Études*, ii, 381.

[105] Sismondi, *Richesse Commerciale*, i, 100; Sismondi, *Nouveaux Principes*, i, 98, 110, 114, 245; Sismondi, *Political Economy*, p. 21; Lauderdale, *Nature and Origin of Public Wealth*, pp. 220, 225, 264; R. D. C. Black, "Parson Malthus, The General and the Captain," *Economic Journal* (March 1967), 67; Ricardo, *Works*, x, 407. For similar analysis without this specific word see Lauderdale, *Three Letters to the Duke of Wellington*, pp. 117, 121; T. R. Malthus, *Principles of Political Economy*, p. 361; Thomas Chalmers, *On Political Economy*, p. 82.

[106] Malthus, *Definitions*, pp. 52, 247; Malthus, *Principles of Political Economy*, p. 317; Sismondi, *Nouveaux Principes*, i, 103–05.

in the short run,[107] so that another way of expressing the existence of a quantity of output above the equilibrium quantity was that the goods would not command enough labor to be reproduced in subsequent periods[108] (implicitly assuming that capital would not continue to accept the unexpectedly low profit rate which had been realized). With Malthus' *definition* of value being labor command,[109] and his measurement of demand being in units of labor command,[110] he could therefore characterize an above-equilibrium income as one in which the quantity of output had increased but not its "value,"[111] and in which aggregate "demand" had declined in the sense that the number of workers who could be hired by employers who expected a given return on their investment had declined.[112] The same proposition could be expressed by saying that the same quantity of capital could not be repurchased together with the labor necessary to operate it—an idea put forth later by Robert Torrens in 1821, with no indication of its essential similarity to the earlier arguments of Sismondi and Malthus.[113]

Sismondi and Malthus often cast their analyses in terms of agricultural examples in which investment took

---

[107] Sismondi, *Nouveaux Principes*, I, 103, 104; Malthus *Principles of Political Economy*, pp. 363, 364.

[108] T. R. Malthus, *Definitions in Political Economy*, p. 52.

[109] *Ibid.*, pp. 117, 193, 220, 222.

[110] *Ibid.*, pp. 58, 210n, 247; T. R. Malthus, *Principles of Political Economy*, pp. 82, 98, 99, 363; T. R. Malthus, *The Measure of Value* (London: John Murray, 1823), p. 55.

[111] T. R. Malthus, *Principles of Political Economy*, pp. 304, 393, 396, 429.

[112] *Ibid.*, p. 317; Malthus, *Definitions*, p. 52; *Quarterly Review* (April 1823), 226–27, 230–31.

[113] Robert Torrens, *An Essay on the Production of Wealth*, p. 344.

the form of wage goods.[114] Malthus ignored the possibility that investment might take the form of fixed capital, which would invalidate his recurrent argument that incremental savings are not self-sustaining if the propertied classes do not purchase the resulting incremental output as consumer goods.[115] The "parsimonious" investors can create a demand for fixed capital instead. But the failure of this subsidiary argument does not invalidate the central logic of the Sismondi-Malthus model. Indeed, in Sismondi fixed capital was a factor prolonging the restoration of equilibrium. He argued that production may be proportioned more to the amount of fixed capital than to the demand in the market,[116] since the firm would lose more by shutting down than by continuing to produce at less than cost-covering prices.[117] Moreover, because education and training were "a sort of fixed capital," skilled workers and businessmen would also continue to supply their services below their long-run equilibrium prices. Insofar as they were striving to maintain a given standard of living, they might even tend to "work with more zeal"[118] during a depression, thereby adding to the difficulties of reestablishing equilibrium.

Despite the emphasis given by Sismondi, Malthus, and other glut theorists to the problems which could exist with overinvestment and overproduction, they nevertheless believed that such overinvestment and overproduction were unlikely to occur in a free market guided by

[114] T. R. Malthus, *Principles of Political Economy*, pp. 318–20; Sismondi, *Nouveaux Principes*, I, 96–98, 114.

[115] T. R. Malthus, *Principles of Political Economy*, pp. 314–15, 322, 323, 404–05.

[116] Sismondi, *Nouveaux Principes*, I, 247, 260, 277; Sismondi, *Political Economy and the Philosophy of Government*, p. 243.

[117] Sismondi, *Nouveaux Principes*, I, 255.

[118] *Ibid.*, p. 260.

individual self-interest.[119] There was no hint of secular stagnation. Sismondi and Malthus both used analogies involving the human body's natural recovery from illness,[120] and both emphasized the suffering experienced until equilibrium was reestablished.[121]

The specific reasons for the initial overinvestment differed somewhat among the glut theorists. Malthus at one point assumed that overinvestment began "when profits were sufficient to encourage it,"[122] but at another point attributed it simply to "unfounded hopes and expectations relating to the employment of capital."[123] Sismondi blamed overproduction on governmental programs designed to force economic growth,[124] and shared Malthus concern over the urging of investment and production by economists[125] and governmental appeals to patriotism toward the same end.[126] Chalmers thought that people paid little attention to such appeals, and objected in principle rather than from practical concern.[127] Lauderdale and later Malthus were worried that governmental fiscal operations might forcibly transform what

[119] Lauderdale, *Nature and Origin of Public Wealth*, pp. 310–11; Lauderdale, *Three Letters to the Duke of Wellington*, p. 121; Sismondi, *Political Economy*, pp. 70, 74; Sismondi, *Études*, I, 107; Malthus, *Principles of Political Economy*, p. 434; Chalmers, *On Political Economy*, pp. 108–09, 110, 116, 126, 131, 148, 344.

[120] Sismondi, *Nouveaux Principes*, II, 303; Sismondi, *Études*, I, 110; Malthus, *Definitions*, pp. 62–63.

[121] Sismondi, *Nouveaux Principes*, II, 148; Malthus, *Principles of Political Economy*, p. 437.

[122] Ricardo, *Works*, IX, 20.

[123] *Quarterly Review* (April 1823), 226.

[124] Sismondi, *Nouveaux Principes*, I, 328–29; II, p. 308.

[125] *Ibid.*, II, 248, 277, 305; Malthus, *Principes of Political Economy*, p. 434.

[126] Sismondi, *Nouveaux Principes*, II, 304; Sismondi, *Études*, I, p. 57; Malthus, *Principles of Political Economy*, p. 434.

[127] Chalmers, *On Political Economy*, p. 148.

would otherwise have been consumption spending into increased investment,[128] presumably without regard to the effect of this on the general profit rate.

POLICY

Although Sismondi has often been represented, in his own time and in the modern literature, as a strong advocate of government intervention in the market, in most cases he argued that government was itself the principal cause of serious disequilibrium and had an obligation to repair its own damage.[129] He also recognized a case for government intervention where social costs differed from private costs.[130] Despite some inconsistencies, Sismondi generally preferred to have the government promote economic progress only "indirectly" through a favorable institutional climate,[131] rather than by direct intervention: "The development of nations proceeds naturally in all directions; it is scarcely ever prudent to obstruct it, but it is no less dangerous to hasten it."[132]

Following this reasoning, Sismondi repeatedly attacked "chrematistics,"[133] which he accused the classical

[128] James Maitland, 8th Earl of Lauderdale, *Observations on the Review of His Inquiry into the Nature and Origin of Public Wealth* (Edinburgh: Arch. Constable and Company, 1804), pp. 75–76; Lauderdale, *Three Letters to the Duke of Wellington,* p. 134; Malthus, *An Essay on the Principle of Population,* Everyman edn. (London: J. M. Dent, 1960), II, 61.

[129] *Nouveaux Principes,* I, 114; *Political Economy,* p. 28; *Études,* I, 108.

[130] *Nouveaux Principes,* II, 242, 245.   [131] *Ibid.,* II, 272.

[132] *Political Economy,* p. 73; *Nouveaux Principes,* II, 193; see also *Political Economy,* p. 28; *Nouveaux Principes,* I, 114–15; *ibid.,* II, 308; *Études,* II, 368.

[133] *Études,* I, 153–54; *ibid.,* II, 145, 229, 235, 263, 312, 328, 343n; *Political Economy and the Philosophy of Government,* pp. 124, 141, 142, 197, 212.

economists of teaching instead of political economy. Chrematistics was "the science of the increase of wealth," conceived of "abstractly and not in relation to man and society."[134] From Sismondi's point of view, by contrast, wealth related to men and not to things.[135] "Wealth is a modification of the human condition,"[136] an "expression of the relationship of things to men";[137] "it is only in relation to man that one can form a clear idea of it."[138] The mere growth of material things was not a true growth of wealth, since "utility" was "the essential character of wealth."[139] This implied a general glut when the growth of things went beyond the point of balance between the utility of consumption and the disutility of production.

Classical economists were accused of "forgetting men for things"[140]—a dichotomy repeated almost endlessly throughout Sismondi's economic writings.[141] Chrematistics often led to "an increase of quantity without an increase of wealth."[142] There is "a growth of national wealth only when there is also a growth of national enjoyments."[143] While this might suggest that wealth increases as long as output has a positive marginal utility, Sismondi implicitly viewed utility in net terms, allowing for the disutility of the production process. The policy implication was that governments' "blind zeal" for

[134] *Études,* I, 4; *Political Economy and the Philosophy of Government,* p. 124.
[135] *Études,* I, 6, 7; *Political Economy and the Philosophy of Government,* p. 127.
[136] *Études,* I, 7.   [137] *Ibid.,* I, 234.   [138] *Ibid.,* I, 7.
[139] *Ibid.,* II, 378.
[140] *Études,* I, 45.
[141] *Nouveaux Principes,* I, 22; *ibid.,* II, p. 94; *Études,* I, 14, 45; *ibid.,* II, 142, 218, 220, 225, 279, 365, 426.
[142] *Études,* II, 235.
[143] *Nouveaux Principes,* I, 67.

"pushing production indiscrminately"[144] should cease: ". . . if it were well understood that the purpose of political economy and of the action of government is the well-being of men and not the accumulation of things, one could indulge oneself in the hope that this disastrous action of government, pushing industrialism, would cease."[145]

Although Sismondi generally advocated only "indirect means" of government influence in the economy,[146] he argued that legislation "must come to the aid" of disadvantaged groups "in a more direct manner"[147] under some conditions. Relying primarily on the social cost argument that some industries are subsidized by having their employees' wages supplemented by public charity (during either employment or unemployment),[148] Sismondi advocated that this cost should be paid by their respective trades, organized corporately.[149] He was content to indicate the principle without attempting "to trace the means of execution."[150] Sometimes Sismondi advocated laissez-faire,[151] but more often he opposed it,[152] and "frequently invoked" the intervention of the government.[153] His inconsistency was perhaps no greater than that of Adam Smith on the same subject, and that is still considerable inconsistency.[154] Perhaps the fairest summary of his position is that he favored the principle

[144] Ibid., I, 260.   [145] Études, II, 365.

[146] Nouveaux Principes, II, 228, 244.

[147] Nouveaux Principes, II, 228.

[148] Ibid., II, 233, 234, 235, 236, 238, 240, 242.

[149] Ibid., II, 240–42.   [150] Ibid., II, 243.

[151] Ibid., II, 305; ibid., I, p. 330; Études, I, 113.

[152] Nouveaux Principes, I, 17, 85; ibid., II, 225; Études, I, 153; ibid., II, 327–28, 370.

[153] Nouveaux Principes, II, 225.

[154] See Jacob Viner, "Adam Smith and Laissez Faire," Journal of Political Economy, XXV (April 1927), 198–232.

of nonintervention but allowed numerous specific exceptions.

Sismondi's discussions of technological unemployment were an Achilles' heel which attracted disproportionate attention from those contemporaries seeking to discredit his entire work. Sismondi sometimes assumed completely inelastic demand for the product whose production costs were lowered by technological advance,[155] ignored the possibility of hours reduction,[156] and arbitrarily assumed that the income saved on one purchase would not be fully spent elsewhere.[157] Sometimes he assumed that prices would not be reduced in proportion to cost reductions,[158] so that employers' profits increased while employment fell. Sismondi's doctrines on technological unemployment were attacked not only by his opponents who supported Say's Law but by Malthus as well.[159] His primary response was to claim that he was not an enemy of technical progress, but merely wished to see it proportioned to demand.[160] In short, he had no fixed, substantive position which he was prepared to defend.

On a more general level, Sismondi was a political liberal but not a democrat,[161] a believer in equal protection and equal opportunities, but not equal conditions.[162]

---

[155] *Political Economy*, p. 129; *Nouveaux Principes*, II, 213, 254.

[156] This was pointed out by McCulloch in the *Edinburgh Review* (March 1821), 105.

[157] *Political Economy*, p. 130.   [158] *Ibid.*, pp. 130–31.

[159] Malthus, *Principles of Political Economy*, p. 366n.

[160] *Nouveaux Principes*, II, 289; *Études*, II, 336.

[161] *Études*, I, vi, x; *Political Economy and the Philosophy of Government*, pp. 214, 286–314, 452; see also Jean-R. de Salis, *Sismondi, 1773–1842* (Paris: Honore Champion, 1932), pp. 239–40.

[162] *Nouveaux Principes*, I, 33–34, 36; *ibid.*, II, pp. 137, 244; *Études*, I, viii, ix, 10.

He carried on a crusade against slavery in various writings[163] and opposed imperialism.[164] He denounced governments for their "gigantic projects" and "pointless wars,"[165] their bias toward the rich,[166] but generally opposed contemporary socialist revolutionaries.[167] Sismondi supported relief under the Poor Laws[168] and denied that the poor made improvident marriages as a result of its availability.[169] In all these liberal leanings, he was at the opposite end of the political spectrum from the conservative British economists, notably Lauderdale, Malthus, and Chalmers, who promoted economic theories of general glut and (implicitly) equilibrium income. He was in fact politically much closer to Say and Ricardo.

SUMMARY AND CONCLUSIONS

Sismondi originated the theory of equilibrium aggregate income which reappeared in the writings of Malthus and other general glut economists. The idea that there could be a theory of aggregate production was one which had appeared in the Physiocrats and which was rejected by the Ricardians. Sismondi's simple but well-defined national income model in *Richesse Commerciale* in 1803 gave way to a much more elaborate and diffuse discussion of equilibrium output and general gluts in his

[163] *Nouveaux Principes*, I, 151, 158; *ibid.*, II, 291; *Études*, I, 1, 5, 35, 93, 367, 377–448; *Richesse Commerciale*, II, 350–51.
[164] *Political Economy*, p. 75; *Nouveaux Principes*, I, 312; *ibid.*, II, 194.
[165] *Nouveaux Principes*, II, 165.
[166] *Ibid.*, II, 104, 301.
[167] *Ibid.*, II, 243, 251.
[168] J. C. L. [Simonde] de Sismondi, [Book Review], *Annales de Legislation et d'économie politique*, Geneva (November 1822), 118.
[169] *Ibid.*, pp. 102, 106, 118.

Nouveaux Principes in 1819. However, the basic continuity of concept between the earlier model and the later analysis is apparent in many ways, including an arithmetic example in *Nouveaux Principes* which reproduces the algebraic model of *Richesse Commerciale,* except that investment could now take the form of fixed capital as well as wages, although current income, Y_t, still equals kW_{t-1} with k now being 5 instead of 2.5 as in the earlier work.[170]

The developed version of the Sismondian theory in *Nouveaux Principes* assumed a rising disutility of labor and consequently a rising supply curve of labor, together with a declining marginal utility of output.[171] Equilibrium implied the simultaneous balancing of the utility of the respective goods and of leisure at their respective margins.[172] This was considered true both of the hypothetical individual on a desert isle[173] and of men in society,[174] with the additional problem that the individual decision-makers in a complex economy lacked knowledge of the social parameters of utility and production functions.[175] The individual producer could not know "the relationship between the wants of society as a whole and the quantity of labor which suffices to satisfy those wants, or better still, which could satisfy them in the future."[176] Sismondi observed: "The kind of glut of the products of human industry which I have sought to explain could scarcely have presented itself in preceding

---

[170] Sismondi, *Nouveaux Principes,* I, 96–97.

[171] *Nouveaux Principes,* II, 265.

[172] *Ibid.,* II, 259, 265; *Études,* I, 73, 106.

[173] *Nouveaux Principes,* I, 75, 110.

[174] *Ibid.,* I, 84; *ibid.,* II, pp. 259, 260, 265; *Études,* I, 68–69.

[175] *Nouveaux Principes,* I, 88, 250, 251; *ibid.,* II, 292; *Études,* I, 68–69, 96; *ibid.,* II, 379.

[176] *Études,* II, 379.

periods of society. In the state of barbarism, when each man laboured only for himself, each man also knew his wants, and it need not be feared that he would impose a useless fatigue on himself in order to create goods which he did not desire."[177]

For Sismondi, "the fundamental question is political economy" was "the balance of consumption with production."[178] By this balance was meant an equilibrium which would permit "reproduction" of the same volume of output in succeeding time periods, not merely the clearing of the market as of a given time. Sismondi repeatedly argued that the mere clearing of the market, when there was excess production, was very deceptive as an indication of the continuance of the same level of output.[179] "Often the convulsions of a dying man seem to indicate more strength than he had when in vigorous health."[180] What matters is whether the market is cleared at such prices, profits, and wages as to "reproduce" the same output under the same conditions.[181] The "false prosperity" of overproduction was repeatedly denounced, whether brought on by miscalculation, monetary manipulation, or war.[182] When goods "can be sold only at a loss" then glut has arrived, though showing "all the characteristics of abundance."[183]

Although the burden of Sismondi's argument was that disequilibrium in aggregate output (not just in internal proportions) was possible, he did not claim that this

---

[177] *Nouveaux Principes*, II, 292; *Études*, I, 95.

[178] *Nouveaux Principes*, II, 293; *Études*, I, 96–97; *Revue encyclopedique* (May 1824), 285.

[179] *Nouveaux Principes*, I, 257; *Études*, II, 233, 420.

[180] *Nouveaux Principes*, I, 257.

[181] *Ibid.*

[182] *Ibid.*, I, 279; *ibid.*, II, 99, 278; *Études*, II, 233, 420.

[183] *Études*, II, p. 233.

was likely—he characterized it as "rare,"[184] in fact—or that it was permanent, in the manner of secular stagnation. Sismondi acknowledged that the economy has recuperative powers to "triumph" over its "derangements,"[185] but stressed "the difficulty encountered in restoring equilibrium."[186] This difficulty included lagged population growth in response to temporarily increased wages during the false prosperity of overproduction,[187] backward-bending supply curves of some workers and entrepreneurs which lead them to produce more as the returns to capital and labor decline,[188] and speculative inventory accumulations.[189] Sismondi said: "A certain equilibrium is re-established, it is true, in the long run, but it is by a frightful suffering."[190]

Despite various attempts (by contemporaries and later commentators) to depict the general glut economists as crude underconsumptionists who simply did not understand national income accounting concepts well enough to see that purchasing power must necessarily equal the value of output, Sismondi recognized that income "must necessarily be equal" to output in his *Richesse Commerciale* in 1803 and repeated this later in his *Nouveaux Principes*.[191] In fact, he gave considerably more attention to national income accounting, including the problems of double counting and transfer payments,[192] than did

---

[184] *Nouveaux Principes,* II, 270.

[185] *Ibid.,* II, 303; *Études,* I, 110.

[186] *Nouveaux Principes,* II, 208.

[187] *Ibid.,* I, 105; *ibid.,* II, 203, 302.

[188] *Ibid.,* I, 296, 254.

[189] *Political Economy,* p. 72.

[190] *Nouveaux Principes,* II, 148.

[191] *Richesse Commerciale,* I, 84–85; *Nouveaux Principes,* I, 103.

[192] *Richesse Commerciale,* I, 84–85; *Études,* II, 448–49; *Political Economy and the Philosophy of Government,* p. 233.

his classical contemporaries. He recognized that "the movement of things which are sold indicates an equal movement, but in the opposite direction, of the money which pays for them."[193] Sismondi's arguments that the national revenue might be insufficient to purchase the national production,[194] that demand might be insufficient for supply,[195] must be understood in the senses in which he used these terms. This was not a naive belief that factor payments added up to less than the value of aggregate output.

Sismondi's simple definition of "revenue" as output minus (labor) cost of production $(P-N)$ in *Richesse Commerciale* gave way to a variety of shifting definitions in his later writings, one example of his general deterioration from the rigor of his earlier work. The original meaning of "revenue" continued to be used,[196] but revenue was also used "in the largest sense" to include all incomes: wages, profits, and rents.[197] It was also used as the sum of property incomes plus the workers' "ability to work"[198]—though Sismondi noted that the latter was "incommensurable"[199] with material wealth. Sometimes revenue was considered capable of purchasing annual production,[200] though at other times

[193] *Nouveaux Principes,* II, 9; see also *Études,* II, 392; *Richesse Commerciale,* I, 127.

[194] *Nouveaux Principes,* I, 276–77, 301, 302, 303; *ibid.,* II, 251–52.

[195] *Ibid.,* II, 254.

[196] *Ibid.,* I, 95; *ibid.,* II, 173; *Political Economy,* p. 5.

[197] *Études,* I, 122–23; *Political Economy and the Philosophy of Government,* p. 224; similarly inconsistent definitions were used in *Richesse Commerciale,* I, 85.

[198] *Nouveaux Principes,* I, 95–96, 102, 104, 109, 112, 120; *ibid.,* II, 173–74.

[199] *Ibid.,* I, 103.

[200] *Ibid.*

production could exceed revenue,[201] or grow faster than revenue,[202] or rise while revenue was falling.[203] Sismondi also confused income *rates* and *aggregates* in a way which suggested that falling rates of return to capital, labor, etc., would reduce aggregate spending,[204] a proposition that was not essential to his argument and he did not use it in his controversies with Say and Torrens.

Yet despite Sismondi's confused exposition, one essential idea ran through these tangled arguments and shifting definitions: equilibrium depended on whether *ex post* returns from a given output were sufficient to pay its *ex ante* supply price. The early growth model in *Richesse Commerciale* concentrated on the supply price of investment and entrepreneurship—"the quantity required in order that the producers not become disgusted and quit their work"[205]—and the return over labor costs ($P-N$) indicated *ex post* returns in relation to this *ex ante* price. In the later writings, revenue was said to equal production when supply prices were paid, causing "a new reproduction."[206] During a glut, it is not money that is lacking but "revenue"—the real supply price of factors of production.[207] Growth occurs when revenue exceeds supply prices, when a "fully paid labor is created either by employing workers who did not exist before or who had remained idle."[208]

[201] *Ibid.,* I, 276–77, 301, 302, 303; *ibid.,* II, 251–52.

[202] *Ibid.,* I, 301–03; *ibid.,* II, 252, 254; *Political Economy and the Philosophy of Government,* p. 243.

[203] *Nouveaux Principes,* I, 262; *ibid.,* II, 218; *Études,* I, 82.

[204] *Nouveaux Principes,* I, 262, 301, 302, 305; *Études,* I, 152; *Political Economy and the Philosophy of Government,* p. 239.

[205] *Richesse Commerciale,* I, 345.

[206] *Nouveaux Principes,* II, 103.

[207] *Ibid.,* II, 16–17; *Political Economy,* p. 82.

[208] *Nouveaux Principes,* I, 269.

Sismondi's "demand" was not simply the quantity demanded, as in the Ricardians, but the quantity demanded at a price sufficient to cover costs of reproduction (the supply price).[209] The "extent of the market" was the quantity for which this condition was fulfilled.[210] In these senses, demand was clearly not necessarily equal to the supply, and the extent of the market was not necessarily coextensive with production. Sismondi was aware that an "overabundance of production" sometimes lead to "a greater consumption because of the lowness of prices"[211] but this was not increased demand.[212] Although Adam Smith had defined "effective demand" in the same way as Sismondi and later Malthus,[213] the Ricardian long-run static equilibrium model made any quantity produced a quantity effectively demanded thereby eliminating the need for the vital distinction between increased demand and increased quantity demanded.

Sismondi's concern over excess savings was not a concern that savings would exceed intended investment, but that each would temporarily be above a sustainable level in view of the rate of return which would be discovered *ex post*. While there are "limits to the accumulation of capital"[214] at a given time, a nation "in a progressive condition" can profitably absorb increasing amounts of capital over time. However, when it is "arrested in its progress" this is no longer true: "A nation which cannot make progress should not make savings."[215]

[209] *Ibid.*, I, 238–39; *ibid.*, II, 213, 254.

[210] *Ibid.*, I, 257; *Richesse Commerciale*, I, 296–97, 348.

[211] *Nouveaux Principes*, I, 111; see also p. 257.

[212] Adam Smith, *The Wealth of Nations*, p. 56; Sismondi, *Nouveaux Principes*, II, 213, 254; Malthus, *Principles of Political Economy*, p. 66n.

[213] *Nouveaux Principes*, I, 248.

[214] *Ibid.*, I, 247.   [215] *Ibid.*, I, 248.

The reception of Sismondi's doctrine was disappointing and continued to be so over the years.[216] It was dismissed by the Ricardians, and even Malthus relegated it to a few passing unfavorable references.[217] Sismondi's loose, rambling style, charged with moralizing fervor, was enough to repel the analytically minded Ricardians[218] and his left-leaning, social-reforming zeal on behalf of the working class isolated him from the socially conservative (if not reactionary) Lauderdale-Malthus-Chalmers school. Sismondi's writings and correspondence reveal an increasing sense of futility and frustration, not only in trying to get his ideas accepted but even in trying to get them understood. In the second edition of *Nouveaux Principles,* he said, "I must expect to be incessantly refuted by people who have not understood me"[219] and "I have not been understood either by those who attack me or by those who defend me."[220] While bitter against his fate, he was never bitter against his adversaries, whom he descirbed as "the men who are today rightly regarded as having produced the most signal progress of the science."[221] He ascribed to their "personal benevolence" the fact that their attacks had not been more severe than they were[222] and spoke with great affection of Ricardo, whose "urbanity, good faith and

[216] *Nouveaux Principes,* I, 17; *ibid.,* II, 274; *Études,* II, 2, 334; *Political Economy and the Philosophy of Government,* pp. 150, 451, 454, 455.

[217] T. R. Malthus, *Principles of Political Economy,* pp. 147, 366.

[218] "Sismondi is too much of a sentimentalist to make a good political economist." Ricardo, *Works,* VIII, 25.

[219] *Nouveaux Principes,* II, 248.

[220] *Ibid.,* II, 289.

[221] *Ibid.,* I, 17.

[222] *Ibid.*

love of truth"[223] he admired. Like Ricardo, Sismondi was a man of great personal generosity who was nevertheless unshakable in his conviction of being right.

The recurrent depressions of the post-Napoleonic war decade caused him to observe that "with all respect to the authority of the Pontiffs of the science, I could say, like Galileo: *Eppur si Muove.*"[224] While Sismondi increasingly relied on "facts" and "experience" instead of arguments for support, he was not wholly unsuccessful intellectually. There was an exchange of polemical articles between Sismondi and J. B. Say in 1824–1826, and the fifth edition of Say's *Traité d'économie politique* in 1826 introduced what Say himself characterized as "restrictions" on the law of markets[225]—a very Sismondian exposition of the theory of equilibrium income which was repeated later in Say's *Cours complet d'économie politique.* Say called attention to the change in letters to Sismondi and Malthus,[226] but it has largely gone unnoticed in the literature, partly because the previous edition of the *Traité* is the one available in English translation and Say's book, *Letters to Malthus,* does not contain the later correspondence. However, even in the

---

[223] *Études,* I, 81n.

[224] *Nouveaux Principes,* I, 18. "Nevertheless, it does move"— Galileo's purported remark after having been forced to recant his doctrine that the earth moves around the sun. The same remark was quoted by J. B. Say in the same manner as Sismondi in a letter to Malthus accepting some of the ideas of Sismondi and Malthus. It seems almost certain that he had seen the quote used in this context in Sismondi, if not in the 2nd edn. of *Nouveaux Principes,* then in the *Revue encyclopedique* (September 1826), 609. Say, *Oeuvres Diverses,* p. 506.

[225] Say, *Oeuvres Diverses,* p. 505.

[226] *Ibid.,* pp. 504–05; Sismondi, *Political Economy and the Philosophy of Government,* p. 449.

French economic journals Sismondi has been largely ignored in historical discussions of Say's Law.[227] Keynes' lauding of Malthus' theories as the forerunners of modern Keynesian analysis undoubtedly contributed to this.

[227] For example, Sismondi's work was scarcely mentioned, and never discussed, in a long series of articles in *Revue d'économie politique* dealing with Say's Law and the controversies which surrounded it (January-February, 1952, November-December 1953, November-December 1962, January-February 1965, January-February 1966). There was an article on Sismondi in *Revue économique* for July 1967, however, the first in any French economic journal in many years.

CHAPTER 3

The British Dissenters

LAUDERDALE, MALTHUS, AND CHALMERS were the major figures in the emergence of a British school of thought which developed parallel to Sismondi on the continent, as far as economic analysis was concerned, though vastly different from him in its sociopolitical outlook. In 1804 Lauderdale published *An Inquiry into the Nature and Origin of Public Wealth and into the Means and Causes of Its Increase,* thereby launching some of the basic ideas common to the glut theorists, but in a highly sketchy and unsystematic manner. Malthus was the major developer of the British version of the glut thesis, with Thomas Chalmers later elaborating and clarifying particular points. A variety of minor figures also joined in the attack on Say's Law, which continued in the intellectual journals of the day long after the major figures on both sides had passed from the scene.[1] Since there are certain common features in this dissenting tradition, it would be possible to speak of a Lauderdale-Malthus "school" as a loose and convenient classification, but not as a living reality in the sense in which there was a united Ricardian school. Malthus not only failed to acknowledge his debt to the earlier work of Lauderdale but gave him the same curt dismissal which he gave Sismondi.[2]

[1] B. J. Gordon, "Say's Law, Effective Demand, and the Contemporary British Periodicals," *Economica* (November 1965), 438–46.

[2] T. R. Malthus, *Principles of Political Economy,* pp. 23, 314, 366n.

Nowhere on the dissenting side was there a central figure such as Ricardo who commanded the respect and loyalty of the others, and whose writings were considered authoritative or definitive.

LAUERDALE

When James Maitland, 8th Earl of Lauderdale (1759–1839), first put forth his economic theories in 1804, Say's Law had not yet developed into an established principle, so the target of his critical fire was Adam Smith's doctrine that saving promotes growth. Like the other glut theorists, Lauderdale was very policy oriented, so that while he attacked Adam Smith on a theoretical level, the main thrust of his writing was directed to the contemporary issue of the merits of a proposed sinking fund, to be built up by budgetary surpluses, for the purpose of retiring the national debt. Lauderdale assumed that the incidence of taxation was such that a budgetary surplus would represent revenue which "would have been expended in the purchase of consumable commodities,"[3] had there been no such taxation. Since the government would automatically invest these funds to earn interest for the eventual retirement of the national debt, the sinking fund represented a conversion of consumption expenditures into investment expenditures—"it effects the *creation*, and not merely the *shifting* of capital"[4]—and raised the question whether there was any limit to profitable investment.

[3] James Maitland, 8th Earl of Lauderdale, *Three Letters to the Duke of Wellington*, p. 134.
[4] The Earl of Lauderdale, *Observations on the Review of His Inquiry into the Nature and Origin of Public Wealth, Published in the VIIIth Number of the Edinburgh Review* (Edinburgh: Arch. Constable and Company, 1804), pp. 75–76.

Capital accumulation via the sinking fund (presumably without regard to its effect on the general profit rate) was for Lauderdale "forced accumulation, by the authority of the government"[5]—a point which he belabored repeatedly[6] which was presumably not immediately offset by private disinvestment. The Ricardian comparative statics model of increased equilibrium investment was clearly irrelevant here, where the question was precisely whether there was an equilibrium limit to investment, and what would happen if it were temporarily exceeded. For Lauderdale there was little danger that private individuals in a free market would over-invest,[7] nor did he believe that the limit to sustainable investment remained fixed over time.[8] He was by no means giving a "mature economy" argument, as suggested in the literature.[9]

Like Sismondi, Malthus, and Chalmers, Lauderdale was concerned not with the static equilibrium question of clearing the market at a given time, but with the problem of sustaining a given level of aggregate output

[5] James Maitland, 8th Earl of Lauderdale, *Nature and Origin of Public Wealth*, p. 232.

[6] *Ibid.*, pp. ix, 245, 254, 267; Lauderdale, *Three Letters to the Duke of Wellington*, pp. 7, 10, 68, 79, 84, 108.

[7] Lauderdale, *Nature and Origin of Public Wealth*, pp. 310–11; Lauderdale, *Three Letters to the Duke of Wellington*, p. 121.

[8] Lauderdale, *Nature and Origin of Public Wealth*, pp. 215, 227, 228.

[9] Frank Albert Fetter, "Lauderdale's Oversaving Theory," *American Economic Review* (June 1945), 281. As so often happens, this and other gross distortions which appear in this article are the result of trying to show "past opinions" which are "reappearing" today and analyzing the "practical pertinence" of this for "contemporary problems" (p. 283). It is a common but nevertheless amazing assumption that good history will be a natural by-product of an attempt to accomplish something else.

in subsequent time periods. He was concerned with "future reproduction,"[10] with "what is subsequently produced,"[11] with whether there will be an "encouragment"[12] or a "discouragement to future production."[13] Far from denying the possibility of purchasing whatever was produced, Lauderdale declared that "nothing is found more nearly commensurate than the expenditure and revenue of every society."[14] The proposition that "the revenue and expenditure of all societies must be equivalent, if left to the natural course of things," was "so generally admitted, as to require no illustration."[15] Any deficiency of aggregate demand could only be a temporary derangement: "Goods, indeed, may appear in a market for which there is no effectual demand; though that is not very probable, as the foresight of mankind generally operates as a preventive check."[16]

The developmental implications of Adam Smith's version of Say's Law were the principal targets of Lauderdale's attack: "Frugality is said to increase, Prodigality to diminish, the public capital. Every prodigal is represented as a public enemy, and every frugal man as a public benefactor."[17]

Here Adam Smith's ambiguous doctrine was taken in the sense of an increased quantity saved rather than an increase of the savings function. Lauderdale argued that despite the capacity of the economy to profitably absorb

[10] Lauderdale, *Nature and Origin of Public Wealth*, p. 220.
[11] *Ibid.*, p. 221.
[12] Lauderdale, *Three Letters to the Duke of Wellington*, p. 120.
[13] *Ibid.*, p. 121.
[14] Lauderdale, *Nature and Origin of Public Wealth*, p. 229.
[15] Lauderdale, *Three Letters to the Duke of Wellington*, p. 121.
[16] Lauderdale, *Nature and Origin of Public Wealth*, p. 311.
[17] *Ibid.*, p. 41; Lauderdale, *Three Letters to the Duke of Wellington*, p. 116.

increasing amounts of capital over time as technology changed, there was a limit to how much capital could be profitably employed at any given time with any given level of technology:

> In every state of society, a certain quantity of capital, proportioned to the existing state of the knowledge of mankind, may be usefully and profitably employed in supplanting and performing labour in the course of rearing, giving form to, and circulating the raw materials produced. Man's invention, in the means of supplanting labour, may give scope, in the progress of society, for the employment of an increased quantity; but there must be, at all times, a point determined by the existing state of knowledge in the art of supplanting and performing labour with capital, beyond which capital cannot profitably be increased, and beyond which it will not naturally increase: because the quantity, when it exceeds that point, must increase in proportion in the demand for it, and its value must of consequence diminish in such a manner as effectually to check its augmentation.[18]

Lauderdale's "demand" here is, in modern terms, quantity demanded, which is to say that in order to clear the market as capital increases beyond some point, its rate of return must fall to a level which will stop net investment. Lauderdale's argument as to the possibility of excess *investment* cannot be automatically assumed to imply excess aggregate *output,* despite the tendency of post-Keynesian interpretation to make that extension.[19] In Lauderdale's theory, there is no logical reason

---

[18] Lauderdale, *Nature and Origin of Public Wealth,* pp. 227–28.
[19] Cf. Morton Paglin, *Malthus and Lauderdale: The Anti-Ricardian Tradition* (New York: Augustus M. Kelley, 1961), p. 99.

why aggregate output must increase, though its division between consumption and investment has changed, nor did he claim that it did. The literature has tended to give Lauderdale's words a Keynesian meaning of shifting investment schedules, though he clearly did not mean an *ex ante* rise in the investment schedule but a government-forced increase in the quantity of investment made—*off the schedule*. Even James Mill recognized that Lauderdale was not discussing "voluntary parsimony."[20]

Lauderdale's distinction between making more savings out of a given income and making more savings as income increased—a distinction repeated (without credit) by Malthus—has been given a modern interpretation of a movement along a savings function versus a movement of the savings function itself.[21] However, Lauderdale's distinction turned on the difference between movement along a savings function and movement off it.

Although the normal tendency was for spending and output to be equal,[22] the circular flow could be reduced by the export of capital as the domestic profit rate declined.[23] However this decline in the profit rate was not the consequence of a decline in the circular flow, but its cause. Why the profit rate would decline in the first place was never adequately explained. A redistribution of relative income shares from capital to labor in the

[20] [James Mill], "Lord Lauderdale on Public Wealth," *The Literary Journal*, IV, No. 1 (July 1804), 14.

[21] Alvin H. Hansen, *Business Cycles and National Income* (New York: W. W. Norton & Company, Inc., 1951), pp. 241, 242.

[22] Lauderdale, *Nature and Origin of Public Wealth*, p. 229; Lauderdale, *Three Letters to the Duke of Wellington*, p. 121.

[23] *Nature and Origin of Public Wealth*, p. 252; *Three Letters to the Duke of Wellington*, p. 74; *Observations on the Review*, pp. 78, 83.

wake of growing investment with an inelastic labor supply, as suggested by Sismondi and made explicit by Malthus, would have accounted for it, but Lauderdale left this a loose end.

Lauderdale's discussion of general glut led him into other areas, including supply and demand (based on utility) as determinants of value,[24] and to suggestions of varying elasticities of demand, in contrast to the unitary elasticity assumption used in the examples of the classical economists.[25] He also suggested that elasticity applied to supply as well.[26] Lauderdale also developed a modern analysis of the national debt, including a rejection of analogies with private debt,[27] a propounding of the doctrine that we owe it to ourselves,[28] and that internal redistribution upon repayment was the main effect of the debt.[29] Like other writers of the period, orthodox and heretical, he wanted to avoid giving money the emphasis which had led to mercantilistic errors.[30] Lauderdale argued that the same results he obtained would come about in "a simple state of society" without "overgrown financial arrangements,"[31] and used Robinson Crusoe examples to illustrate.[32]

Lauderdale advanced the proposition, which later became prominent in Malthus, that increased agricultural output would create—through population growth—the

[24] *Nature and Origin of Public Wealth*, pp. 12, 15–17, 18 21, 38, 78, 109, 167.
[25] *Ibid.*, pp. 60, 71, 94.   [26] *Ibid.*, pp. 78, 85.
[27] Lauderdale, *Three Letters to the Duke of Wellington*, pp. 31, 33, 39, 77, 79, 82, 84, 85, 125, 126.
[28] *Ibid.*, pp. 32, 33, 34, 44, 45, 80n.
[29] *Ibid.*, pp. 34, 39, 59, 77, 80.
[30] Lauderdale, *Nature and Origin of Public Wealth*, pp. 3–4.
[31] *Ibid.*, p. 212.
[32] *Ibid.*, pp. 304–05; Lauderdale, *Observations on the Review*, pp. 64–65.

increased demand which would eventually make its current level a new equilibrium level.[33] Agricultural output alone "appears capable of unlimited increase" in this way.[34] Say's Law was later to be interpreted by Malthus as a generalization of this principle to all kinds of output,[35] and the fact that Say himself resorted to this line of reasoning to defend his Law on one occasion[36] facilitated the misunderstanding.

The rational parts of Lauderdale's arguments were interspersed with gross errors. For example, a sudden shift in demand from one commodity to another was regarded as reducing aggregate demand, simply because he traced out the downward multiplier effects of the reduction in the demand for one commodity, but not the similar, offsetting upward multiplier effects in the increased demand for the other.[37] Like the writings of the other glut theorists, Lauderdale's writings were seldom marked by analytical rigor, and were not concentrated in economics, as were the writings of the supporters of Say's Law.

While Lauderdale did not reach the crucial concept of an equilibrium income, he did develop the concept of an equilibrium level of investment and a theory of economic adjustments to temporary displacements from it. There was no necessary linkage between the quantity of investment and aggregate output because his argu-

---

[33] Lauderdale, *Nature and Origin of Public Wealth*, pp. 224–25.
[34] *Ibid.*, p. 224.   [35] Ricardo, *Works*, VI, 168.
[36] J. B. Say, *Letters to Malthus*, pp. 27–28.
[37] Lauderdale, *Nature and Origin of Public Wealth*, pp. 88–89. Yet the literature claims that there were *no* multiplier effects in Lauderdale: J. J. Spengler and W. R. Allen, eds., *Essays in Economic Thought*, p. 185; B. A. Corry, *Money, Saving and Investment in English Economics, 1800–1850* (New York: St. Martin's Press, 1962), p. 119.

ments did not refer to movements of schedules but of quantities off the schedules. Lauderdale did not deny that aggregate output could vary (it might well decline after abnormally low domestic profits resulting from over-investment had driven capital abroad) but his theory was simply not a theory of aggregate output variation, except in the negative sense that he denied that increased quantities of savings would necessarily increase sustainable output.

SPENCE

William Spence (1783–1860) acquired a small but secure place in history when his *Britain Independent of Commerce* in 1808 provoked James Mill's *Commerce Defended,* which became a landmark in the development of Say's Law. However, neither this pamphlet of Spence's nor his later writings approached the level of analysis of Sismondi, Malthus, or Chalmers, or even the understandably imperfect pioneering efforts of Lauderdale. Spence is commonly lumped with the Malthusian school because of pro-agricultural biases, a general concern over aggregate demand, and Spence's own references to Lauderdale as the inspiration of his ideas. Yet despite the similarity of social views and conclusions, the basic reasoning of Sismondi and the Lauderdale-Malthus school was totally absent from Spence, who was, after all, primarily concerned with showing that foreign trade was less important than agriculture in the British economy. Spence's rejoinder to Mill complained, with some justice, that the argument had wandered far afield from his basic point of contention.[38]

Spence's discussion of the national debt and the sinking fund added nothing to Lauderdale's discussion, from

[38] William Spence, *Tracts on Political Economy,* p. xxv.

which it was expressly taken. The discussion of demand in Spence's tracts simply arbitrarily picked landlords as a link in the circular flow and showed how their failure to spend would reduce aggregate demand[39]—but, of course, so would anyone else's failure to spend. Spence alone among the glut theorists suggested that there might be deliberate *ex ante* hoarding.[40] But this potential bombshell played no significant role in his analysis, and he specifically disavowed any practical implications of it in his next pamphlet.[41] Even Spence's objection to excessive capital accumulation had none of the significance which might be expected in the light of contemporary or modern thinking along these lines; industrial capital was simply considered to be excessive relative to capital in agriculture.[42]

Spence's reply to James Mill—*Agriculture, the Source of the Wealth of Britain*—cannot be considered part of the general glut controversy because it was almost wholly devoid of references to those parts of Mill's book which dealt with the issues involved in Say's Law. A great part of Spence's reply simply deprecated foreign trade as bringing in frivolous luxuries,[43] or argued for describing the operations of the economy in Physiocratic terminology, although "in no respect do I deduce any practical rule from it."[44] In short, Spence was a living straw man. James Mill chose to attack him at length in preference to giving similar attention to Lauderdale's more formidable work which was well known to him at the time.[45]

---

[39] *Ibid.*, p. 29.   [40] *Ibid.*, p. 78n.   [41] *Ibid.*, p. 153.
[42] *Ibid.*, pp. 160–61, 120.
[43] *Ibid.*, pp. 170–73.   [44] *Ibid.*, p. 142.
[45] James Mill, *Commerce Defended*, p. 96n. The fact that it was substantial was also well known. [James Mill], "Lord Lauderdale on Public Wealth," *The Literary Journal* (July 1804), 17–18.

The existence of people like Spence is not merely a complication to present day students of the general glut controversy. At the time, they provided an opportunity for the proponents of Say's Law to answer vulgarized underconsumptionist theories and Physiocratic illusions instead of coming to grips with the major arguments of their major adversaries.

MALTHUS ON DEMAND AND GROWTH

While the literature on the general glut controversy has followed Keynes in depicting Malthus as the major figure among the opponents of Say's Law,[46] the basic features of the Malthusian analysis have been shown to have been present also in Sismondi's *Nouveaux Principes,* which was not only published a year before Malthus' *Principles of Political Economy,* but which Malthus had read before completing the latter work.[47] However this was not a case of plagiarism. Although Sismondi was the originator of this analysis in an objective sense,

[46] John Maynard Keynes, *Essays in Biography,* ed. Geoffrey Keynes (New York: Horizon Press, 1951), pp. 81–124; John Maynard Keynes, *The General Theory of Employment, Interest and Money* (New York: Harcourt, Brace and Co., 1936), pp. 362–64; Paul Lambert, "The Law of Markets Prior to J. B. Say and the Say-Malthus Debate," *International Economic Papers,* No. 6 (1956), pp. 7–22; Paul Lambert, "Malthus et Keynes: Nouvel Examen de la Parenté Profonde des Deux Oeuvres," *Revue d'économie politique,* 72, No. 6 (November-December, 1962), 783–829; James J. O'Leary, "Malthus and Keynes," *Journal of Political Economy,* L, No. 6 (December 1942), 901–19; Morton Paglin, *Malthus and Lauderdale: The Anti-Ricardian Tradition* (New York: Augustus M. Kelley, 1961), p. 13; B. A. Corry, *Money, Savings and Investment in English Economics, 1800–1850* (London: St. Martins Press, 1962), p. 125.

[47] Ricardo, *Works,* VIII, 108–09; Malthus, *Principles,* p. 323, the latter work commenting on the review of *Nouveaux Principes* in the *Edinburgh Review.*

89

Malthus' subjective originality is established by the appearance of most of their common ideas in his correspondence with Ricardo[48] prior to the publication of *Nouveaux Principes* in 1819. Moreover, Malthus' analysis developed two important additional ideas not found in Sismondi: (1) a schedule concept of supply and demand, and (2) a growth theory and growth-promotion policy interwoven with his discussion of equilibrium income and general gluts.

Supply and Demand

A number of important features of the Sismondi-Malthus analysis are difficult to express without schedule concepts to distinguish an increase in quantity along a given function and an upward shift of the function itself. For example, an increase in "demand" was for both an increased willingness to make a "sacrifice"[49] to obtain the desired good. An increased quantity demanded, as during a period of overproduction, was not for them an increase in demand.[50] They also distinguished between increased investment at a given level of technology—where it "is in the nature of all such means of employing capital to become less and less advantageous"[51]—and in-

---

[48] For example, the emphasis on future rather than present produce (Ricardo, *Works*, VI, 111–12), on the fact that though the market can "always" be cleared, "it makes an infinite difference" whether this is done under conditions which "encourage production" or "discourage it" (*ibid.*, p. 303), a rejection of the insatiable wants argument as irrelevant (*ibid.*, p. 142; *ibid.*, VII, 122), and discussion of excess investment. (*ibid.*, VI, 155–56.)

[49] Malthus, *Principles*, pp. 366, 384, 403; *Nouveaux Principes*, II, 254, 259; see also *Richesse Commerciale*, I, 347.

[50] *Études*, II, 233, 403; Malthus, *Quarterly Review* (April 1823), 226–27; Malthus, *Principles*, p. 68.

[51] Ricardo, *Works*, VI, 167.

creased investment in response to technological advance;[52] in short, they distinguished a downward movement along the marginal product of capital curve and a shift outward of that curve. This idea had, of course, also appeared earlier in Lauderdale. Malthus further distinguished increased saving out of a given income and increased saving out of an increased income.[53] While condemning "excess saving" as a quantity, Malthus nevertheless wished to maximize the savings function in order to promote sustainable growth.[54]

As early as 1814, Ricardo observed to Malthus that "we do not attach the same meaning to the word demand."[55] The Ricardian meaning—quantity demanded—was referred to by Malthus as the "extent" of demand or the "effectual demand," sharply contrasted with the "intensity" of demand.[56] The extent of demand was simply the "quantity of commodity purchased."[57] Malthus said: ". . . it is not in the sense of mere extent of consumption that demand raises prices, because it is almost always when prices are lowest, that the extent of demand and consumption is the greatest."[58] By contrast, the "intensity" of demand was defined as: "The sacrifice which the demanders are able and willing to make in order to satisfy their wants. It is this species of demand alone which, compared with the supply, deter-

---

[52] Malthus, *Principles,* pp. 351–52; *Nouveaux Principes,* I, 247–48.

[53] Malthus, *Principles,* pp. 365, 367, 430.

[54] *Ibid.,* p. 60; see also [Samuel Bailey], *An Inquiry into those Principles respecting the Nature of Demand and the Necessity of Consumption lately advocated by Mr. Malthus,* pp. 53, 65.

[55] Ricardo, *Works,* VI, 129.

[56] Malthus, *Principles,* pp. 65n–66n; Malthus, *Definitions,* pp. 244–45.

[57] Malthus, *Definitions,* p. 244.

[58] Malthus, *Principles,* p. 68.

mines prices and values."[59] The meaning of an *increased* demand in these terms was a willingness "to make a greater sacrifice than before" to obtain a desired good,[60] or as a contemporary paraphrased Malthus, "a disposition to give more for the quantity actually taken, or to buy more at the same rate"[61]—a shift outward of the demand schedule.

Similarly, supply was defined in terms of the necessary "conditions" of the supply, or in schedule terms.[62] Malthus noted that cost of production as a condition of supply was usually an important factor in price determination,[63] but that supply was the more general principle, which applied even in cases where cost of production was irrelevant for one reason or another.[64] The Ricardian determination of value by cost of production for competitively produced commodities in long-run equilibrium was seen by Malthus as only a special case of the more general determination of value by supply and demand, the latter principle holding for monopolized as well as competitively produced commodities,[65] and in the "intervals" of adjustment as well as in long-run equilibrium.[66]

Malthus' conception of demand was not only in schedule terms but was in essence based on utility. J. B. Say has generally been credited with being the leading early pioneer in the development of the utility theory of value.

[59] Malthus, *Definitions,* p. 245.

[60] Malthus, *Principles,* pp. 65n–66n.

[61] [Samuel Bailey], *Observations on Certain Verbal Disputes,* p. 65.

[62] Malthus, *Principles,* pp. 71, 73, 74; Malthus, *Definitions,* pp. 242, 243; Malthus, *Measure of Value,* pp. 17, 19.

[63] Malthus, *Principles,* pp. 71, 72, 74.

[64] *Ibid.,* pp. 70, 71, 74.

[65] *Ibid.,* pp. 70, 71.

[66] *Ibid.,* pp. 65n–66n, 72; *Definitions,* p. 221; *Measure of Value,* p. 44.

However, he was characteristically shifting in his concept of utility, so that it sometimes represented the economic agent's own subjective evaluation and sometimes Say's own idea of what was "really" useful.[67] Malthus' "estimation" corresponds more closely with the modern concept of utility, since it depends entirely on the economic agent's own subjective feelings.[68] Malthus objected to the *word* "utility" and to its ambiguous usage in Say's theory of value,[69] but was by no means opposed to the utility theory of value in substance. Rather, he added a needed clarification of its meaning as wholly subjective. Malthus also derived macroeconomic conclusions similar to those of Sismondi: "Unless the estimation in which an object is held, or the value which an individual or the society places on it when obtained, adequately compensates the sacrifice which has been made to obtain it, such wealth will not be produced in future."[70]

Value therefore had two meanings for Malthus, or could be viewed in two ways: (1) the exchange-ratio between goods, and/or (2) the estimation in which a

[67] Say began by defining utility as the "capability of certain things to satisfy the various wants of mankind." *Treatise on Political Economy*, p. 66. Yet utility was later used to mean "objects of rational desire" rather than "artificial wants," *ibid.*, p. 208; see also pp. 402, 413, 414n.

[68] Malthus, *Principles*, pp. 300, 301; *Definitions*, pp. 207–08, 235.

[69] *Definitions*, pp. 22, 250, 251; *Quarterly Review* (January 1824), 298, 304; letter to Say in J. B. Say, *Oeuvres Diverses de J. B. Say*, p. 507. Say defended himself by reverting to his original definition of subjective utility, *ibid*, pp. 503, 504, 512; [J. B. Say], *"Definitions in Political Economy, etc.,"* *Revue encyclopedique*, XXXIII (February 1827), 495. The basis for ascribing the latter article (identified only by initials) to Say is his stated intention to review this book in this journal: *Oeuvres Diverses*, p. 506.

[70] Malthus, *Principles*, pp. 361, 302.

single good was held, relative to the disutility of obtaining it.[71] He rejected the idea of value as solely relating one commodity to another, since "in a country where there were only deer, and no beavers or other products to compare them with," the esteem in which deer were held could nevertheless be indicated by the fact that "any man would willingly walk fifty miles in order to get one."[72] In short, "if the real value of a commodity be considered as synonymous with the estimation in which it is held, such value must be measured by the quantity of labour which it will command."[73] This enabled him to introduce the concept of the value of *aggregate* output—"the value of the whole produce"[74]—which was to prove important in his discussion of general gluts and which was to puzzle and exasperate his critics.[75]

Obviously values defined as exchange ratios cannot rise or fall as a whole—a truism which Malthus repeatedly acknowledged.[76] But to "confine the term value" to "the mere relation of one commodity to another" would be "to render it pre-eminently futile and useless,"[77] at least for his purposes. While an increased quantity of output normally tended to represent an increased "value" or labor command, this was not so during a period of overproduction or glut when "a mere abundance of commodities" would not be capable of "em-

[71] Malthus, *Definitions,* pp. 235, 251.

[72] *Ibid.,* p. 128.   [73] *Ibid.,* p. 117.

[74] Malthus, *Principles,* pp. 362, 365, 388, 394, 413, 426; Ricardo, *Works,* VI, 131; *Quarterly Review* (January 1824), 315.

[75] [John Stuart Mill], "Political Economy," *Westminster Review* (January 1825), 224; [Samuel Bailey], *Observations on Certain Verbal Disputes in Political Economy,* pp. 22, 59.

[76] Malthus, *Definitions in Political Economy,* p. 64, for example.

[77] *Ibid.,* p. 186.

ploying the same number of workmen"[78] that produced it. At such times "the produce of a country estimated in the labour which it will command falls in value."[79] There is thus an "insufficiency of demand"[80] without any leakage from the circular flow. A general glut in these terms is a simple extension of a partial glut: ". . . it is quite obvious that this mass of commodities, compared with the labour with which it is to be exchanged, may fall in value from a glut just as any one commodity falls in value from an excess of supply."[81]

Disproportionality (the cause of temporary depressions in the Ricardian system)[82] is unnecessary for Malthus' denial of the proposition that an increased quantity supplied will necessarily entail an increased quantity demanded:

> It is asserted that effectual demand is nothing more than the offering of one commodity in exchange for another, which has cost the same quantity of labour. But is this all that is necessary to effectual demand? Though each commodity may have cost the same quantity of labour in its production, and they may be exactly equivalent to each other in exchange, yet why may not both be so plentiful as not to command more labour, than they have cost, that is, to yield no profit, and in this case would the demand for them be effectual? Would it be such as to encourage their continued production? Unquestionably not. Their relation to each other may not have changed; but their

[78] Malthus, *Principles,* p. 396.
[79] *Ibid.,* p. 364.
[80] Malthus, *Definitions,* p. 247.
[81] Malthus, *Principles,* p. 316.
[82] Ricardo, *Works,* II, 305, 306, 366, 413, 415; *ibid.,* VIII, 277, 334n.

relation to the wants of society, and their relation to labour, may have experienced a most important change.[83]

Malthus has been credited, first by Keynes and then by later interpreters, with developing a monetary analysis which enabled him to expose the weakness of the barter analysis of the supporters of Say's Law.[84] However, none of Malthus' major works contained any systematic monetary analysis, and his assertions of the importance of money went little further than pointing out that classical analysis was descriptively inadequate without it.[85] In essence his analysis was as nonmonetary as that of the supporters of Say's Law, or of Sismondi, Lauderdale, Spence, and Chalmers, all of whom strongly emphasized their nonmonetary approach. The only difference was that the latter continued Adam Smith's denunciations of popular misconceptions of money,[86] whereas Malthus felt that economists' "zeal to correct the absurd notions of the mercantile classes"[87] was overdone. It was little more than a matter of taste.

Despite the glut theorists' statements (paralleling those of the orthodox) that there was no hoarding,[88] that money was "immediately" respent,[89] that the velocity of

[83] Malthus, *Principles*, p. 317.

[84] J. M. Keynes, *Essays in Biography*, p. 116; Paul Lambert, *L'Oeuvre de John Maynard Keynes*, I, 78.

[85] Malthus, *Principles*, p. 324n; *Definitions*, pp. 54, 60n.

[86] Lauderdale, *Nature and Origin of Public Wealth*, p. 4; *Nouveaux Principes*, I, 54, 120, II, 15, 51, 52; *Political Economy*, pp. 81, 82; *Études*, II, 317, 318, 357, 358, 360, 395, 428.

[87] Ricardo, *Works*, VI, 21.

[88] Chalmers, *On Political Economy*, p. 96; Malthus, *Definitions*, p. 238; Malthus, *Principles*, p. 38; Spence, *Tracts on Political Economy*, pp. 30–31.

[89] *Nouveaux Principes*, I, 278; *Political Economy*, p. 79.

96

circulation was constant,[90] they also referred to idle balances accumulating during a general glut. Their approach to money, like that of the orthodox, tended to be one of formal de-emphasis in implicity long-run terms combined with ad-hoc recognitions of the role of its short-run fluctuations. While Sismondi thought it would be irrational to allow "useless stagnation" of funds because of the "lost interest,"[91] nevertheless during a crisis circulating money contracts because "anyone prefers to lose the interest on a certain sum" rather than risk the principal during a period of great temporary uncertainty.[92] His statements implying a (long-run) stability of monetary velocity[93] did not prevent Sismondi from saying that velocity declined during crises,[94] or from advocating a controlled reflation at such times.[95] Lauderdale likewise presented analysis which proceeded in real terms in order to avoid the complications of "overgrown financial arrangements,"[96] but he too observed that money might "for a time" be "allowed to lie dormant" in banks.[97] Malthus also denied hoarding as a general behavioral characteristic,[98] but mentioned in passing idle balances during depressions.[99] The reasons for this apparently inconsistent treatment of money require some elaboration.

[90] *Nouveaux Principes*, II, 82, 95; *Political Economy*, p. 92.

[91] *Nouveaux Principes*, II, 82; see also *Richesses Commerciale*, I, 133n.

[92] *Nouveaux Principes*, II, 83; *Études*, II, 394.

[93] *Ibid.*, II, 10, 44, 80, 82, 95.

[94] *Ibid.*, II, 83.

[95] *Ibid.*, II, 84.

[96] Lauderdale, *Nature and Origin of Public Wealth*, p. 212.

[97] Lauderdale, *Three Letters to the Duke of Wellington*, p. 75.

[98] Malthus, *Principles*, pp. 38, 325; *Definitions*, p. 238.

[99] *Definitions*, p. 66.

Both the orthodox and the dissenting economists of the period under consideration put much more emphasis than do modern economists on causation in a sequential sense rather than in the sense of simultaneous determination of the values of related variables. Thus, for example, Ricardo was very much concerned, in viewing commodities which had changed in value relative to each other, to discover which one had "really" changed, i.e., where the change had *originated* in some change of production costs, etc.[100] The glut theorists approached money in much the same way. Money movements were not an "original cause" or the "mainspring" of the phenomena under discussion,[101] because "the variations have originated in the supplies of commodities, and not in the supplies of the currencies."[102] Money might lie idle *after* a general glut because the rate of return on real capital was below its long-run supply price, tending to keep the interest rate on money capital also below its long-run supply price. Another reaction might be an export of capital[103] if the glut were purely domestic. But these were peripheral monetary *effects,* not causes, the "necessary consequences" of "overproduction and overtrading."[104]

The possible further consequences of these idle balances and international money movements were not traced out, and this minor role of money was not a point of contention with the supporters of Say's Law. J. B. Say, Robert Torrens, and John Stuart Mill also referred to

[100] *Ricardo,* Works, I, 17–18.

[101] [T. R. Malthus], "Depreciation of Paper Currency," *Edinburgh Review,* XVII, No. XXIV (February 1811), 359, 343; see also 342, 344.

[102] Ricardo, *Works,* VI, 41.

[103] George William Zinke, "Six Letters from Malthus to Pierre Prevost," *Journal of Economic History* (November 1942), 178.

[104] Malthus, *Definitions,* p. 66.

credit contraction or idle money balances during depressions.[105] The latter's early essays also dealt with deficient money demand, and the effect of increased spending in activating unemployed resources[106]—arguments which might have more claim to being forerunners of Keynesion economics than did those of the glut theorists.

Money was assumed by Malthus to represent a relatively stable labor command,[107] even though commodities did not, so that money was symptomatic of "estimation"[108] and changes in the money price of the aggregate output would indicate whether its "value" changed proportionally with its quantity, that is, whether it was a sustainable level of production. But again money was an effect or derivative symptom rather than a causal factor that changed the ultimate result.

Development, Consumption, and Saving

For Malthus economic development was "the grand object of all inquiries in Political Economy."[109] The discussion of equilibrium and the possibility of general gluts in the final chapter of his *Principles* was only part, and not the main part, of the purpose of that chapter. The "principal object of the present inquiry," according to Malthus, was to explain the "progress of wealth," and

---

[105] J. B. Say, *Letters to Malthus*, pp. 45n–46n; J. B. Say, *Cours Complet*, I, 475; John Stuart Mill, *Essays on Some Unsettled Questions of Political Economy*, p. 72; Robert Torrens, *An Essay on the Production of Wealth*, p. 421.

[106] John Stuart Mill, *Essay on Some Unsettled Questions of Political Economy*.

[107] Malthus, *Definitions*, pp. 164, 171; Malthus, *Principles*, pp. 385, 393.

[108] Malthus, *Principles*, pp. 393–94; *Definitions*, pp. 166, 178–79.

[109] Ricardo, *Works*, VII, 122.

as a practical matter to discover "the most immediate and effective stimulants to the continued creation and progress of wealth."[110] The discussion of saving and consumption must be understood in the context of this concern. For example: "But we have yet to inquire what is the state of things which generally disposes a nation to accumulate; and further, what is the state of things which tends to make that accumulation the most effective and lead to a further and continued increase of capital and wealth."[111]

A mere addition to the quantity saved might "tend prematurely to diminish the motive for accumulation,"[112] i.e., "profits" or interest, whereas Malthus was concerned with promoting "the permanent increase of wealth,"[113] with maintaining "the motive to further accumulation,"[114] and with the "causes which encourage or discourage the increase of wealth."[115] He made an analogy between population growth and capital growth (later repeated and elaborated by Thomas Chalmers) which argued that (1) an equilibrium increase of either promoted economic development and well-being, but that (2) an increase beyond limits of sustainability existing at any given time would lead only to reduced earnings and subsequent contraction of the quantity supplied even though (3) what was an "excessive" quantity at one time might be a sustainable or even a deficient quantity at a later period under more favorable conditions.[116]

Despite the "obvious desirableness" of increasing the size of the population, it would be "useless and foolish

[110] Malthus, *Principles*, p. 310.   [111] *Ibid.*, p. 314.
[112] *Ibid.*, p. 328; Ricardo, *Works* IX, 20.
[113] Malthus, *Principles*, p. 330.   [114] *Ibid.*, p. 398.
[115] *Quarterly Review* (January 1824), 332.
[116] *Ibid.*, p. 328; Chalmers, *On Political Economy*, Chapter IV, passim.

directly to encourage the birth of more children" without a sufficient demand for labor, since this would only result in "increased misery and mortality with little or no final increase of population"; and "the same kind of reasoning ought, I think, to be applied to the rate of profits and the progress of capital."[117] Therefore it "is equally vain, with a view to a permanent increase of wealth, to push saving to excess, as to push population to excess."[118] Reasoning strongly suggesting the cobweb theorem was applied to both population and capital.[119] Yet Malthus was in favor of increasing the *desired* saving, for having "the greatest permanent annual increase in the value of the materials of capital."[120] This should not be obscured by his attacks on excess quantities saved.

Consumption, or "unproductive consumption" to distinguish it from investment ("productive consumption"), must also be viewed within a growth-oriented framework, and as a function rather than a quantity. Malthus regarded the "prosperity to spend what is actually possessed" as a minor consideration, in the context of his concern for growth: "The main part of the question respecting the wants of mankind, relates to their power

[117] Malthus, *Principles,* p. 328.

[118] *Ibid.,* 1st edn., p. 573; see also p. 375.

[119] T. R. Malthus, *An Essay on the Principle of Population,* Everyman edn. (London: J. M. Dent, 1958), I, 15–16, 17; *ibid.,* II, 36–37.

[120] *The Measure of Value,* p. 60. "The central preoccupation of Malthus is therefore to maximize the rate of saving." Translated from B. J. Gordon and T. S. Jilek, "Malthus, Keynes et l'apport de Lauderdale," *Revue d'économie politique,* 75, No. 1 (January-February, 1965), 120. Gordon and Jilek have been mistakenly criticized for this conclusion by R. D. C. Black, "Parson Malthus, The General and the Captain," *Economic Journal,* LXXVII, No. 305 (March 1967), 62, and by Paul Lambert, "Lauderdale, Malthus et Keynes," *Revue d'économie politique* (January-February 1966), 56.

of calling forth the exertions necessary to acquire the means of expenditure."[121]

Malthus could therefore call for both greater consumption and greater savings, not as quantities nor as functions of current income, but as alternatives to leisure or "indolence."[122] In short, Malthus wished to increase the marginal rate of substitution of both consumption and saving (i.e., real income), for leisure. The *ex post* quantity consumed (productive plus unproductive) would always equal the quantity produced, but Malthus could nevertheless refer to the possibility that production could be "in great excess above consumption" in an *ex ante* sense, this latter sense being clearly indicated by the phrases "will to consume" and "power to produce" used in the same context.[123]

Malthus agreed with James Mill's proposition that consumption (aggregate demand) was coextensive with production could be maintained if one "strictly adhered" to the definition of consumption as "quantity consumed" (both productively and unproductively), but this was "a truism equally obvious and futile."[124] The question to which Malthus addressed himself was not the clearing of the market at a given time but the maintenance of the ongoing process of economic growth.[125]

[121] Malthus, *Principles,* p. 403.

[122] "The tendency to consume is powerfully counteracted by the love of indolence. . . . It is true that wealth produces wants; but it is still a more important truth that wants produce wealth." *Ibid.,* 1st edn., p. 586; see also pp. 468–70, and 2nd edn., pp. 401–02.

[123] *Ibid.,* p. 7.   [124] Malthus, *Definitions,* p. 47.

[125] The interpretation which appeared in an earlier paper has been criticized on grounds that Malthus believed consumption to be less than production (R. D. C. Black, *op. cit.,* p. 62). However, it should be apparent from the statements cited in notes 123 and 124 that Malthus did not mean that the quantity

Malthus' desire to maintain "unproductive consumers" such as absentee landlords, tax-supported sinecurists, etc., was not based on a naive belief that a mere transfer of demand from productive workers and entrepreneurs was a net increase of aggregate demand, as his critics seemed to assume.[126] Malthus, like Sismondi, regarded the workers as unwilling to submit to much continued labor beyond the point where their conventional necessities could be obtained.[127] He regarded entrepreneurs as similarly disposed to weigh the utility of goods and the disutility of work.[128] However, the weighing of goods against leisure at the margin does not enter the calculations of those living on "fixed money revenue, obtained by inheritance, or with little or no trouble,"[129] and their uninhibited spending tends to keep the customary standard of living higher than it would be otherwise. Moreover, the taxes and other transfer payments to them from the producing classes make it necessary for the latter to work harder in order to reach this standard.[130] Thus in the Malthusian system the income of unproductive con-

---

consumed would be less than the quantity produced, which was the substance of my argument even though my phrasing was not as precise as it should have been. Thomas Sowell, "The General Glut Controversy Reconsidered," *Oxford Economic Papers,* November 1963, pp. 198–99.

[126] J. B. Say, *Letters to Malthus,* p. 30; J. B. Say, *Treatise on Political Economy,* p. 141; [John R. McCulloch], *Edinburgh Review* (March 1821), 122–23; Ricardo, *Works,* II, 207, 423, 436, VIII, 301.

[127] *Nouveaux Principes,* I, 84, 110, II, 265; Malthus, *Principles,* p. 334; see also Malthus, *An Essay on the Principle of Population,* Everyman edn., II, 25.

[128] Malthus, *Principles,* p. 335.   [129] *Ibid.,* p. 379.

[130] *Ibid.,* p. 409. Similar reasoning appeared in McCulloch, *Principles of Political Economy,* pp. 62–63. Malthus' argument was objected to on moral grounds in [Samuel Bailey], *Observations on Certain Disputes,* pp. 66–67.

sumers is not an economic rent, but is rather a necessary supply price of productive efforts, though not the efforts of the recipients. Malthus recognized the offsetting disadvantage of keeping potential producers idle but regarded the optimum proportions of these transfers as an empirical question.[131]

Unproductive consumption was important in still another sense. Because total output equaled total spending and the latter consisted of productive and unproductive consumption (investment and consumption in modern terms), unproductive consumption, as the only alternative to investment, was necessary to continue "uninterrupted" the "motives to production,"[132] that is, to prevent excess savings from driving down the rate of return below the supply price of loanable funds.

Population and Employment

While the logic of the Sismondi-Malthus glut theories can be illustrated with a model in which equilibrium prevails initially in both capital and labor markets, Malthus shared the prevailing opinion derived from Adam Smith that wages were in fact usually above the "subsistence" level that represented long-run equilibrium.[133] This meant that continuous growth, with continuously increasing demand for labor, was necessary to sustain the existing wage level with full employment. Although the long-run supply curve of labor was infinitely elastic at the subsis-

[131] George William Zinke, "Six letters from Malthus to Pierre Prevost," *Journal of Economic History* (November 1942), 180–81; Malthus, *Principles*, pp. 409–10.

[132] Ricardo, *Works*, IX, 20.

[133] T. R. Malthus, *Principles*, pp. 223–24; Adam Smith, *The Wealth of Nations*, Modern Library edn., pp. 69–71, 74–75; Ricardo, *Works*, I, 94–95.

tence level (S_L in Figure 2), the time lag necessary for a new generation of workers to grow up (or for reduced mortality to make the existing generation larger than it would be otherwise) creates a rising short-run supply curve of labor at any given point on the long-run curve:

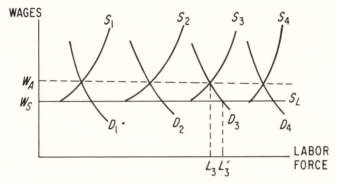

Figure 2

(S_1, S_2, S_3, S_4). With demand for labor continuously increasing (D_1, D_2, D_3, D_4) the actual short-run wages (W_A) may remain above the long-run subsistence wages (W_S) indefinitely. When economic development slows down or stops—permanently in the Ricardian "stationary state" or temporarily in the Sismondi-Malthus glut theory—the labor force continues to increase (the short-run supply curve flattens out to coincide with the long-run curve). The wages fund per capita declines, implying either reduced wages for all or unemployment with downward wage rigidity. Sismondi argued that "the wages of each worker diminish"[134] although he also inconsistently referred to unemployment at such times.[135] For Malthus, however, unemployment was "a most painful but almost unavoidable preliminary to a fall in the

[134] *Nouveaux Principes*, I, 247.   [135] *Ibid.*, II, 271.

105

money wages of labor."[136] Therefore, for a time, the employed workers might receive above-subsistence and above-equilibrium wages, while other workers were unemployed.[137] The important point is that in the Malthusian system the mere cessation of growth causes unemployment among a population which is growing "under its former impulse"[138] in response to the above-subsistence wages of an earlier period, and has increased beyond the point where it can be employed at prevailing wages. Therefore "this stagnation must throw the rising generation out of employment."[139] The problem is one of "employing an increasing population" under these conditions.[140] If the demand for labor stopped at D_3 and wages remained rigid at W_A, then unemployment L_3L_3' would exist, assuming D_3 to be a rectangular hyperbola as suggested by the wages fund doctrine.[141]

The contrast between the Malthusian population theory, in which the population was pressing against the means of subsistence, and the later general glut theory, in which "a country is always liable to an increase in the funds for the maintenance of labour faster than the increase of population,"[142] was pointed out by contempo-

---

[136] Malthus, *Principles,* p. 393.

[137] George William Zinke, "Six Letters from Malthus to Pierre Prevost," *Journal of Economic History* (November 1942), 185; Malthus, *An Essay on the Principle of Population,* Everyman edn., II, 138.

[138] Malthus, *Principles,* p. 417.

[139] Ricardo, *Works,* IX, 20.   [140] *Ibid.,* p. 10.

[141] That is, the aggregate real wages received by the employed workers would be equal to the aggregate real wages which would have been received if the total labor force were employed, and this is sufficient to support a population L_3', which is the population which will tend to exist if the less than reproductive population produced by the unemployed is offset by the more than reproductive population produced by those employed at above-subsistence wages.

[142] Malthus, *Principles,* p. 320.

rary critics as well as by subsequent commentators.[143]
Despite the apparent symmetry between population
growth and capital growth in Malthus and Chalmers,
the Malthusian population theory turned precisely on an
asymmetry between them: that the former's potential
rate of increase was always greater than that of the latter.
For wages to remain above subsistence in the manner
set forth by Adam Smith (Figure 2) does not in itself
invalidate the Malthusian population theory. But if, a
generation later, wages continue above subsistence it
means that, contrary to Malthus, population growth was
not limited by the means of subsistence during the inter-
vening period, which was sufficient for any increment
to population to reach labor force age and force wages
back down again through competition. Yet Malthus'
Principles gave examples from history in which a rise
in living standards persisted for more than a single
generation.[144]

Sismondi was more consistent. He rejected the Malthusian population theory as containing both "error" and
"confusion."[145] Sismondi accepted the classical doctrine
of an infinitely elastic long-run supply of labor at subsistence,[146] but argued that people may continue living
"in happiness and abundance" indefinitely,[147] which
would be impossible in the long run if population grew
faster than the food supply whenever there was room to
do so. The infinitely elastic supply of labor says that population will continue to grow as long as wages are above
the subsistence level, but says nothing about the *rate* at

[143] J. B. Say, *Letters to Malthus,* pp. 27–28, for example.
[144] Malthus, *Principles,* pp. 228, 229, 250.
[145] Sismondi, *Political Economy,* p. 116; Sismondi, *Nouveaux Principes,* II, 181.
[146] Sismondi, *Political Economy,* p. 114; Sismondi, *Political Economy and the Philosophy of Government,* p. 228.
[147] Sismondi, *Nouveaux Principes,* II, 193.

which it will grow, either absolutely or relative to the rate of increase of the food supply. The Malthusian geometrical increase of population and arithmetical increase of food was dismissed by Sismondi as "completely sophistical" because it compared "the possible increase" of population with "the positive increase of food."[148] Comparing them on the same bases, the *actual* growth of population was restrained by the will so as not to exceed that of the means of subsistence,[149] and the *abstract potential* of food growth was greater than that of the population (since the other living things which served as man's food usually had more offspring and shorter reproductive cycles).[150] On a *probabilistic* basis, Sismondi argued, the means of subsistence tend to increase faster than the population.[151] He saw the fatal ambiguities in the Malthusian discussions of "tendencies" (in historical, potential, and probabilistic senses) long before Whately or Senior, to whom this discovery is usually credited.[152]

---

[148] Sismondi, *Political Economy,* p. 114; Sismondi, *Nouveaux Principes,* II, 182.

[149] Sismondi, *Nouveaux Principes,* II, 169, 170, 183.

[150] *Ibid.,* pp. 181–82; Sismondi, *Political Economy,* pp. 117–18.

[151] Sismondi, *Political Economy,* p. 23n; Sismondi, *Nouveaux Principes,* I, 97.

[152] The later writings of Whately and Senior on this point were, however, somewhat clearer and more systematic. Richard Whately, *Introductory Lectures on Political Economy* (London: B. Fellowes, 1832), pp. 248–50; Nassau W. Senior, *Two Lectures on Population,* pp. 36, 56, 58, 77. Among those crediting Whately and/or Senior with having discovered this ambiguity in Malthus are Edwin Cannan, *A History of the Theories of Production and Distribution in English Political Economy from 1775 to 1848* (London: Rivington, Percival & Co., 1894), pp. 159n, 170–71; Mark Blaug, *Ricardian Economics,* pp. 111, 112, 113; Kenneth Smith, *The Malthusian Controversy,* pp. 183, 183n, 184–89, 213.

Thomas Chalmers

Thomas Chalmers (1780–1847) did not set out to expound a system of economics,[153] but only to clarify various points and issues, and his chief work, *On Political Economy* (1832), reflected the strengths and weaknesses of that approach. It was more successful in apt illustrations of particular aspects of the general glut argument than in developing its logical structure or in showing how its constituent parts fitted together. Chalmers made no claims to originality, and was, in fact, a follower of Malthus not only in the theory of general glut but in population theory and policy and in the desire to promote economic development by overcoming "indolence" with new "desires." His contribution was primarily one of clarification and elaboration, which was needed in view of the ambiguities and missing links in Malthus' exposition.

A central feature of Chalmers' writing was the development of Malthus' analogy between population growth and capital accumulation. After chapters on "the increase and limit of food" and "the increase and limit of employment," there was a chapter on "the increase and limit of capital" followed with one demonstrating "the parallel between population and capital, both in respect of their limits and their powers of expansion."[154] Just as population is limited "by the impossibility of labourers being subsisted beneath a certain rate of wages" so investment "is limited by the impossibility of capital being supported beneath a certain rate of profit."[155] The maintenance of the supply price of either was dependent upon not exceeding a given quantity of

[153] Thomas Chalmers, *On Political Economy*, pp. 551, 553.
[154] *Ibid.*, pp. 1, 30, 75, 106.
[155] *Ibid.*, p. 107.

either at a given time. Chalmers was more explicit than Malthus had been in showing that "unproductive consumption" was simply a means of keeping up the profit rate by restraining the rate of investment, just as the desire for a high standard of living by workers would tend to restrain the rate of population growth: "We are abundantly familiar with the idea, that the rate of wages is dependent on the average standard of enjoyment among labourers. But we have not been so accustomed to think of the rate of profit, as depending on the average standard of enjoyment among capitalists. Nevertheless, it is actually so."[156]

While the maximum quantity of population or capital consistent with the maintenance of its supply price was limited as of a given time, this limit itself tended to expand over time with economic development. Though "both are greatly short, at present, of that magnitude which they may yet attain in the course of ages; both may press at all times on a slowly retiring limit."[157] To exceed this limit was to produce an "insufficient wage" in the one case and "insufficient profit" in the other.[158] However, this was unlikely in the case of capital to produce secular stagnation because capitalists would not "continue" and "persist" in extending their investment and production after they "come to find" that it is unprofitable.[159] Chalmers' reasoning was in terms of short-run period analysis: "If this return be not an adequate one, the capital is not replaced; and, after a single revolution of the economic cycle, it again starts in diminished magnitude."[160]

[156] *Ibid.*, pp. 90–91.
[157] *Ibid.*, p. 136. ". . . capital is hemmed on all sides by a slowly receding boundary." *Ibid.*, p. 105.
[158] *Ibid.*, p. 136; also 80, 82, 110.
[159] *Ibid.*, p. 146.   [160] *Ibid.*, p. 82.

In his frequently repeated references to the analogy between population growth and capital growth,[161] Chalmers argued that "it is not the object of wise policy, to stimulate, beyond the natural incitements to their production, the increase of either."[162] There were such "checks and stimulants" in the markets that "the economic machine might, with all safety, be left to its own movements."[163] There should be "no artificial fostering" of growth, which can "be left to itself,"[164] to "spontaneous forces,"[165] and to "the guidance of individual interest."[166] His objection to the "delusive confidence"[167] inspired by Say's Law was that it provided a rationale for deliberately trying to increase capital and output "to the uttermost."[168] Any attempt to move toward "indefinite parsimony" was an attempt to achieve something that "never can be realized,"[169] not in the paradox-of-thrift sense sometimes attributed to this argument in Malthus, but explicitly because "it would speedily be checked" by falling profits.[170] With Chalmers, as with the other glut theorists, there were no losses from the circular flow such as those necessary for a paradox of thrift. Money was not hoarded, and whatever was not used for consumption was used for investment and was "equally spent in either way."[171] Failure to cover cost was the key element in Chalmers: "We shall at length come to a limit, beyond which the expense incurred in the fabrication must exceed the expense of the thing fabricated."[172] No distinction was made here between *ex*

---

[161] *Ibid.*, pp. 80, 81, 83, 90–91, 92, 108–09, 130, 136, 559, 562.
[162] *Ibid.*, p. 108.   [163] *Ibid.*, p. 116.   [164] *Ibid.*, p. 125.
[165] *Ibid.*, pp. 125, 126.   [166] *Ibid.*, p. 131.
[167] *Ibid.*, pp. 157, 161.   [168] *Ibid.*, p. 168.
[169] *Ibid.*, p. 145.   [170] *Ibid.*, p. 146.   [171] *Ibid.*, p. 96.
[172] *Ibid.*, p. 158.

post expenses actually incurred and *ex ante* supply prices, though it is clear from other parts of the argument that the latter were intended. But the failure to make this unmistakably clear was a crucial weakness in an argument which had no leakages from the circular flow.

Say's Law, for Chalmers, was "the idea that capital may, by the operation of parsimony and good management, be extended *ad infinitum,*"[173] and that "the simple act of preparing commodities, and placing them as it were on one side of an exchange, will, through the operation of stimulus, call forth into existence equivalent commodities on the other side of it."[174] Like most economists who discussed the issue of the indefinite expansion of investment during the classical period, Chalmers did not distinguish its short-run meaning, with given technology and tastes, from its meaning in a longer historical period with changing technology and tastes. However, it is clear from his discussions in other contexts within the same work that he understood this basic distinction and that his condemnation applied to the short-run doctrine. He failed, however, to see that others could have meant it in a longer run historical sense, or, more likely, not have thought it through enough to have specified any given span.

Unlike Lauderdale, Sismondi, and Malthus, who were concerned about the policy implications of Say's Law, Chalmers said that "it is not in opposition to any apprehended practical evil, but in opposition to a theory" that he opposed it.[175] Chalmers had "no alarm for the effect of economic theories on the habits of individuals" although he observed that it would be regrettable if such

[173] *Ibid.,* p. 35.
[174] *Ibid.,* pp. 60–61.
[175] *Ibid.,* p. 146.

theories "led our capitalists to spend more, or to spare more, than they would spontaneously."[176]

Chalmers attacked the belief that an increased quantity supplied would automatically create an increased (schedule of) demand, which in turn would mean that any initially given level of output was permanently sustainable. This interpretation of Say's Law, which has already been encountered in Lauderdale and Malthus, was held by Chalmers to apply only to the supply of food:

> Unlike to all other articles of merchandise, an increased supply of food is surely and speedily followed by an increased demand for it. It may be a drug in the market for a year or two; but though it should continue to be sent, in the same or in superior abundance, season after season, it will not remain so. The reason is, that, unlike to other commodities, it creates a market for itself. Through the medium of the stimulus given to population, it does what no other articles of merchandise can do—it multiplies its own consumers . . . for, whatever the additional number may be which it can feed, that number will rise to be fed by it.[177]

While this conception of the idea that supply creates its own demand appears grotesque to modern eyes, the classical exposition of Say's Law was by no means sufficiently clear or consistent to preclude it, or indeed, to avoid suggesting it.

Although Chalmers staunchly rejected hoarding as an explanatory variable (in a sequential causation sense), he nevertheless developed the idea that demand for money and "money illusion" were essential parts of the

[176] *Ibid.,* p. 148. [177] *Ibid.,* p. 65.

general glut theory: "When a consumer refuses certain commodities, it is not always, as has been assumed, because he wants to purchase others in preference but because he wants to reserve entire the general power of purchasing."[178] The capitalist as well as the consumer may also be interested in money as such: "The great object of the monied capitalist, in fact, is to add to the nominal amount of his fortune. . . . The importance of this object to him is not affected by fluctuations in the currency, or by a change in the real value of money."[179]

However, nothing was made of all this analytically, nor was it squared with his other statements that what was not spent in one way would be spent in another,[180] or that consideration of money merely "obscured" the analysis "without essentially changing it."[181] Like some other dissenting economists, he contributed more in the way of isolated insights than he did in systematic economics.

[178] *Ibid.*, p. 164.   [179] *Ibid.*, p. 165.
[180] *Ibid.*, p. 96.   [181] *Ibid.*, p. 158.

CHAPTER 4

The General Glut Controversy

THE CONTROVERSIES over Say's Law and the possibility of general gluts reached a peak of intensity and volume of output in the 1820's, involving every major economist of the period, in a way unrivaled until the Keynesian revolution of the 1930's. There were also earlier and later controversies on the same issues which extended well beyond the major figures covered here,[1] in addition to the later Marxian and other challenges which involved different issues. Like the later Keynesian controversies, the general glut controversy involved not only clashes of substantive propositions, but also clashes over empirical assumptions and policy views, misunderstandings, tautologies, shifting views—and some progress.

The supporters of Say's Law tended to interpret their critics as crude underconsumptionists, and repeatedly

[1] Lauderdale was criticized earlier by James Mill and by Henry Brougham, and replied to the latter; Spence was criticized by Mill and replied to him. In addition, a considerable journal literature on the subject continued on into the 1840's, by which time most of the major protagonists were dead. [James Mill], "Lord Lauderdale on Public Wealth," *Literary Journal,* IV, No. 1, (July 1804), 1–18; [Henry Brougham] "Lord Lauderdale on Public Wealth," *Edinburgh Review* (July 1804), 343–77; The Earl of Lauderdale, *Observations on the Review of His Inquiry into the Nature and Origin of Public Wealth.* James Mill, *Commerce Defended;* William Spence, *Agriculture the Source of the Wealth of Britain.* B. J. Gordon, "Say's Law, Effective Demand, and the Contemporary British Periodicals, 1820–1850," *Economica* (November 1965), 438–46.

pointed out to them that savings were not lost from the circular flow, being merely a transfer and not a net reduction of demand,[2] that what was saved would be as readily spent as what was consumed.[3] None of this was relevant to the arguments actually advanced by Lauderdale, Sismondi, and Malthus. The controversy over the role of consumption ("unproductive consumption") was also largely at crosspurposes. Malthus wished to increase the *desire* for consumption relative to the desire for leisure or "indolence,"[4] seeking through international trade, for example, to find additional goods which would "excite people to work" more and thereby promote development.[5] The proponents of Say's Law interpreted Malthus in simple quantity terms—an increased amount of consumption with a corresponding reduction of savings— and argued that (1) increased consumption spending was simply a transfer from investment spending, not a net increase of aggregate demand,[6] that (2) wants were "insatiable," so that no additional quantity of consumption need be urged, for whatever was produced would always be consumed,[7] that (3) there is no "indisposition to consume" but only an indisposition to produce,[8] and that (4) international trade presents no additional outlet

[2] James Mill, *Commerce Defended,* p. 76; Say, *Treatise on Political Economy,* p. 141; [John Stuart Mill], "War Expenditure," *Westminster Review,* II, No. III (July 1824), 38–39; Ricardo, *Works,* II, 309, 449; *ibid.,* VI, 133.

[3] James Mill, *Commerce Defended,* pp. 76–77, 92; James Mill, *Elements of Political Economy,* p. 226; [John Stuart Mill], "War Expenditure," *Westminster Review* (July 1824), 39.

[4] Malthus, *Principles,* 1st edn., p. 586; see also pp. 469–70.

[5] *Ibid.,* 2nd edn., p. 359.

[6] J. S. Mill, *Essays on Some Unsettled Questions of Political Economy,* p. 48.

[7] *Ibid.*

[8] *Edinburgh Review* (March 1821), 107; Say, *Treatise,* p. 143.

for production, but merely permits a lower cost of production to be attained or a different assortment of goods to be consumed.[9] None of this was relevant to the argument actually advanced by Malthus, which was that supply and demand would balance at a higher level of output when emulative motives were added to the desire for goods as such, and that additional new commodities would probably have a higher marginal utility than more of the old commodities;[10] he did not claim that aggregate demand would somehow be increased merely by being transferred, either domestically or internationally.

The belief that wants, as such, were insatiable was common to both sides in the general glut controversy.[11] But Sismondi and Malthus considered people's desires for goods precisely in relation to their willingness to make the "sacrifices"[12] which were necessary to produce them. In this sense, wants were clearly not insatiable, and sustainable output was therefore not unlimited, nor limited only by the marginal cost of subsistence, as in the Ricardian model. John Stuart Mill at one point inadvertently adopted the dissenters' approach by adding the proviso that goods be not only desired but that people "would work to possess them."[13] However, he showed

[9] James Mill, *Commerce Defended*, p. 116; Ricardo, *Works*, II, 395, 402–03.

[10] Malthus, *Principles*, pp. 359, 388.

[11] Ricardo, *Works*, I, 290–91, 387; Say, *Letters to Malthus*, p. 23; J. S. Mill, *Principles of Political Economy*, Ashley edn., p. 68; *ibid.*, Toronto edn., 67–68; Lauderdale, *Nature and Origin of Public Wealth*, pp. 309, 315; William Spence, *Tracts on Political Economy*, p. 187; *Nouveaux Principes*, II, 274; *Études*, I, 64; Sismondi, *Political Economy*, p. 20; Malthus, *Principles*, p. 47; Chalmers, *On Political Economy*, p. 185.

[12] Malthus, *Principles*, pp. 302, 303, 366, 384, 403; *Nouveaux Principes*, II, 254, 259; *Richesse Commerciale*, I, 347.

[13] J. S. Mill, *Essays on Some Unsettled Questions of Political Economy*, p. 73.

no awareness that this completely changed the conclusion that there were no limits (other than the Ricardian ones) to investment and output.

One of the curious by-products of the debates over the developmental role of consumption and savings was a model in which the propertied classes would forego all consumption above the level of "necessaries"—as the workers were assumed to do already—in order to maximize capital accumulation. Economists on both sides of the controversy used this model,[14] and reached the same analytical conclusions, though each side regarded these conclusions as a victory for its viewpoint. Each side assumed that the additional savings took the form of wage goods rather than fixed capital,[15] that—in Ricardo's words—"the funds for the maintenance of labour increase much more rapidly than population," in the short run, leading to "a fall of profits," after which producers "would cease to produce" on the same scale.[16] However, this did not "impugn the general principle" of Say's Law because it was a "temporary" situation (Ricardo), because supply and demand were still definitionally equal (James Mill), because the lowered rate of return on capital would automatically tend to reduce the excessive rate of investment (J. B. Say).[17]

While admitting that output would be above a sustainable level—under these very peculiar conditions—Ricardo asked, what of "the other question" whether the

[14] Williams Spence, *Tracts on Political Economy*, p. 157; *Nouveaux Principes*, I, 86–87; Malthus, *Principles*, pp. 319–20; Chalmers, *On Political Economy*, pp. 99, 139, 140; James Mill, *Elements of Political Economy*, pp. 235–36.

[15] Malthus, *Principles*, p. 323; Sismondi, *Political Economy*, p. 23; *Études*, I, 81n; Ricardo, *Works*, I, 293.

[16] Ricardo, *Works*, I, 293.

[17] Say, *Letters to Malthus*, p. 37.

commodities would "find purchasers" without a change of relative prices.[18] In short, the proponents of Say's Law tended to regard the central question as whether the market could always be cleared, given that goods were in the proper proportion to each other (as indicated by their unchanged relative prices), whatever might be their aggregate quantity. Sismondi and Malthus, on the other hand, argued repeatedly that the real question was not the ratio of goods to each other, but the ratio of goods as a whole to human desires,[19] or to the labor which people would expend to acquire them,[20] that is, the marginal utility of real income versus the marginal disutility of labor. This in turn meant that their central concern was not in clearing the market but in sustaining the existing level of production.

SUPPLY EQUALS DEMAND

The doctrine that supply creates its own demand was bound to have varied meanings in a period when there was no generally accepted definition of supply or demand, when schedule and quantity concepts were used by different economists and by the same economists at different times. This basic statement of Say's Law was interpreted in at least four distinct ways in the general glut controversy: (1) that quantity supplied equals quantity demanded, that (2) an increment to the quantity supplied would lead to an equal increment to the quantity demanded, that (3) an increment in quantity supplied

[18] Ricardo, *Works*, ii, 303–04.
[19] Malthus, *Definitions*, pp. 127, 128, 208, 208n; Malthus, *Principles*, p. 317; Malthus, *Measure of Value*, p. 7; *Nouveaux Principes*, ii, 255, 256.
[20] Malthus, *Definitions*, pp. 64, 208n; *Measure of Value*, p. 7; Malthus, *Principles*, pp. 316, 317, 384; *Quarterly Review* (April 1823), 232n; *Nouveaux Principes*, ii, 259–60.

would lead to a corresponding shift of the demand curve, and that (4) an increase in the supply function would lead to a corresponding increase in the demand function, so as to lead to a proportionate increase in realized aggregate output.

Quantity Supplied Equals Quantity Demanded

Supply obviously equals demand in quantity terms if only those goods actually traded are considered and any unsold excess ignored. This *ex post* accounting identity appeared in James Mill's *Commerce Defended,* where it was argued that "annual purchases and sales" will "always balance."[21] The difference between the *ex ante* and *ex post* meanings of such statements was later noted in Mill's *Analysis of the Human Mind,*[22] but without any reference to his own doctrine. McCulloch likewise declared that there cannot "be any *selling* without an equal *buying*," as part of his defense of Say's Law.[23] To Torrens supply and demand were "convertible" terms[24] and John Stuart Mill stated that the equality of supply and demand "is not a deduction of probability," but "possesses all the certainty of a mathematical demonstration," because it depends on "the very meaning of the words, demand and supply."[25] He continued to argue this way throughout his writings. The equality of supply and demand was true "by the metaphysical necessity of the case,"[26] and any

[21] James Mill, *Commerce Defended,* p. 82.
[22] James Mill, *Analysis of the Phenomena of the Human Mind,* ed. John Stuart Mill (London: Longmans, Green Reader and Dyer, 1869), II, 41.
[23] *Edinburgh Review* (March 1821), 108.
[24] *Ibid.* (October 1819), 470.
[25] *Westminster Review* (July 1824), 41.
[26] John Stuart Mill, *Essays on Some Unsettled Questions of Political Economy,* p. 69.

other view involved "inconsistency in its very conception" and was "essentially self-contradictory."[27]

J. B. Say's version of the doctrine that quantity supplied equals quantity demanded was somewhat different and emerged later in the controversy. Where supply exceeded demand *ex ante* and some goods had to be sold at less than cost-covering prices (i.e., below their supply prices), these latter goods were simply excluded from Say's definition of "production," which included sale at cost-covering prices.[28] Leaving aside those things which were "made inconsiderately" without really "producing" anything, Say concluded that "my doctrine on markets becomes complete."[29]

The point here is not to claim that Say's Law was purely an identity to its supporters. On the contrary, they did not clearly distinguish an identity from a behavioral equation, and drifted unconsciously back and forth between the two concepts, tending under polemical pressure to adopt the impregnable tautology.

Incremental Quantity Supplied Equals Incremental Quantity Demanded

This version of Say's Law, though apparently deducible from the first version, had in fact a separate rationale and a different substantive meaning. The supporters of

[27] John Stuart Mill, *Principles of Political Economy,* Ashley edn., pp. 557, 562, Toronto edn., pp. 571, 575.

[28] Say, *Cours Complet,* I, 345–46, II, 209; Say, *Traité d'économie politique,* 5th edn., p. 195. In earlier writings, "production" was simply the production of utility, but in the later writings, where the possibility of an above-equilibrium output was considered, it was made clear that production meant a *net* production of utility, deducting the disutility represented in the various costs of production.

[29] Say, *Oeuvres Diverses de J. B. Say,* p. 513.

121

Say's Law argued that when a producer increased his quantity supplied, it was because of, and to the extent of, the increased quantity of other goods which he desired. This was not an accounting identity but a behavioral theory in which the incremental quantity supplied equaled the incremental quantity demanded *ex ante*. This was true on the individual level, and therefore in the aggregate as well.[30]

In the Sismondi-Malthus model, in which labor is paid during production while capital receives a residual return which will be "realized" later,[31] the aggregate expectations of capital-suppliers can obviously exceed what they will in fact receive. This argument does not assume, as the Ricardians claimed, that producers produce "without a motive,"[32] or that they will "continue" the existing level of production,[33] but only that their initial anticipations may be disappointed. The Ricardian approach which tended to treat "costs of production" as cost actually incurred for past production ignored the possibility that these might differ from supply prices. This was not unreasonable in a Ricardian long-run model. The problem was that the Ricardians interpreted *others'* ideas in these Ricardian terms.

[30] James Mill, *Elements of Political Economy*, pp. 228, 231, 232; James Mill, *Commerce Defended*, p. 83; [John Stuart Mill], "War Expenditure," *Westminster Review* (July 1824), 41–42; [John Stuart Mill], "Political Economy," *Westminster Review* (January 1825), 230–31.

[31] *Nouveaux Principles*, I, 113.

[32] *Westminster Review* (July 1824), 42; Robert Torrens, *An Essay on the Production of Wealth*, pp. 228–29, 231; Ricardo, *Works*, I, 290; J. R. McCulloch, *Principles of Political Economy*, p. 144; J. S. Mill, *Essays on Some Unsettled Questions of Political Economy*, pp. 49, 53; *Edinburgh Review* (March 1821), 105.

[33] J. S. Mill, *Principles of Political Economy*, Ashley edn., p. 560; Toronto edn., p. 573.

Incremental Quantity Supplied Shifts the Demand Function

Lauderdale first advanced the argument that an increment to *agricultural* output "has a direct tendency to increase population," which in turn will increase the demand for food, and therefore "it is this branch of the property of mankind that alone appears capable of unlimited increase."[34] Say's Law was later to be interpreted by Malthus and Chalmers as an incorrect generalization of this reasoning to production as a whole. After reading Say's *Traité d'économie politique,* Malthus wrote to Ricardo: "I think the source of his error is, that he does not properly distinguish between the necessaries of life and other commodities,—the former create their own demand the latter not."[35] The same reasoning reappeared in Malthus' published writings, and later in Thomas Chalmers.[36]

Strange as it may seem today to have the proposition that supply creates its own demand interpreted in this way, J. B. Say did in fact generalize this reasoning to output as a whole in his polemics against Malthus.[37] Malthus also interpreted this version of Say's Law to mean that a *decrease* in quantity supplied—as in the wake of wartime devastation—would reduce the aggregate demand function, a result "directly opposite to all experience, which shows with what rapidity losses are recovered."[38]

Malthus argued also that make-work schemes for em-

[34] Lauderdale, *Nature and Origin of Public Wealth,* pp. 224–5.

[35] Ricardo, *Works,* vi, 168; Malthus, *Principles,* pp. 140, 150.

[36] Chalmers, *On Political Economy,* p. 65.

[37] Say, *Letters to Malthus,* pp. 3–4, 27–28.

[38] *Quarterly Review* (April 1823), 230; See also Malthus, *Principles,* p. 315; Ricardo, *Works,* vi, 111, 114, 123.

ploying the unemployed in producing goods increased the quantity of output supplied without increasing the demand—and that opposition to such programs was therefore more in keeping with his analysis than with Say's or Ricardo's,[39] although Ricardo had, in fact, expressed his opposition.[40] Malthus emphasized that current schemes were financed by converting revenue into capital (consumption spending into investment),[41] so the question of unlimited investment opportunities was raised by implication. Ricardo replied that (1) if the net effect of such programs were simply to transfer capital from private production for the market to government make-work projects, he was opposed to it as lowering efficiency, but that (2) if there were a net increase of capital in the country (Malthus' real argument), then there would be an "increased demand" as well as supply[42]— completely ignoring the point which had been emphasied by Malthus and others, that this was a forcible increase of investment by the government beyond the amount which the market had desired or would be willing to continue to sustain.

Increased Supply Function Increases the Demand Function

Sismondi and Malthus interpreted Say's Law to mean that increased productivity, or a shift outward of the supply curve, would necessarily lead to a corresponding shift outward of the demand function, so as to produce a proportionally increased realized quantity supplied and demanded. Say's Law was an assertion that "mankind al-

[39] P. Sraffa, "Malthus on Public Works," *Economic Journal*, ixv, No. 259 (September 1955), 543–44.

[40] Ricardo, *Works*, vii, 116, 121.

[41] P. Sraffa, "Malthus on Public Works," *op. cit.*, p. 544.

[42] Ricardo, *Works*, vii, 121.

ways produces and consumes as much as they have the power to produce and consume," according to Malthus,[43] who opposed "those who think that the power of production is the only element of wealth, and, who consequently infer that if the means of production be increased, wealth will certainly be increased to proportion."[44] The same interpretation appeared in a contemporary journal, *The British Critic,* which said that "the tastes and wants of mankind cannot be supposed to rise and fall with the ebbs and flows of invention or with the improvement of manufacturing apparatus."[45] Sismondi likewise opposed the idea that an increased "power to produce" was necessarily followed by an increased "power to consume."[46]

This interpretation had no substantial basis in the writings of the supporters of Say's Law, except as one possible meaning of the general proposition that supply creates its own demand. Ricardo expressed his astonishment at Malthus' position: ". . . for what are all his attacks on Say and on me, surely not because we have said that in all cases there would be motives sufficient to push production to its utmost extent, but because we have said, that, when produced, commodities would always find a market."[47]

SIMULTANEOUS CAPITAL-LABOR "REDUNDANCY"

Ricardo regarded it as mere inconsistency in Malthus that the latter sometimes depicted gluts as causing wages

---

[43] Malthus, *Principles,* p. 424.   [44] *Ibid.,* p. 419.

[45] B. J. Gordon, "Say's Law, Effective Demand and the Contemporary British Periodicals, 1820–1850," *Economica,* XXXII, No. 128 (November 1965), 439.

[46] *Nouveaux Principes,* II, 252, 272, 250n.

[47] Ricardo, *Works,* IX, 13; see also [McCulloch], *Edinburgh Review* (March 1821), 105.

to rise and at other times as causing them to fall.[48] In a comparative statics model it could have one effect or the other, but not both. But Malthus' period analysis frame of reference was obvious in this case. He spoke of "first an unnatural demand for labour, and then a necessary and sudden diminution of such demand."[49] There would be an "increased produce awarded at first to the labourers."[50] Savings beyond a "certain point" would cause profit decline "at first" and a reduction of output and employment "afterwards."[51]

During the glut, "the labourer who is employed earns more corn than usual" though others "are out of work."[52] Wage rates did not move downward readily: "We know from repeated experience that the money price of labour never falls till many workmen have been for some time out of work."[53] Ricardo would not accept this assump-

[48] Ricardo, *Works,* II, 308.   [49] *Ibid.,* IX, 20.
[50] *Quarterly Review* (January 1824), 327.
[51] Malthus, *Principles,* p. 326.
[52] George William Zinke, "Three Letters from Malthus to Pierre Prevost," *Journal of Economic History* (November 1942), 185; Malthus, *Essay on the Principle of Population,* Everyman edn., II, 138; *Quarterly Review* (January 1824), 327.
[53] Ricardo, *Works,* IX, 20. See also Malthus, *Principles,* p. 393. Malthus' argument here was not an after-thought which he had to "introduce" to "fend" Ricardo's attack, or something he had to "resort to" during his polemics with Ricardo, as suggested in the literature (George J. Stigler, "Sraffa's Ricardo," *American Economic Review* [September 1953], 597; Mark Blaug, *Ricardian Economics,* p. 86n). It was present from the first edition of Malthus' *Principles* and was implicit in examples used in his *Essay on Population* (Everyman edn., II, 65, 138), just as a lag in upward wage adjustments was implicit in his earlier discussion of forced savings (*Edinburgh Review* [February 1811], 364). How long the "preliminary" unemployment was supposed to last before wages fall was never explained by Malthus, so it is not surprising that some of the arguments in his writings imply wage flexibility (*Essay,* I, 61; *Principles,*

126

tion. Insufficient demand for labor "must mean a diminishing reward for the labourer, and not a diminishing employment of him"—although elsewhere he referred to an instance of downward wage rigidity.[54] Malthus' argument that unemployment was "an unavoidable preliminary to a fall in the money wages of labour"[55] meant that for a time there could be simultaneous unemployment or "redundancy" of labor and capital—at existing disequilibrium wage rates and profit rates,[56] though Ricardo repeatedly denied this possibility,[57] which he considered "a contradiction in terms."[58] It was of course impossible with the assumptions of the Ricardian model, as were so many of the (disequilibrium) situations posed by Malthus, but this did not in itself mean that empirically the disequilibrium situations were less common. Malthus assumed that they were in fact more common.[59]

"Quantity" Versus "Value"

Ricardo repeatedly opposed Malthus' policy position that it was desirable to increase the "value" rather than the "quantity" of aggregate output.[60] Again it was simply a question of translating another economist's words into Ricardian terms and then refuting the new substantive

---

1st edn., pp. 370–71) while others do not (*Principles*, 1st edn., p. 321; 2nd edn., p. 393; *Essay on Population*, ii, 65, 138), the time span being unspecified in both cases. Permanent rigidity was never claimed. It is inexplicably denied that Malthus believed in downward wage rigidity in Mark Blaug, *Economic Theory in Retrospect*, p. 149.

[54] Ricardo, *Works*, viii, 316.   [55] See footnote 53.

[56] Malthus, *Principles*, p. 402; *Journal of Economic History* (November 1942), 181–82.

[57] Ricardo, *Works*, ii, 241, 426; vii, 181, 185, 278.

[58] *Ibid.*, ii, 426.   [59] *Ibid.*, vii, 215.

[60] *Ibid.*, i, 319, ii, 373, vii, 215; cf. Malthus, *Principles*, pp. 393, 396.

argument thus created. Value in Ricardo's system was cost of production and quantity was equilibrium quantity. Clearly there was no reason to increase the cost of production of output, and certainly not to give this a priority over increasing the level of sustainable production. But value in Malthusian terms was utility or "estimation"[61] and a rising utility of aggregate output was necessary for maintaining the pace of economic growth. Production of more of the same commodities would lead to problems of declining marginal utility and substitution of leisure for potential output as productivity increased. In the context of this concern, international trade was important primarily because it introduced new commodities with a higher marginal utility, which tended to maintain the process of development.[62] Ricardo saw in international trade only a means of producing goods more cheaply.[63]

INDEPENDENT CONTEMPORARIES

The general glut controversy was not limited to a few prominent economists lining up unequivocally on one side or the other. It embraced lesser known economists,[64] popular journals,[65] and some economists who took one side on some points and the opposite side on others, or

[61] Malthus, *Principles,* pp. 300, 361; *Definitions,* pp. 207–08, 235.

[62] Malthus, *Principles,* pp. 359, 388.

[63] Ricardo, *Works,* II, 403, 407, 408.

[64] B. A. Corry, *Money, Saving and Investment in English Economics, 1800–1850,* pp. 139–53; R. D. C. Black, "Parson Malthus, The General and the Captain," *Economic Journal* (March 1967), 59–74.

[65] B. J. Gordon, "Say's Law, Effective, Demand, and the Contemporary British Periodicals, 1820–1850," *Economica* (November 1965), 438–46.

whose whole position shifted substantially over time. Perhaps the most important of the latter group was Robert Torrens.

Robert Torrens

Although it was Torrens who launched the attack on Sismondi in 1819 which precipitated the polemical outpourings of the next decade, by 1821 he was beginning to have misgivings:

> To M. Say and to Mr. Mill belong the merit of having been the first to bring forward the very important doctrine, that as commodities are purchased with commodities, one half will furnish a market for the other half, and increased production will be the occasion of increased demand. But this doctrine, though it embraces the very key-stone of economical science, is not correct in the general and unqualified sense in which these distinguished writers have stated it. Though one half of our commodities should be of the same value as the other half, and though the two halves should freely exchange against each other, it is yet possible that there may be an effectual demand for neither. It is quite obvious that there can exist no reciprocal effectual demand, unless the interchange of two different sets of commodities replaces, with a surplus, the expenditure incurred in the production of both.[66]

For Torrens, supply was said to equal demand only when commodities "may be readily and profitably exchanged" for each other.[67] Supply is "redundant" when the profit rate is less than that required and "deficient"

[66] Robert Torrens, *An Essay on the Production of Wealth*, p. ix.
[67] *Ibid.*, p. 341.

when it is more.[68] Torrens rejected the argument that "the quantity of other commodities" constituted the demand,[69] or that an "alteration" of these quantities affected "the relations between supply and demand,"[70] as suggested by those who claimed that disproportionality, or the lack of complementary commodities, was the cause of gluts. Nevertheless, Torrens argued that a reduction of the profit rate was not the same thing as reducing demand, as long as profit remained above a level "sufficient to stimulate the capitalist to produce."[71] Apparently he did not conceive of the capitalist's supply schedule as having any elasticity; the capitalist would either produce or not produce, but would not vary the quantity of production according to the rate of return. This was consistent with the classical economists' implicitly horizontal cost curves in manufacturing. Moreover, Torrens reverted to the classical argument that a "want of effectual demand, or profitable vend, would be occasioned, not by an excess, but by the deficiency of products."[72] The complementary commodity concept of demand which had been explicitly rejected was thus implicitly accepted later in the same work.

Torrens advanced beyond the classical school, however, in arguing that a general glut was possible, not in the sense of Sismondi or the Malthusian school, but due to monetary phenomena. Internal disproportionality of production was the first step in a chain of events which ended with "a suspension of production, not merely of the commodity which first exists in excess, but of all the other commodities brought to market."[73] Those in the overproducing sectors of the economy, who are suffering

[68] *Ibid.*, pp. 360–61.   [69] *Ibid.*, p. 363.
[70] *Ibid.*   [71] *Ibid.*, p. 390.
[72] *Ibid.*, p. 391; see also pp. 392, 396.   [73] *Ibid.*, p. 414.

losses, have an increased demand for money,[74] while others have an increased supply,[75] but the "multiple failures" of the period "strike a panic into the holders of floating capital," so that they refuse loans which, under normal circumstances, "they would be disposed to consider unobjectionable."[76]

While this reasoning is suggestive of later Keynesian economics, it was no concession to the Sismondi-Malthus theory of an equilibrium real aggregate income. And although it was at variance with the prevailing deprecations of the role of money by both the dissenters and the orthodox, J. B. Say had already (inconsistently) referred to the depressing effects of idle balances in his *Lettres à M. Malthus* in 1820.[77] Torrens was, however, well in advance of his contemporaries in developing this analysis, for which John Stuart Mill is sometimes erroneously credited with being the originator, and which reappeared (without credit) in Karl Marx. Torrens also had suggestions of multiplier analysis.[78]

Samuel Bailey

An anonymous pamphlet of 1821, probably written by Samuel Bailey,[79] challenged Say's Law without accepting the dissenting doctrine of Sismondi and Malthus. *An Inquiry into those Principles Respecting the Nature of Demand and the Necessity of Consumption Lately Advocated by Mr. Malthus* correctly saw Malthus' concern

---

[74] *Ibid.*, pp. 420–21.   [75] *Ibid.*, p. 419.   [76] *Ibid.*, p. 424.

[77] J. B. Say, *Oeuvres Diverses de J.-B. Say* (Paris: Chez Guillaumin et Cie, 1848), p. 477n. See J. B. Say, *Letters to Malthus*, pp. 45n–46n.

[78] Robert Torrens, *An Essay on the Production of Wealth*, pp. 414–15.

[79] Thomas Sowell, "Samuel Bailey Revisited," *Economica* (November 1970), 402–08.

to be with the increase of national wealth,[80] with a growth which proceeds "steadily, and free from reverse or fluctuation."[81] The practical aspect of the Malthusian glut doctrines was seen more clearly than by the classical economists and expressed more clearly than in Malthus: "Production, in the long run, we must remember is the object he has in view; and if he fears an excess of it at one time, it is only as tending permanently to cripple the future progress of it."[82]

The author of the *Inquiry* saw the question of a general glut to turn not on clearing the market but on profitable sale: "Nobody denied, that a new product will always, or almost always, find a *market:* the question is, at what price? Whether a profitable market? Whether its production and sale will bring in what were before the usual average profits of stock or less?"[83] Say's Law as expressed was considered inadequate even as a posing of the question: ". . . with regard to the maxim of M. Say, it does not necessarily follow that because increased production may be said to find a *market* for itself, it finds *such* a market as affords an undiminished rate of profit."[84]

The doctrine of unlimited capital investment outlets was likewise attacked as "useless," since obviously no one ever denied that capital "might *'be employed'* if you did not care what profits it brought."[85] Moreover, the secular fall of the profit rate, for which Smith, Ricardo, and others sought theories, was dismissed as an illusion based on the declining risk premium component of inter-

[80] [Samuel Bailey], *An Inquiry into those Principles respecting the Nature of Demand and the Necessity of Consumption Lately advocated by Mr. Malthus* (London: R. Hunter, 1821), p. 2.
[81] *Ibid.,* p. 3.   [82] *Ibid.,* p. 65.   [83] *Ibid.,* p. 14.
[84] *Ibid.,* p. 18.   [85] *Ibid.,* p. 19.

est rates as markets became better established.[86] The author of the *Inquiry* also saw that the crucial variable was the marginal efficiency of capital: "the gain of *new* capitalists, or of capitalists considered as owners of *added* capital."[87]

Marginal and schedule concepts occur repeatedly in the *Inquiry*. It described a declining marginal efficiency of capital,[88] a rising supply curve of labor,[89] and a savings *function,* which clarified much of the dispute over the role of "savings": "To say that people are more disposed to save and gain, *means* that *more* persons are disposed to lay out capital in the hope of the former profits; or else that the same person, who laid out capital in the hope of the former profits, now think it worth while to lay out more in the hope of somewhat *less* than the former profits; probably both."[90] In these terms, Malthus' arguments on the glut-producing effects of increasing "parsimony" among the rich capitalists was rejected: "If these rich people are become more parsimonious, then, even if it be true that there is not so great inducement to accumulate, they do not *want* so great an inducement."[91]

This exposes the ambiguity of Malthus' language rather than reaches the real substance of Malthus' argument. Malthus did not argue that rises in the savings schedule, which he advocated, caused gluts, but that increases in the quantity saved—off the schedule, due to miscalculation of returns—caused lagged reductions of the rate of return below the supply price. Malthus' unfortunate use of the word "permanently" in discussing the lagged reduction of investment was denounced in the *In-*

---

[86] *Ibid.,* pp. 10–13. [87] *Ibid.,* p. 28.
[88] *Ibid.,* p. 19. [89] *Ibid.,* p. 21.
[90] *Ibid.,* p. 30. [91] *Ibid.,* p. 40; see also pp. 30–31.

quiry and changed in the second edition of Malthus' *Principles*.[92] The author of the *Inquiry* apparently realized that Malthus was in fact thinking of short-run dynamic changes.[93] He also realized the need to "disentangle" Malthus' theory of equilibrium income from his theory of growth-promotion through unproductive consumption.[94]

William Blake

A variety of writers in the post-Napoleonic war period argued that the government's wartime expenditures had represented a net increase of aggregate demand, and that the reconversion to peacetime expenditure patterns therefore represented a net reduction in aggregate demand, which had led to the observed increase in unemployment and unsold goods.[95] They did not attempt to develop a general theory of equilibrium, like Sismondi, Lauderdale, or Malthus, but attempted to account for the immediate problem and to propose solutions. Perhaps the most interesting of these was William Blake, whose *Observations on the Effects Produced by the Expenditure of Government during the Restriction of Cash Payments* (1823) drew the critical fire of Ricardo, James Mill, and John Stuart Mill.[96]

Blake, a friend of Ricardo, was well acquainted with

[92] *Ibid.*, pp. 33, 57; T. R. Malthus, *Principles of Political Economy*, 2nd edn., p. 326, where "permanently" (1st edn., p. 369) became "afterwards."

[93] [Samuel Bailey], *An Inquiry* . . . , pp. 43, 45. 51.

[94] *Ibid.*, p. 70.

[95] Jacob Viner, *Studies in the Theory of International Trade*, pp. 185–93.

[96] Ricardo, *Works*, IV, 323–56; James Mill, *Elements of Political Economy*, p. 237 (Blake's name was omitted in the 1844 edition cited here, but had appeared—amid the same arguments—in the 1824 edn., p. 231); [John Stuart Mill], "War Expenditure," *Westminster Review* (July 1824), 27–48.

the classical argument that government expenditures represented a transfer, and not a net change, in demand.[97] He recognized that if capital is always fully employed ("in the fullest activity"), then "no extra production can take place in any one employment of it, without a corresponding diminution of production" elsewhere.[98] But "the error lies in supposing, first, that the whole capital of the country is fully occupied; and, secondly, that there is immediate employment for successive accumulations of capital as it accrues from saving."[99] But some capital is always "lying wholly dormant" and "if these dormant portions could be transferred into the hands of government in exchange for its annuities, they would become sources of new demand, without encroaching upon the existing capital."[100] This dormant capital argument was later to be incorporated (without crediting the source) into John Stuart Mill's celebrated essay on Say's Law,[101] but at the time it was simply dismissed in J. S. Mill's attack on Blake, since it involved "the fallacy of the universal glut"[102] and supported "refuted, and now almost forgotten errors."[103]

Blake's idle-capital theory was one of the few arguments of the period which could be considered a forerunner of Keynesian analysis. He argued that funds which were unavailable for private investment at the going rate of return were nevertheless available for the

---

[97] William Blake, *Observations on the Effects Produced by the Expenditure of Government during the Restriction of Cash Payments* (London: John Murray, 1823), p. 44.

[98] *Ibid.*, p. 50.   [99] *Ibid.*, p. 54.   [100] *Ibid.*, pp. 54–55.

[101] John Stuart Mill, *Essays on Some Unsettled Questions of Political Economy*, pp. 54–60.

[102] [John Stuart Mill], "War Expenditure," *Westminster Review* (July 1824), 40, 47.

[103] *Ibid.*, p. 48.

purchase of government bonds at the same rate of return, since the lenders "prefer the security of government to that of private borrowers," thus allowing the monetary counterpart of the idle capital to pass into the hands of the government, which will "devote them to expenditure."[104] The long-run effect of this was put aside by Blake, who argued in dynamic fashion that "during its continuance" it would tend "to increase both prices and profits."[105]

Unfortunately, like other glut theorists, Blake interspersed gross errors among his insights, and these errors became the main targets of the supporters of Say's Law, who were thus able to dismiss or ignore the troublesome questions raised. For example, Blake claimed that the empirical existence of idle capital which had been activated by the war against Napoleon could be proved by a process of *reductio ad absurdum:* fully employed capital would have meant that wartime deficit financing had simply transferred civilian investment into military consumption, and the continuance of this process for a period as long as that of the war must eventually reduce output and wages well before the return of peace.[106] But this was "at absolute variance" with the actual course of events, which showed growing output, investment, and wages throughout the war.[107] This argument presupposed not only a full-employment economy, but also that government bonds were always purchased at the expense of investment rather than consumption expenditures. If government expenditures were financed from an annual flow representing a disposable surplus—Sismondi's "revenue" or the Physiocrat's *produit net*—rather than from a preexisting capital stock, then it could, of course,

---

[104] William Blake, *Observations*, p. 62.   [105] *Ibid.,* p. 63.
[106] *Ibid.,* pp. 48–53.   [107] *Ibid.,* pp. 53–54.

continue indefinitely without reducing output, employment, or wages.

Ricardo and John Stuart Mill rebutted Blake by simply assuming that government expenditures were *not* at the expense of investment, because private savings overbalanced government expenditure,[108] which amounts to saying that government military expenditures represented transfers from civilian consumption. The important theoretical question as to what would happen if, or to the extent that, this was *not* true empirically was simply side-stepped.

Blake was familiar with the classical argument that "demand and supply are correlative terms and must always balance each other," that for every case of excess production in the economy, "there must be a corresponding deficiency in other things."[109] But he raised the question whether by "miscalculation on the part of the producers"[110] there might not be a general excess. To this J. S. Mill replied that if a man "continues" to produce, it shows his consumption desires are unsatisfied, for why would he "continue to take the trouble of producing for no purpose?"[111] It was, of course, never alleged by Blake that such a glut of production would *continue;* he explicitly argued in several places that it would *not* continue.[112] As often happened with the Ricardians, Mill did not answer Blake's question but merely transformed it from one of dynamics to one of comparative statics. Ricardo was even more remote from understanding Blake's proposition, taking the "glut arising from miscal-

[108] Ricardo, *Works,* iv, 399; [John Stuart Mill], "War Expenditure," *op. cit.,* pp. 40, 43.

[109] William Blake, *Observations,* p. 59.

[110] *Ibid.,* p. 60.

[111] [John Stuart Mill], "War Expenditure," *op. cit.,* p. 42.

[112] William Blake, *Observations,* pp. 61, 91, 95.

culation" to refer to a glut of "particular commodities" rather than of output in general.[113]

Blake emphasized the monetary aspects of the post-Napoleonic war depression and traced out the monetary accompaniments of his real analysis to a greater extent than any of the major advocates of a general glut theory, but like other economists of the period, he conceived of causation in a sequential sense and argued that changes in the money supply and/or its "rapidity of circulation" were consequences rather than causes of fluctuations.[114] Blake also did not deny Say's Law as an equilibrium condition (Say's Equality), and in fact considered it "unanswerable" in these terms.[115] He did not deny that the market could be cleared, but asserted only that during a glut it would be cleared at less than cost-covering prices.[116]

G. P. Scrope

Although Robert Torrens had in 1821 made an argument in which an excess demand for money was sequentially involved in the causation of gluts in a particular way, it was left to George Poulett Scrope in 1833 to make the argument that an excess demand for money was *logically implied* in any excess supply of goods. It was the first explicit assertion of the version of Say's Law now called Walras' Law.[117] According to Scrope, "such epochs of general embarrassment and distress" (which he called "a general glut") were real phenomena "in spite

[113] Ricardo, *Works,* IV, 344, 345.
[114] William Blake, *Observations,* p. 81.
[115] *Ibid.,* p. 59n; see also pp. 58–59.
[116] *Ibid.,* p. 91n.
[117] "General Glut of Goods Supposes A General Glut of Money,": page title, George Poulett Scrope, *Principles of Political Economy* (London: Longman, Rees, Orme, Brown, Green & Longman, 1833), pp. 214–15.

of what theory may urge as to their impossibility."[118]
He said:

> Bearing in mind this instability of value inherent in
> money of all kinds, we cannot fail to perceive that
> a general glut—that is, a general fall in the *prices* of
> the mass of commodities below their production
> cost—is tantamount to a rise in the general exchange-
> able value of money; and is a proof, not of excessive
> supply of goods, but of a deficient supply of money,
> against which the goods have to be exchanged.[119]

The writers discussed here—Torrens, Bailey, Blake,
and Scrope—were doubtful allies of the general glut theorists (all except Blake made devastating attacks on the
latter at one point or another), though they punctured
particular arguments of the orthodox. The equilibrium
income model of Sismondi and Malthus depicted excessive aggregate output as not only a possibility, but as
the initiating force in the chain of events, including
monetary phenomena, which led to depression; Torrens,
Bailey, Blake, and Scrope saw the chain of causation
beginning with monetary and fiscal actions. John Stuart
Mill was later to incorporate Blake's idle-capital and de-
ficient-money arguments into his discussions of Say's
Law,[120] without acknowledgment and with an explicit
denial that they represented anything new on the
subject.[121]

RECONCILIATION

After years of controversy with Malthus, Ricardo came
finally to see the basic reasoning behind the glut theory.

[118] *Ibid.*, p. 214.   [119] *Ibid.*, p. 215.
[120] John Stuart Mill, *Essays on Some Unsettled Questions of
Political Economy*, pp. 54–60.
[121] *Ibid.*, p. 74.

While criticizing the manuscript of James Mill's *Elements of Political Economy*, Ricardo commented on the section presenting Say's Law: "This does not answer the objection usually made . . . . The supply above the demand would produce such a glut, that with the increased quantity you could command no more labour than before. All motive to save would cease."[122]

Even more dramatic results came from a controversy between Say and Sismondi on the continent. After an exchange of polemical articles[123] in 1824–1826, Say added several new paragraphs to the end of his celebrated chapter, "Des Débouchés," in the fifth (1826) and subsequent editions of his *Traité d'économie politique,* additions which Say later characterized as "restrictions" of his law of markets,[124] and which he elaborated in his *Cours Complet d'économie politique* after informing Sismondi of the "concessions" he planned to make.[125]

After repeating the previous arguments for Say's Law in the chapter, "Des Débouchés," Say raised an additional question as to "the limit of a growing production . . . since it is only in abstract quantities that there are infinite progressions" and "we are studying practical political economy here."[126] As "needs become less and

---

[122] Ricardo, *Works,* IX, 131.

[123] J. C. L. Simonde de Sismondi, "Sur la balance des consommations avec les productions," *Revue encyclopedique,* XXII, (May 1824), 264–98; Jean-Baptiste Say, "Sur la balance des consommations avec lec productions," *Revue encyclopedique,* XXIII, (July 1824), 18–31; J. C. L. Simonde de Sismondi, "Note sur l'article de M. Say, intitulé 'Balance des consommations avec les productions,' " *Nouveaux Principes d'économie politique,* II, 306–09.

[124] Say, *Oeuvres Diverses,* p. 505.

[125] Sismondi, *Political Economy and the Philosophy of Government,* p. 449.

[126] J. B. Say, *Traité d'économie politique,* 5th edn., (Paris: Rapilly, 1826), I, 194–95.

less pressing," people "would make gradually less sacrifices in order to satisfy them," implying that "it would be more and more difficult to find in the price of the products a full compensation for their costs of production."[127] In his later *Cours Complet,* Say said that beyond some point, "products become too dear for the utility which is in them" to "indemnify" the "sacrifice" necessary to obtain them, adding: "They cease from that time to be able to be produced, to be able consequently to offer markets for new products by their sale."[128] In short, it was no longer necessarily true, as originally claimed in Say's Law, that "production . . . opens a demand for products."[129] Excess production could not offer markets for new products at prices which would continue their production. But rather than distinguish the short-run limit to sustainable output and the long-run increase of that limit, Say chose to maintain that there could be no overproduction—in either the short run or the long run—by simply defining production above the equilibrium level as not being truly "production."[130]

Aside from semantic difficulties, Say's Law was now reconciled with the theory of an equilibrium income. "Our discussion on markets begins to be no more than a dispute over words," Say wrote in 1827 to Malthus,[131] who had said that his objection had been to "your doctrine as it was first presented."[132] Logically, this should have been the end of the general glut controversy, with each side able to claim victory on the essentials of its argument. Historically, the debate not only continued but suffered a retrogression from which it has never fully recovered.

[127] *Ibid.,* p. 196.   [128] *Cours Complet,* I, 346–47.
[129] Say, *Treatise,* p. 137.   [130] *Cours Complet,* I, 345–46.
[131] *Oeuvres Diverses,* p. 513.   [132] *Ibid.,* p. 508.

CHAPTER 5

The Counterrevolution of John Stuart Mill

D ESPITE the advances in mutual understanding
finally achieved by some of the main participants
in the general glut controversy, John Stuart Mill's
Principles of Political Economy in 1848 proceeded with
precisely the same arguments—and precisely the same
misinterpretation of the general glut theories—that the
supporters of Say's Law had put forth in the beginning,
nearly three decades earlier. The long, unchallenged
dominance of Mill's *Principles* as the leading work in
economics effectively put an end to the questioning of
Say's Law, and turned the clock back to a position
which remained largely unchallenged by respectable
economists until Keynes' *General Theory*.

Mill ascribed to Sismondi, Malthus, and Chalmers a
belief in a "permanent" glut,[1] despite all their statements
to the contrary. Malthus' argument that values ("estimation" or labor command) might fall generally was met
by the assertion that it was "a sheer absurdity that all
things should fall in value"[2]—defined as relative prices.
Mill claimed that Chalmers "inculcates on capitalists the
practice of moral restraint in reference to the pursuit of
gain,"[3] when in fact Chalmers—like the other glut theorists—urged that saving be "left to itself," or to indi-

[1] John Stuart Mill, *Principles of Political Economy,* Ashley
edn., p. 561; Toronto edn., p. 575.
[2] *Ibid.,* Ashley edn., p. 558; Toronto edn., p. 572.
[3] *Ibid.,* Ashley edn., p. 557; Toronto edn., p. 571.

vidual self-interest, with neither fostering or retarding, institutionally or by exhortation.[4] Mill repeated the classical arguments of decades before that purchasing power necessarily equals output,[5] that savings are merely transfers and not net reductions of demand,[6] that wants are insatiable[7]—all points on which there was no disagreement. The idea of an equilibrium income underlying the theory of a general glut was implicitly denied: "production is not excessive, but merely ill-assorted."[8]

Fortunately, the level of Mill's understanding of his opponents was not indicative of the level of his understanding of the issues raised by Say's Law. Here his ideas evolved in a more sophisticated way which defies easy characterization, and his treatment of the subject in his *Essays on Some Unsettled Questions of Political Economy* was perhaps the clearest and most advanced presentation in classical economics. In the related area of value theory, he also made advances of his own while undoing the progress made by others.

CRISES

Mill's position on the miscalculation of demand shifted somewhat over time. In 1824 he admitted the possibility of such miscalculation, but denied that this affected the equality of aggregate supply and demand:

Men miscalculate, it is true; but it is concerning the desires of others, never concerning their own. Every

[4] Thomas Chalmers, *On Political Economy*, p. 125.

[5] J. S. Mill, *Principles*, Ashley edn., pp. 557–58; Toronto edn., pp. 571–72.

[6] *Ibid.*, Ashley edn., pp. 68, 71, 560; Toronto edn., pp. 67–68, 70–71, 573–74.

[7] *Ibid.*, Ashley edn., 558–59; Toronto edn., pp. 572–73.

[8] *Ibid.*, Ashley edn., p. 559; Toronto edn., p. 573.

man knows what he himself wishes for. If any man produces more, it must be because he desires more; not more cloth, or corn, perhaps, but more of something: and if all produce more, it is because all desire more. The requisites for demand are, the wish to consume, and the means of purchasing. By increasing their supply, they prove themselves to have the desire, and they obtain the means, of consuming.[9]

Mill's statement does not take account of the possibility that, while the supply of each individual producer's efforts and outputs may be a monotonically increasing function of other goods (real income) that will be supplied to him, any such function implies some projected ratio at which his particular product will exchange for others' output, and that this ratio need not prove to coincide with other producers' projected ratios or either set of ratios with *ex post* reality. In short, there is no reason why aggregate expectations of real returns to factor inputs must prove to be simultaneously realizable. Writing in another context (not against the general glut theorists) just two years later, Mill traced out the consequences of "the universal propensity of mankind to overestimate the chances in their own favour" and of the "extensive miscalculation" which, "upon a sufficiently extensive scale, will terminate in the ruin of multitudes."[10]

Every merchant, who remembers the commercial revulsions of 1810–11, and 1815–16, will testify that

[9] [J. S. Mill], "War Expenditure," *Westminster Review* (July 1824), 43.

[10] John Stuart Mill, *Essays on Economics and Society,* ed. J. M. Robson (Toronto: University of Toronto Press, 1967), I, 77. The original article appeared in the *Parliamentary Review, Session of 1826* (London: Longman, Rees, Orme, Brown and Green, 1826), pp. 630–62.

such are the events which always follow the opening of new markets, the expectation of deficient supplies, every thing, in short, which excites a confident hope of rapid gains. The additional supplies necessary are enormously over-estimated, enormous over-production and over-trading take place, the market is glutted, the holders suffer immense losses, many of them become insolvent, and their ruin draws along with it the ruin of many others, who have given them credit, confiding in the enormous wealth which they appeared to have the power of realizing during the continuance of those high prices of which their own purchases were in a great measure the cause.[11]

A later description (1833) of the same events by Mill again suggested that he believed a general overproduction in real terms had occurred, with the accompanying monetary phenomena being an effect rather than a cause:

From the impossibility of exactly adjusting the operations of the producer to the wants of the consumer, it always happens that some articles are more or less in deficiency, and others in excess. To rectify these derangements, the healthy working of the social economy requires that in some channels capital should be in full, while in others it should be in slack, employment. But in 1825, it was imagined that *all* articles, compared with the demand for them, were in a state of deficiency. An unusual extension of the spirit of speculation, accompanied rather than caused by a great increase of paper credit, had produced a rise of prices, which not being supposed to be connected with a depreciation of the currency, each merchant or manufacturer considered to arise from an increase

[11] J. S. Mill, *Essays on Economics and Society,* p. 76.

145

of the effectual demand for his particular article, and fancied there was a ready and permanent market for almost any quantity of that article which he could produce. Mr. Attwood's error is that of supposing that a depreciation of the currency *really* increases the demand for all articles, and consequently their production, because, under some circumstances, it may create a *false opinion* of an increase of demand, which false opinion leads, as the reality would do, to an increase of production, followed, however, by a fatal revulsion as soon as the delusion ceases. The contraction in 1825 was not caused, as Mr. Attwood fancies, by a contraction of the currency; the only cause of the real ruin, was the imaginary prosperity. The contraction of the currency was the consequence, not the cause, of the revulsion.[12]

Mill's argument here strongly suggests that he was discussing cases where production had been "excessive" and not merely "ill-assorted," where real output went above an equilibrium level *before* there was a monetary contraction, where, in short, the general glut theory applied. He was open to Marx's indictment of the whole classical school on Say's Law, that it "admits the same phenomenon as present and necessary when it is called A, but denies it when it is called B," denying it "in a form in which it comes up against prejudices, and admitting it only in a form in which no one bothers about it."[13] Mill took substantively different positions when arguing against the glut theories than when considering cyclical phenomena on their own, arguing that there could be no such thing as a real above-equilibrium output in the

[12] *Ibid.*, p. 191.
[13] Karl Marx, *Theories of Surplus Value*, p. 375.

146

one case, and explaining how it came about in the other. He was consistent, however, in never admitting the possibility of a general glut in a barter economy, which meant not confronting the Sismondi-Malthus theory of a real equilibrium income or the related notion of a simultaneous balance among the respective utilities of various goods and of leisure.

In his well-known essay on Say's Law in his *Essays on Some Unsettled Questions of Political Economy,* Mill limited the principle of the necessary equality of supply and demand to a barter economy:

But there is this difference—that in the case of barter, the selling and the buying are simultaneously confounded in one operation; you sell what you have, and buy what you want, by one indivisible act, and you cannot do the one without doing the other. Now the effect of the employment of money, and even the utility of it, is, that it enables this one act of interchange to be divided into two separate acts or operations; one of which may be performed now, and the other a year hence, or whenever it shall be most convenient. Although he who sells, really sells only to buy, he need not buy at the same moment when he sells; and he does not therefore necessarily add to the *immediate* demand for one commodity when he adds to the supply of another. The buying and selling being now separated, it may very well occur, that there may be, at some given time, a very general inclination to sell with as little delay as possible, accompanied with an equally general inclination to defer all purchases as long as possible.[14]

[14] John Stuart Mill, *Essays on Some Unsettled Questions of Political Economy,* p. 70.

Insofar as Mill here uses terms in their classical senses, it is clear that the equality of supply and demand is basically an *ex ante* equality of desired purchases and sales by each individual, not a mere accounting identity which views each transaction as being, *ex post,* both a purchase and a sale. Similar reasoning reappeared in Mill's *Principles,* where he was at pains to deny that a general glut, in the Sismondi-Malthus sense of an above-equilibrium real income, could occur, despite what he had said in his articles of the 1820's and 1830's. Economists had been "led to embrace so irrational a doctrine" because they were "deceived by a mistaken interpretation of certain mercantile facts" and thereby "imagined that the possibility of general over-production was proved by experience."[15] According to Mill, "the true explanation" of the observed phenomena was "totally different":[16]

I have already described the state of the markets for commodities which accompanies what is termed a commercial crisis. At such times there is really an excess of all commodities above the money demand: in other words, there is an under-supply of money. From the sudden annihilation of a great mass of credit, every one dislikes to part with ready money, and many are anxious to procure it at any sacrifice. Almost everybody therefore is a seller, and there are scarcely any buyers; so that there may really be, though only while the crisis lasts, an extreme depression of general prices, from what may be indiscriminately called a glut of commodities or a dearth of money. But it is a great error to suppose, with Sismondi, that a commercial crisis is the effect of a general excess of production.[17]

[15] J. S. Mill, *Principles,* Ashley edn., p. 560; Toronto edn., p. 574.

[16] *Loc. cit.*

[17] *Ibid.,* Ashley edn., p. 561; Toronto edn., 574.

While Mill's statement here accurately expresses the issue between himself and Sismondi, it also, like much of Mill's work (1) walks a thin line between accepting and denying the possibility of a general glut, leaning much more toward denial than had his articles of 1826 and 1833, and (2) advances toward modern monetary explanations of cyclical downturns while denying the fundamental theory of an equilibrium aggregate income.

Mill's correspondence gives some clues to his ambivalent or inconsistent treatment of the issues raised in the controversies over Say's Law. Although he wrote to a friend in 1834 that there was "much new speculation" on the subject which would be "added to" his then-unpublished essay on gluts,[18] when the essay actually appeared, it claimed that *nothing* was "added to" or "subtracted from" Say's Law as it had been previously presented in the classical tradition.[19] Either Mill had ignored the new speculation after all, or was not being completely candid. In another letter he expressed a fear of "giving a handle to the enemies of the science; which such men as Torrens and Malthus and even Senior are constantly doing, and which I systematically avoid."[20] He urged this course upon others: "I am even anxious that in your article on the theory of a 'glut of capital,' you should avoid the phrase 'glut' or any other word which will bring you into seeming collision (through not real) with my father's and Say's doctrine respecting a general glut."[21]

This attitude of loyal defense of an embattled classical tradition may go far toward explaining Mill's efforts to

[18] John Stuart Mill, *The Earlier Letters of John Stuart Mill,* ed. Francis E. Mineka (Toronto: University of Toronto Press, 1963), I, 231.

[19] J. S. Mill, *Essays on Some Unsettled Questions of Political Economy,* p. 74.

[20] J. S. Mill, *The Earlier Letters of John Stuart Mill,* p. 236.

[21] *Ibid.*

add his own original ideas (in value theory as well as on Say's Law) to Ricardian doctrines to which they were at best awkward appendages, rather than attaching them to dissenting doctrines with which they were more consonant.

Capital Accumulation

The definition of "capital" in Mill's *Principles* turns not on its material constituents, but on its being "destined" by its owner for investment purposes,[22] but he inconsistently included unintended inventory ("unsold goods" not currently "marketable")[23] as well. In short, Mill confounded *ex ante* investment and *ex post* investment, and this turned out to affect his substantive conclusions. Among his "fundamental propositions respecting capital" was that capital may be "indefinitely increased, without creating an impossibility of finding them employments"[24]—a proposition which he considered to be in opposition to the theories of Malthus, Chalmers, and Sismondi.[25] He did not directly confront the issue raised in Bailey's *Inquiry,* whether such statements meant that the rate of profit did or did not decline with successive increments of capital at a given time with a given level of technology. Lauderdale, Sismondi, and Malthus had said that it did. Mill himself said, sometimes, that it did,[26] and that profit rates sank to the verge of the minimum supply price of capital:

> . . . the rate of profit is habitually within, as it were, a hand's breadth of the minimum, and the country

[22] J. S. Mill, *Principles,* Ashley edn., p. 56; Toronto edn., p. 57.

[23] *Ibid.,* Ashley edn., pp. 50, 57; Toronto edn., p. 57.

[24] *Ibid.,* Ashley edn., p. 66; Toronto edn., p. 66.

[25] *Ibid.,* Ashley edn., p. 67n; Toronto edn., p. 67n.

[26] *Ibid.,* Ashley edn., p. 731; Toronto edn., pp. 738–39.

therefore on the very verge of the stationary state. By this I do not mean that this state is likely, in any of the great countries of Europe, to be soon actually reached, or that capital does not still yield a profit considerably greater than what is barely sufficient to induce the people of those countries to save and accumulate. My meaning is, that it would require but a short time to reduce profits to the minimum, if capital continued to increase at its present rate, and no circumstances having a tendency to raise the rate of profit occurred in the meantime. The expansion of capital would soon reach its ultimate boundary, if the boundary itself did not continually open and leave more space.[27]

The last sentence was little more than a paraphrase of Chalmers' earlier assertion that "capital is hemmed on all sides by a slowly receding boundary,"[28] but Mill denied that this implied the possibility of a general glut:

The difficulty would not consist in any want of a market. If the new capital were duly shared among many varieties of employment, it would raise up a demand for its own produce, and there would be no cause why any part of that produce should remain longer on hand than formerly. What would really be, not merely difficult, but impossible, would be to employ this capital without submitting to a rapid reduction of the rate of profit.[29]

Except for terminological preferences, Mill was now substantively within a hand's breadth of Chalmers and

[27] *Ibid.*
[28] Thomas Chalmers, *On Political Economy,* p. 105.
[29] J. S. Mill, *Principles,* Ashley edn., p. 732; Toronto edn., pp. 739–40.

the other general glut economists. While arguing that the market could be cleared (never an issue), he agreed that profits could fall to a point at which net investment was zero; they argued that profits could fall to a point where net disinvestment took place. Actually, for Malthus' model with lagged population growth and downwardly rigid wages, all that was necessary for unemployment to occur was that capital stop growing. At times Mill's arguments were in substance identical with those of Lauderdale, Sismondi, and Chalmers on excess investment. For example, Mill said:

> . . . unless a considerable portion of the annual increase of capital were either periodically destroyed, or exported for foreign investment, the country would speedily attain to the point at which further accumulation would cease, or at least spontaneously slacken, so as no longer to overpass the march of invention in the arts which produce the necessaries of life. In such a state of things as this, a sudden addition to the capital of the country, unaccompanied by any increase of productive power, would be of but transitory duration; since, by depressing profits and interest, it would either diminish by a corresponding amount the savings which would be made from income in the year or two following, or it would cause an equivalent amount to be sent abroad, or to be wasted in rash speculations.[30]

But though Mill's *Principles* at some points proceeded as if there were a downward sloping marginal product of capital curve, at other points it proceeded as if this were not the case. For example, even if by fiscal operations (such as those suggested by Lauderdale) there

---

[30] *Ibid.,* Ashley edn., p. 740; Toronto edn., p. 747.

should be an increased investment which was "not spontaneous, but imposed by law or opinion" on the investors, it would nevertheless be sustainable.[31] Presumably this could mean that if the same law or force of public opinion continued to force the investment to be made, there was no impossibility of continuing to clear the market. But Mill did not make this argument, and it would be completely irrelevant to the arguments on general glut if he had.

The idea that incremental investment can be made only at declining rates of return also conflicts with Mill's well-known doctrine that "demand for commodities is not demand for labour."[32] In arguing that demand for products is not demand for labor, Mill's central point was that a shift of demand from goods to services means an increase in the aggregate demand for labor, not merely a transfer.[33] The new demand for services directly employs additional labor while the capital which formerly employed the labor which produced the goods from which the demand was transferred is "set free"[34] to continue employing labor in producing some other commodity. Mill's argument was *not* that commodity-sector employment declines less than service-sector employment rises (different labor-intensities),[35] but rather that there is no offsetting decline in the commodity-producing

[31] *Ibid.,* Ashley edn., p. 67; Toronto edn., p. 67.
[32] *Ibid.,* Ashley edn., pp. 79–90; Toronto edn., pp. 70, 78–90. This doctrine and its meaning were debated in A. C. Pigou, "Mill and the Wages Fund," *Economic Journal* (June 1949), 171–80, and Harry G. Johnson, "Demand for Commodities Is Not Demand for Labour," *Economic Journal* (December 1949), 531–36.
[33] J. S. Mill, *Principles,* Ashley edn., pp. 85n–86n; Toronto edn., pp. 81n, 85n–86n.
[34] *Ibid.,* Ashley edn., p. 83; Toronto edn., p. 82.
[35] H. G. Johnson argues different capital-labor intensities, *op. cit.*

sector; all of the employment increase in the service sector is a net increase of total employment. The no longer needed portion of the capital in the commodity sector is "ready for a new employment, in which it will maintain as much labour as before."[36]

The crucial assumption on which this conclusion depends is that goods are paid for after being produced while services are paid for in advance,[37] so that what is involved is (in money terms) the activation of an otherwise idle transactions balance or (in real terms) the movement of wage goods out of the inventory pipeline and into the wages fund earlier than otherwise.[38] What is important here is not so much the validity of this conclusion in the labor market as the implication of it for the capital market. If capital investment is effectively increased (by the growth of the wages fund), the profit rate should be expected to fall. Mill can say that the capital "set free" in the commodity sector is "ready for a new employment" only if it is "destined" for use as capital in some fatalistic sense, independently of its rate of return. Again, his doctrine of the closeness of the profit rate to a stationary state level was not allowed to influence his discussion of the unlimited investment opportunities for capital.

VALUE

There were significant anticipations of modern value theory in Lauderdale, Say, Malthus, and Senior—all rejecting the labor cost theory of value in favor of some

[36] J. S. Mill, *Principles*, Ashley edn., p. 80; Toronto edn., p. 79.
[37] *Ibid.*, Ashley edn., pp. 85n–86n; Toronto edn., pp. 84n–86n.
[38] A. C. Pigou, *op. cit.*

essentially utility-based theory,[39] perhaps best expressed in Malthus' schedule concept of demand based upon subjective "estimation." John Stuart Mill opposed both the schedule concept of demand and the subjective utility theory on which it was based.

Sixteen years before the publication of Mill's *Principles,* Nassau Senior had developed the concept of utility per unit as a variable magnitude inversely related to the quantity consumed.[40] Mill ignored this and dealt with the utility theory of value by conceiving of utility in the same way Ricardo had conceived of it: the utility of having one unit of a commodity as against not having the commodity at all. Given this premise, Mill logically derived all the familiar Ricardian conclusions: while utility was necessary for value, it formed the limit of value but did not determine where, within those limits, the actual value would be.[41] Utility, as Mill illustrated, would determine the value only of a monopolized product, of which the monopolist was content to sell a single unit.[42] In short, Mill did not confront the utility theory of value as it existed; he merely perpetuated a misconception of it.

Similarly, Mill repeatedly objected to the use of the

[39] Lauderdale, *Nature and Origin of Public Wealth,* pp. 12, 23; T. R. Malthus, *Principles of Political Economy,* pp. 60–69; J. B. Say, *Treatise of Political Economy,* pp. 66, 288, 292, 293; N. W. Senior, *An Outline of the Science of Political Economy,* pp. 6, 7, 11, 13, 15–16, 23–24.

[40] N. W. Senior, *op. cit.,* pp. 11–12. Indeed, Galiani had done the same thing in the preceding century. Arthur E. Monroe, ed., *Early Economic Thought* (Cambridge: Harvard University Press, 1951), p. 288.

[41] J. S. Mill, *Principles,* Ashley edn., p. 437; Toronto edn., p. 457.

[42] *Ibid.,* Ashley edn., p. 449; Toronto edn., pp. 468–69; see also J. S. Mill *Essays on Economics and Society,* I, 400.

words "supply" and "demand" in any sense other than that of quantities supplied and quantities demanded.[43] Again he simply followed Ricardo faithfully.[44] Given this conception, it was true, as Mill (and Ricardo) argued, that supply and demand determine only the direction of the fluctuation of price, not the level around which these fluctuations take place.[45] Excess quantities supplied reduce prices and excess quantities demanded raise prices, but the level at which they are equated is determined by the cost of production. If there were 600 apples supplied and 700 apples demanded, prices would rise, and if there were 600 automobiles supplied and 700 automobiles demanded, prices would also rise, but the apples and the automobiles would not reach equilibrium at the same price.

Supply and demand, in the Ricardian sense of quantities, could determine prices by themselves only where supply was a fixed quantity and the quantity demanded would necessarily have to equate itself to this fixed amount, price settling at the level necessary to accomplish this. This was clearly an "exceptional case," as Mill said.[46] The "small class" of commodities which are "limited to a definite quantity" have "their value entirely determined by demand and supply, save that their cost of production (if they have any) constitutes a minimum below which they cannot permanently fall."[47] Actually

[43] J. S. Mill *Principles,* Ashley edn., pp. 446, 447, 449; Toronto edn., pp. 466, 467, 469; John Stuart Mill, "Notes on N. W. Senior's *Political Economy,*" *Economica* (August 1945), 134, 145.

[44] Ricardo, *Works,* I, 382, VI, 129.

[45] J. S. Mill *Principles,* Ashley edn., p. 448; Toronto edn., pp. 475–76; Ricardo *Works,* II, 39n, 40n–41n, I, 384–85.

[46] J. S. Mill *Principles,* Ashley edn., p. 448; Toronto edn., p. 468.

[47] *Ibid.,* Ashley edn., p. 469; Toronto edn., p. 488.

cost of production would be irrelevant in this case, since sunk costs are sunk, and reproduction costs are ruled out by hypothesis. This analysis would, however, be correct in a related case, where the supply was fixed only in the short run.

Mill's *Principles* carefully distinguished three cases of value determination: (1) with perpendicular supply curves, (2) with horizontal supply curves, and (3) with upward sloping supply curves. These were covered in different chapters. The table of contents showed supply and demand to be the "law" for commodities "which are absolutely limited in quantity," cost of production as the law for commodities "which are susceptible of indefinite multiplication without increase of cost," and rising marginal cost (costs "in the most unfavorable existing circumstances") as the law for commodities "which are susceptible of indefinite multiplication, but not without increase of cost."[48] It is necessary to emphasize that Mill did *not* treat supply and demand as *general* determinants of prices because his "exceptional case" has sometimes been presented as general, thereby making Mill a contributor to the development of modern value theory.[49] In fact, Mill was implacably opposed to the schedule concepts of supply and demand, and to the conclusions derived from them.

Nassau Senior argued that a deficient harvest of wheat would cause an increased demand for such substitutes as oats or barley, even though there could be no increase in the actual quantity purchased of the latter (their amounts, presumably, having been fixed by their harvest)—but it was still true to say that "the demand for

[48] *Ibid.,* Ashley edn., p. xli; Toronto edn., pp. xi–xii.
[49] George J. Stigler, "The Nature and Role of Originality in Scientific Progress," *Economica* (November 1955), 298.

157

them was increased."[50] Mill objected to this passage because demand "must" be used "in the sense of quantity of the commodity," that is, the "quantity for which at the market price, purchasers can be found."[51] This was a step backward from Adam Smith and the glut theorists, for whom the "effectual demand" was the quantity which consumers were willing to buy at cost-covering prices. There could be an excess or deficient aggregate demand in this sense, while there could be none, by definition, in Mill's sense.

Mill's *Principles* rejected the implicitly schedule concept of demand as the "will and power" to purchase, where an increased demand meant an increased willingness or ability to purchase.[52] The schedule concept of demand was rejected, not because of defects of its own, but because it was inconsistent with references to a "ratio" between supply and demand which sometimes occurred in the writings of the proponents of supply and demand theory. "Demand, to be capable of comparison with supply, must be taken to mean, not a wish, nor a power, but a quantity."[53] Instead of dismissing the notion of a ratio, Mill dismissed the schedule concept of demand.

It is important here to distinguish substantive from terminological differences and to distinguish limitations from errors. Mill did not deny the proposition that the quantity demanded varied inversely with the price, but neither was his terminological preference without consequences. Mill's Ricardian terminology was adequate for explaining price determination in a stationary economy;

[50] N. W. Senior, *An Outline of the Science of Political Economy*, p. 15.
[51] J. S. Mill, "Notes on N. W. Senior's *Political Economy*," *Economica* (August 1945), 134.
[52] J. S. Mill, *Principles,* Ashley edn., pp. 445–46; Toronto edn., pp. 465–66.
[53] J. S. Mill, *Essays on Economics and Society,* II, 635.

it failed to make the crucial distinction between movement along a curve and movement of the curve itself,
which was the heart of Malthus' argument, and which
was necessary for discussing a market which was cleared
at disequilibrium prices. There could be increased demand in Mill's sense without an increased demand in
the sense used by the glut theorists and modern economists. On a microeconomic level, Mill accurately described the role of shortages and surpluses in producing
an equilibrium price, but this showed no originality in
1848; J. B. Say had done the same thing in 1803, and
had characterized his own discussion as familiar to the
point of being "trivial" even then.[54] A similar discussion
had in fact appeared in Adam Smith.[55]

Mill did not deny a theory, he dismissed a conception.
By defining the elements of the conception in alien
Ricardian terms he was able to make the whole notion
of supply-and-demand look untenable as a *general* theory
of prices. He acknowledged its role in special situations,
but treated these situations as very rare, and (sometimes)
made supply-and-demand and cost-of-production theories of value mutually exclusive: "Wherever cost of production does *not* regulate the price, there demand and
supply *do* regulate it."[56]

As in the case of Say's Law, Mill's effective silencing
of dissent through unconscious misinterpretation was accompanied by significant contributions of his own which
fitted in more with the dissenters' ideas than with the
ideas of the classical tradition that he was defending.

[54] J. B. Say, *Traité d'économie politique*, 1803 edn., II, 58.
[55] Adam Smith, *The Wealth of Nations*, p. 57.
[56] J. S. Mill, *Essays on Economics and Society*, I, 400; see
also p. 401. Sometimes Mill argued that all determinants of
value operate through supply and demand: [J. S. Mill], "The
Quarterly Review—Political Economy," *Westminster Review*
(January 1825), 221.

In discussing international values, he not only used numerical examples which are readily translatable into schedule concepts in Edgeworth-Bowley diagrams,[57] but also introduced the concept of elasticity—"the proportionality of demand to cheapness" or the "extensibility" of demand.[58] But throughout his life he remained blind to similar ideas when expressed in terms offensive to the Ricardian system. His youthful impatience with Malthus' "insignificant disputes about value"[59] was a forerunner of the more celebrated statement in his *Principles:* "Happily, there is nothing in the laws of value which remains for the present or any future writer to clear up."[60]

POPULATION

John Stuart Mill was as steadfast in his defense of the third pillar of classical orthodoxy—the Malthusian population theory—as he was in defending Say's Law or the cost of production theory of value. Among economists, Nassau Senior had led the attack on the Malthusian population theory in the 1820's and 1830's, though Sismondi had anticipated some of his arguments. Senior stated that the theory was in principle empirically verifiable, but that the shifting use of the word "tendency" had hitherto allowed it to escape refutation.[61] The

[57] J. S. Mill, *Principles,* Ashley edn., pp. 584–91; Toronto edn., pp. 596–600.

[58] *Ibid.,* Ashley edn. p. 603; Toronto edn., p. 614.

[59] [J. S. Mill], "The Quarterly Review—Political Economy," *Westminster Review* (January 1825), 218.

[60] J. S. Mill, *Principles,* Ashley edn., p. 436; Toronto edn., p. 456.

[61] N. W. Senior, *An Outline of the Science of Political Economy,* pp. 43, 47, 50; see also N. W. Senior, *Two Lectures on Population* (London: Saunders and Otley, 1829), pp. 46, 76–77, where the same point is made more obliquely and politely in letters to Malthus.

potentiality of population to increase faster than the food supply was widely accepted, and had been long before Malthus; the significant issue was the *likelihood* of this happening with every advance in food production. Senior argued from history that the opposite had in fact happened. He believed that in the probabilistic sense, "food has a tendency to increase faster than population, because, in fact, it has generally done so."[62]

Although Malthus balked when confronted with this terminology,[63] he later in a different context observed that it was "true, as Mr. Senior says, that there is a tendency to improvement in the condition of the lower classes."[64] Malthus' *Principles of Political Economy* even provided examples from history where wage increases had not been negated by subsequent population growth.[65] He observed that either of "two very different results might follow" from "higher real wages": faster population growth or "improvements in the modes of subsistence."[66] Malthus still maintained that population growth was more probable, but the apparently airtight syllogism of his *Essay on Population* had been quietly abandoned.

Mill's answer in his *Principles* to those who had pointed out the fateful ambiguity in Malthus' use of the word "tendency" was that the correction of "mere language" did not change the real problem, which was that population presses "too" closely on the means of subsis-

---

[62] N. W. Senior, *Two Lectures on Population*, p. 58.

[63] *Ibid.*, pp. 60–64.

[64] Quoted in R. N. Ghosh, "Malthus on Emigration and Colonization: Letters to Wilmot-Horton," *Economica* (February 1963), 53.

[65] T. R. Malthus, *Principles of Political Economy*, pp. 228, 229, 231.

[66] *Ibid.*, p. 226.

tence.[67] Similarly, in a direct criticism of Senior, Mill argued that population bore "too" great a ratio to capital.[68] Mill simply shifted from the analytical question whether a particular theory was valid (or even meaningful as formulated) to a policy position that fewer workers (relative to food or capital) would be a good thing. He gingerly referred to population's "power of increase" and "capacity of multiplication"[69]—potentialities—but proceeded as if he had demonstrated a *probable* Malthusian course of events. In fact, population and food statistics available in the early nineteenth century had repeatedly gone against the classical population doctrine, causing a number of economists, including McCulloch, to repudiate Malthus.[70] Mill himself acknowledged these facts,[71] and then proceeded as if he had not acknowledged them.

Mill's alarm over the dangers of overpopulation seemed to override all other policy considerations. He was, for example, hesitant to condemn exclusionary labor unions because they might indirectly contribute to popu-

[67] J. S. Mill, *Principles,* Ashley edn., p. 359; Toronto edn., p. 353; see also J. S. Mill *Essays on Economics and Society,* I, 368, 449.

[68] J. S. Mill, "Notes on N. W. Senior's *Political Economy,*" *Economica* (August 1945), 135; J. S. Mill, *Principles,* Ashley edn., p. 359; Toronto edn., p. 353.

[69] J. S. Mill, *Principles,* Ashley edn., pp. 156, 157; Toronto edn., pp. 154, 155; see also J. S. Mill, *Essays on Economics and Society,* I, 367.

[70] Mark Blaug, "The Empirical Content of Ricardian Economics," *Journal of Political Economy* (February 1956), 45.

[71] "Subsistence and employment in England have never increased more rapidly than in the last forty years, but every census since 1821 showed a smaller proportional increase of population than that of the period preceding." J. S. Mill, *Principles,* Ashley edn., p. 161; Toronto edn., p. 159.

lation restriction;[72] he considered it a "recommendation" of communism that it might prescribe "penalties" for those who contributed to excessive population growth;[73] even in *On Liberty* he defended laws which "forbid marriage unless the parties can show that they have the means of supporting a family";[74] peasant agriculture was likewise to be judged according to the "cardinal point"—whether it tended to lead to an "increase of population."[75] Ricardo had used, as an analytical device, a wage which would allow workers "to subsist and perpetuate their race, without either increase or diminution,"[76] while denying that wages actually were at this low level.[77] J. S. Mill, however, claimed that population pressure kept wages "habitually" at this cultural subsistence level.[78] Even Malthus had declared, twenty years earlier, that such a level of wages was in fact "rare" and "most unnatural."[79] But Mill remained more Malthusian than Malthus.

SUMMARY AND CONCLUSION

Probably only a man with Mill's massive reputation for an open and forward-looking mind could have so

[72] *Ibid.*, Ashley edn., p. 402; Toronto edn., p. 397; see also J. S. Mill, *Dissertation and Discussions*, Vol. 5, p. 87.

[73] J. S. Mill, *Principles*, Ashley edn., p. 287; Toronto edn., p. 206.

[74] John Stuart Mill, "On Liberty," in *Utilitarianism, Liberty, and Representative Government* (London, J. M. Dent and Sons, Ltd., 1951), p. 220.

[75] J. S. Mill, *Principles*, Ashley edn., p. 287; Toronto edn., p. 283.

[76] Ricardo, *Works*, I, 93.

[77] *Ibid.*, pp. 93–94.

[78] J. S. Mill, *Principles*, Ashley edn., p. 689; Toronto edn., p. 696.

[79] T. R. Malthus, *Principles of Political Economy*, p. 223.

successfully turned the clock back on fundamental developments in economics and perpetuated a population doctrine which had been discredited theoretically and empirically. His victory was not one of logic—he did not come to grips with the real arguments of his adversaries—but of what Jevons called "the noxious influence of authority."[80] Nothing could have been further from Mill's precepts or usual practices than to have sought such a victory on such grounds. It was more characteristic of Mill to eagerly seek out divergent views (his correspondence and association with intellectual opponents such as Comte, Coleridge, and Carlyle being obvious examples) and to publicly change his mind (his celebrated "recantation" of the wages fund doctrine) when presented with convincing arguments to the contrary. One possible explanation of Mill's peculiar role and pattern was suggested by Schumpeter:

> . . . Mill, however, modest on his own behalf, was not at all modest on behalf of his time. "This enlightened age" had solved all problems. And if you knew what its "best thinkers" thought, you were in a position to answer all questions . . . this attitude, besides being ridiculous, made for sterility and—yes—superficiality. There is too little attention to groundwork. There is too little thinking-things-through and much too much confidence that most of the necessary thinking had been done already.[81]

Thus Mill's seeking out of intellectual diversity and opposition was not irreconcilable with his reliance on

[80] W. Stanley Jevons, *The Theory of Political Economy* (New York: Kelley & Millman, 1957), pp. 275–77.
[81] J. A. Schumpeter, *History of Economic Analysis* (New York: Oxford University Press, 1954), p. 530.

prevailing opinions. The dissenting doctrines with which Mill concerned himself were the *accredited* dissenting doctrines, the intellectual equivalents of "His Majesty's loyal opposition." This is nowhere better illustrated than in his deliberately setting out to familiarize himself with "the best socialistic writers"[82] (according to current opinion), which did not include Karl Marx. Nothing in Mill's voluminous writings and correspondence, which dealt extensively with socialism and communism, indicates that he had any inkling that such a person existed.[83]

Similarly, Mill wasted little time on economic doctrines which the Ricardians had long since drummed out of the regiment. His first discussion of the Malthusian glut doctrine in the 1820's treated it as a subject worthy only of heavy-handed satire,[84] and it remained in his later economic *Essays* of 1844 and *Principles* of 1848 merely an obvious "absurdity"[85] involving "inconsistency in its very conception"[86] and amounting to no more than a "chimerical supposition."[87] Despite these sweeping rejections of the general glut doctrine, there was never a single quotation or page reference in Mill's published writings or correspondence to any discussion of general gluts in Sismondi, Lauderdale, or Malthus—even though his *Principles* abounded in such references to almost every

---

[82] John Stuart Mill, *Autobiography* (London: Oxford University Press, 1949), p. 198.

[83] I am indebted to Professor Francis E. Mineka of Cornell University for confirming that the later letters of John Stuart Mill, which he is in the process of editing, contain no reference to Marx.

[84] *Westminister Review* (July 1825), 213–32.

[85] J. S. Mill, *Essays on Some Unsettled Questions of Political Economy*, p. 73.

[86] J. S. Mill, *Principles*, Ashley edn., p. 557; Toronto edn., p. 571.

[87] *Ibid.*, Ashley edn., p. 562; Toronto edn., p. 575.

leading economist of the period, including the glut theorists on other subjects.[88]

Mill declared that his *Principles* was intended to incorporate "new ideas and new applications of ideas"[89] from the recent literature of economics, but it was clear from his correspondence that the new applications were the predominant element. The point was to show how various new practical schemes which Mill favored—such as Wakefield's colonization plan—"do not contradict but *fit into*" the classical theory.[90] On the theoretical level, Mill considered himself to be "sticking pretty close to Ricardo," and added: "I doubt if there will be a single opinion (on pure political economy) in the book, which may not be exhibited as a corollary from his doctrines."[91] There was no apparent intention here of rethinking the basic principles of economics, much less of reexploring old heresies.

Given Mill's limited objectives, it is possible to understand the breakneck speed with which this huge book was written.[92] He frankly intended it as a vehicle for his policy pronouncements, in which he would make use of the reputational "capital" which he had recently earned with his *System of Logic*.[93] In short, another element in

[88] *Ibid.*, Toronto edn., pp. 1097–1155.
[89] *Ibid.*, Ashley edn., p. xxvii.
[90] J. S. Mill, *The Earlier Letters of John Stuart Mill*, p. 642.
[91] *Ibid.*, p. 731.
[92] "The Political Economy . . . was commenced in the autumn of 1845, and was ready for the press before the end of 1847. In this period of little more than two years there was an interval of six months during which the work was laid aside, while I was writing articles." J. S. Mill, *Autobiography*, p. 199. Mill was also a full-time official of India House during this period.
[93] J. S. Mill, *The Earlier Letters of John Stuart Mill*, pp. 708–09.

Mill's negative role was his desire to "do good" in his analytical work rather than to pursue purely intellectual goals. The long-run damage that he did included stamping out the early beginnings of basic concepts of modern economics: the utility theory of value, the schedule concept of supply and demand, and the theory of equilibrium income—all of which had to be rediscovered and redeveloped later as if their early pioneers had never lived.

CHAPTER 6

The Marxian Challenge

THE LAST GREAT CHALLENGE to Say's Law in classical economics, though not a challenge heard in respectable circles, was that of Karl Marx. As in the case of the general glut theorists, the Marxian attack on Say's Law entailed a challenge to the classical theory of value as well. An analysis of disequilibrium and the dynamic forces it sets in motion cannot accept a theory of price determination which holds only in long-run equilibrium. Marxian value and business cycle theory are intimately related, and not overly complicated in themselves, but both must be disentangled from an elaborate mythology which has grown up around them. Marx had no labor theory of value, for example.[1] His business cycle theory is equally remote from popular beliefs about it. As in other areas of Marxian thought, prevailing interpretations and their origins must be analyzed along with Marx's own theories.

UNDERCONSUMPTION VERSUS DISPROPORTIONALITY

The general glut controversy was already history by the time Marx's first writings appeared in the early 1840's, and John Stuart Mill's *Principles* had consolidated the classical defense of Say's Law long before the

[1] See Thomas Sowell, "Marx's *Capital* After One Hundred Years," *Canadian Journal of Economics and Political Science* (February 1967), 50–74.

168

first volume of Marx's *Capital* was published in 1867. In short, there were clearly established positions on Say's Law to which Marx could relate his own ideas, and the manner in which he did so provides important clues to his own position.

The basic dichotomy was between those economists who attributed crises or depressions to internally disproportionate output and those who attributed them to excess aggregate output. The latter may be further divided into those who believed that the value of output somehow exceeded purchasing power (crude underconsumptionists such as Owen and Rodbertus) and those who saw real output exceeding a sustainable level even with markets being cleared—the glut theorists. From his earliest writings to the posthumous volumes of *Capital* and *Theories of Surplus Value,* Marx saw disproportionality as the initiating force in crises. His manuscripts of 1844 show him dismissing the Lauderdale-Malthus position, in opposition to the Say-Ricardo position, which he also did not accept, but which at least represented "clarity about the nature of wealth."[2] In his first published economic writing, *Wage Labour and Capital* in 1845, Marx followed the classical argument that aggregate supply necessarily equaled aggregate demand: "If the price of a commodity rises considerably because of inadequate supply or disproportionate increase of the demand, the price of some other commodity must necessarily have fallen proportionately . . ."[3]

Later, in *Capital* Marx answered the underconsumptionists by arguing repeatedly that consumption or de-

[2] Karl Marx, *Economic and Philosophic Manuscripts of 1844* (Moscow: Foreign Languages Publishing House, 1961), p. 128.

[3] Karl Marx, "Wage Labour and Capital," Karl Marx and Frederick Engels, *Selected Works* (Moscow: Foreign Languages Publishing House, 1955), i, 86.

mand tends to *increase* immediately before a cyclical downturn.[4] He rejected the whole underconsumptionist position with contempt:

> It is purely a tautology to say that crises are caused by the scarcity of solvent consumers, or of a paying consumption . . . . If any commodities are unsaleable, it means that no solvent purchasers have been found for them, in other words, consumers (whether commodities are bought in the last instance for productive or individual consumption). But if one were to attempt to clothe this tautology with a semblance of a profounder justification by saying that the working class receive too small a portion of their own product, and the evil would be remedied by giving them a larger share of it, or raising their wages, we should reply that crises are precisely always preceded by a period in which wages rise generally and the working class actually get a larger share of the annual product intended for consumption. From the point of view of the advocates of "simple" (!) common sense, such a period should rather remove a crisis.[5]

Engels denounced the underconsumptionists again in *Anti-Duhring:*

> But unfortunately the underconsumption of the masses, the restriction of the consumption of the masses to what is necessary for their maintenance and reproduction, is not a new phenomenon . . . . Therefore, while underconsumption has been a constant feature of history for thousands of years, the general shrinkage of the market which breaks out in crises as the result of a surplus of production is a phenomenon only of the last fifty years . . . . The

[4] Marx, *Capital,* II, 86, 362, 475, III, 359, 528, 567.
[5] *Ibid.,* II, 475–76.

underconsumption of the masses is a necessary condition of all forms of society based on exploitation, consequently also of the capitalist form, but it is the capitalist form which first produces crises. The underconsumption of the masses is therefore also a necessary condition of crises, and plays in them a role which has long been recognised; but it tells us just as little why crises exist today as why they did not exist at earlier periods.[6]

Marx and Engels thus dismissed underconsumption as either the precipitating factor or a sufficient condition for cyclical downturns. It should now be considered in what sense it was a necessary condition, as Engels termed it, or the "last cause" of all crises, as Marx termed it.[7] Marx rejected the "insatiable wants" defense of Say's Law by arguing that wants as such are irrelevant in a capitalist economy, where workers lack the means of translating their wants into market demand: "If overproduction could only occur after all members of the nation had satisfied even their most essential needs, in the history of bourgeois society up to the present not only no general overproduction, but even no partial overproduction, could have occurred."[8]

In short, the "limit of production is the *capitalist's profit* and not at all the *needs of the producers*." Production "comes to a standstill at a point determined by the production and realisation of profit, not by the satisfaction of social needs."[9] Whatever the validity of these arguments, it is clear that Marx's statements are statements about the basic institutional nature of capitalism rather

[6] Frederick Engels, *Herr Eugen Duhring's Revolution in Science* (New York: International Publishers, 1939), p. 312.
[7] Marx, *Capital*, III, 568.
[8] Marx, *Theories of Surplus Value*, p. 394.
[9] Marx, *Capital*, III, 303.

than statements about the behavior of economic variables (sequentially or simultaneously) within an implicitly given institutional framework. He had no underconsumption theory in this sense, and explicity rejected it in this sense. Interpreters who have viewed Marx as an underconsumptionist have been driven to the farcical expedient of quoting each other and ignoring Marx.[10]

From the earliest writings of Marx and Engels, fluctuations in the relative prices of individual commodities—symptoms of disproportionality—were linked to crises:

> The economists say that the *average price* of commodities is equal to the cost of production; that this is a *law*. The anarchical movement, in which rise is compensated by fall and fall by rise, is regarded by them as chance. With just as much right one could regard the fluctuations as the law and the determination by the cost of production as chance. . . . But it is solely these fluctuations, which, looked at more closely, bring with them the most fearful devastations and, like earthquakes, cause bourgeois society to tremble to its foundations.[11]

Just as it was here "solely" the price fluctuations brought on by disproportionality which precipitated crises, so in *The German Ideology* (1845) "overproduction causes crises only through its influence on the exchange-value of products"[12] and in *The Poverty of*

[10] For example, Martin Bronfenbrenner cites Paul M. Sweezy, who in turn cites a number of other economists—not including Karl Marx. M. Bronfenbrenner, *"Das Kapital* for the Modern Man," *Science & Society* (Fall 1965), 419–38; P. M. Sweezy, *The Theory of Capitalist Development* (New York: Monthly Review Press, 1956), Chapter XI.

[11] Marx, "Wage Labour and Capital," *op. cit.,* p. 87.

[12] Karl Marx, *The German Ideology* (New York: International Publishers, 1947), p. 163.

Philosophy (1847) "overproduction and many other features of industrial anarchy"[13] result from stresses on the price-allocational mechanism due to disproportionality. Engels likewise stated in 1844 that "the fluctuations of competition and its tendency to crisis would be impossible" if producers would "organize production" and "share it out amongst themselves,"[14]—a prescription which is in keeping with the disproportionality theory of crises but one which would be meaningless if a deficiency of aggregate demand were the basic problem. In Marx's later writings, as in the earlier ones, price fluctuations and disproportionality continued to be linked to crises: "Violent fluctuations of price . . . cause interruptions, great collisions, or even catastrophes in the process of reproduction."[15] While there are tendencies toward equilibrium by the competitive market process, "the continuity of the process itself equally presupposes the constant disproportionality, which it has continuously, often violently, to even out."[16]

The dialectical notion that "necessity" and "accident" are not polar opposites, as commonly assumed, runs through the writings of Marx and Engels,[17] including

[13] Karl Marx, *The Poverty of Philosophy* (New York: International Publishers, 1963), p. 44.

[14] F. Engels in appendix to Karl Marx, *Economic and Philosophic Manuscripts of 1844*, p. 196.

[15] Marx, *Capital,* III, 140.

[16] Marx, *Theories of Surplus Value*, p. 368.

[17] F. Engels "Ludwig Feuerbach and the End of Classical German Philosophy," Karl Marx and Friedrich Engels, *Basic Writings on Politics and Philosophy,* ed. L. S. Feuer (Garden City: Doubleday & Co., Inc., 1959), p. 226; Engels, "The Origin of the Family, Private Property and the State," Marx and Engels, *Selected Works,* II, p. 322; Marx and Engels, *Selected Correspondence* (New York: International Publishers, 1942), pp. 484, 518; F. Engels, *Dialectics of Nature* (Moscow: Progress Publishers, 1964), pp. 38, 223.

173

their analysis of disproportionality and the price-deter-mination process. Dialectics, according to Engels, deals with laws which "assert themselves unconsciously, in the form of external necessity in the midst of an endless series of seeming accidents."[18] This applied to the ultimate necessity of resource allocation which imposed itself on the individually uncontrolled producers through fluctuations in the prices of their products. There was "no necessary, but only an accidental, connection between the volume of society's demand for a certain article and the volume represented by the production of this article,"[19] or—looked at another way—the "mutual confluence and intertwining of the reproduction or circulation processes of different capitals is on the one hand necessitated by the division of labour, and on the other is accidental."[20] Price fluctuations in disequilibrium are symptoms of the external necessity which asserts itself in this particular pattern of seeming accidents:

> . . . the law of the value of commodities ultimately determines how much of its disposable working-time society can expend on each particular class of commodities. But this constant tendency to equilibrium, of the various spheres of production, is exercised, only in the shape of a reaction against the constant upsetting of this equilibrium. The *a priori* system on which the division of labour, within the workshop, is regularly carried out, becomes in the division of labour within the society, an *a posteriori*, nature-imposed necessity, controlling the lawless caprice of the producers, and perceptible in the barometrical fluctuations of the market prices.[21]

[18] F. Engels, "Ludwig Feuerbach," *op. cit.*, p. 226.
[19] Marx, *Capital*, III, 220.
[20] Marx, *Theories of Surplus Value*, p. 385.
[21] Marx, *Capital*, I, 391.

174

The equalization postulated in classical theory was almost never an empirical reality, according to Marx, occurring so seldom that it might, for all practical purposes be "considered as not happening."[22] There were compensating deviations which produce a "prevailing tendency, in a very complicated and approximate manner, as a never ascertainable average of ceaseless fluctuations."[23] It was only in this "vague and meaningless form" that "the value of the commodities is determined by the labor contained in them."[24]

The Marxian concept of value as "socially necessary labor time" implied equilibrium allocation of labor as well as technically efficient labor.[25] The "concrete" or "individual" labor actually performed was sharply distinguished from the "abstract," "social," or "socially necessary" labor representing value. The market evaluated the individual labor as social labor,[26] accepting it only at a discount if too much was expended, either in terms of demand or technological necessity, and at a premium if insufficient labor was devoted to a particular sector.[27] In the language of the later Marxian writings, the divergence between the two kinds of labor—disproportionality—led to crises.[28]

Marx followed Robert Torrens (without acknowledgment) in arguing that overproduction in particular sectors led to liquidity crises and thus to general overpro-

---

[22] *Ibid.*, III, 223.   [23] *Ibid.*, III, 190.   [24] *Ibid.*, III, 203.

[25] *Ibid.*, I, 120; Marx, *Theories of Surplus Value*, pp. 398–99; F. Engels, *Herr Eugen Duhring's Revolution in Science*, p. 338; Marx, *The Poverty of Philosophy*, p. 15; Marx, *Critique of Political Economy*, p. 59; Marx, *Capital*, III, 214–15.

[26] Marx, *Capital*, I, 84; Marx, *Critique of Political Economy*, pp. 47, 63–64.

[27] Marx, *Capital*, III, 221.

[28] Marx, *Theories of Surplus Value*, pp. 381–408; Marx, *Critique of Political Economy*, p. 80; Engels, *Herr Eugen Duhring's Revolution in Science*, p. 338.

duction relative to the contracting supply of money and credit. He was not as explicit as Torrens, who had indicated that increased demands for liquidity in sectors experiencing losses were not offset by increasing supplies of liquidity from sectors experiencing unusually high profits, because of the crisis psychology. Like J. S. Mill, Marx argued that there can be an excess demand for money: aggregate supply can exceed aggregate demand because "the demand for the general commodity, money, exchange value, is greater than the demand for all particular commodities."[29]

Marx was well aware that the insufficiency of demand was an insufficiency only at given prices: "The excess of commodities is always relative, that is, it is an excess at certain prices. The prices at which the commodities are then absorbed are ruinous for the producer or merchant."[30] The lower prices are ruinous because the whole price structure cannot deflate smoothly: "The fixed charges . . . remain the same, and in part cannot be paid."[31] Even commodities which were not among those which had been overproduced "are now suddenly in *relative* overproduction, because the means to buy them, and therewith the demand for them, have contracted."[32] Thus "in times of general overproduction, the overproduction in some spheres is always the *result,* the *consequence,* of overproduction in the leading articles of commerce."[33]

The Marxian sequence did not begin with overproduction in the Sismondi-Malthus sense of an above-equilibrium real output, though it ended with an above-equilibrium output at current money prices. Against those who tried "to argue away the possibility of a general glut,"

[29] Marx, *Theories of Surplus Value,* p. 392.
[30] *Ibid.,* p. 393.   [31] *Ibid.,* pp. 390–91.
[32] *Ibid.,* p. 401.   [33] *Ibid.,* pp. 393, 408.

Marx declared: "For a crisis (and therefore also overproduction) to be general, it is sufficient for it to grip the principal articles of trade."[34]

CYCLES AND "BREAKDOWNS"

Marx's theory of individual downturns was developed in greater detail than his theory of the business cycle as a whole. The periodicity of cyclical fluctuations was attributed to capital replacement cycles, reinforced by bunched new investments brought on by the crises themselves—presumably in their aftermath, when conditions have become favorable again.[35] The particular periods of the replacement cycles varied in the writings of Marx and Engels,[36] and in *Capital,* where the period was assumed to be ten years, it was pointed out that the specific time period was not crucial.[37] After Marx's death, Engels moved to the view that periodic depressions had given way to chronic stagnation,[38] but without any elaboration of reasons or evidence.

Marx is often interpreted as having a theory of a "breakdown" of the capitalist economy, corresponding to the classical stationary state. This breakdown is sometimes linked to the underconsumptionist interpretation of Marx, so that it means that the economy ultimately reaches a point at which it cannot purchase its own output, nor recover the power to do so. Thorstein Veblen

[34] *Ibid.,* p. 393.   [35] Marx, *Capital,* II, 211.
[36] F. Engels, *The Condition of the Working-Class in England in 1844* (London: George Allen and Unwin, 1952), pp. x, xiv; Marx, *Economic and Philosophic Manuscripts of 1844,* p. 195; Marx, *Capital,* II, 211.
[37] Marx, *Capital,* II, 211.
[38] Engels in Marx, *Capital,* III, 574n–575n; Engels, "Preface," Karl Marx, *The Poverty of Philosophy,* p. 20n; Engels, *The Condition of the Working-Class in England in 1844,* p. xvi.

pointed out in 1906 that there was simply *no such theory* in Marx;[39] later commentators have neither cited such a theory nor relinquished this interpretation. Three indirect pieces of evidence are usually referred to in defense of this interpretation:

1. *The Marxian "law" of the tendency of a falling rate of profit*—As in the classical theory, this could lead to a level of profit which would not encourage any additional net investment. However, Marx was at pains to point out the distinction between secular profit declines and "temporary" declines for other reasons,[40] such as play a role in his cycle theory. He also did not discuss the long-run end result of such falls, but considered instead the offsetting actions which such a tendency would call forth, and the social tensions these offsetting actions would generate.[41] Obviously, this was much more central to the question of revolution, which was Marx's ultimate concern.

2. *The ever-increasing severity of crises mentioned in various writings of Marx and Engels*—This idea first appeared in an early article by Engels (later cited approvingly by Marx).[42] In this article, and in a later discussion by Engels, crises had an ever-widening scope for their operation as all sectors of the traditional, precapitalist economy tended to become more and more drawn into the capitalist market system over

[39] Thorstein Veblen, "The Socialist Economics of Karl Marx and His Followers," *Quarterly Journal of Economics* (August 1906), 591.

[40] Marx, *Capital,* III, 249.

[41] See Thomas Sowell, "Marx's *Capital* After One Hundred Years," *Canadian Journal of Economics and Political Science* (February 1967), 63.

[42] Engels in appendix to Marx, *Economic and Philosophic Manuscripts of 1844,* pp. 175–209; Marx and Engels, *Selected Correspondence,* p. 232.

time. Engels declared that each crises was "worse" than the last in that it was "more universal" in its scope,[43] ultimately embracing the world market.[44] In these early writings, as in the later Marxian works, crises lead eventually to "social revolution"[45] through their effect on men, not to permanent economic breakdown of the capitalist economy. This conception was in keeping with the role later ascribed to crises in the *Communist Manifesto,* where "the commercial crises . . . by their periodical return put the existence of the entire bourgeois society on its trial, each time more treateningly."[46] Similarly, in *Capital,* the "knell of capitalist private property sounds" when the "expropriators are expropriated"[47]—a deliberate act of men, not a mechanistic self-destruction by the economy.

3. *The Marxian assertion that capitalism destroys itself by its own internal contradictions*—These are Hegelian "contradictions"—internal conflicting forces which transform the entity of which they are part—and, as such, are, in Hegel's words, "the very moving principle of the world," rather than something which is "unthinkable."[48] Marx used the term contradiction to refer to "conflicting elements" in his *Theories of*

[43] Engels in appendix to Marx, *Economic and Philosophic Manuscripts of 1844,* p. 196.

[44] Engels, *The Condition of the Working-Class in England in 1844,* p. 82.

[45] Engels in Marx, *Economic and Philosophic Manuscripts of 1844,* p. 195.

[46] Marx and Engels, "The Communist Manifesto," *A Handbook of Marxism,* ed. Emil Burns (New York: Random House, 1935), p. 29.

[47] Marx, *Capital,* I, 837.

[48] G. W. F. Hegel, *The Science of Logic* (London, 1892), trans. W. Wallace, p. 223. See also J. A. Schumpeter, *History of Economic Analysis,* p. 438n.

Surplus Value, and his use of the same term in designating his own theories in *Capital* obviously indicates that he was not using it in the usual sense of logical impossibility.[49] The underlying concept of Hegelian contradiction helps explain the repeated presence in Marxian writings of analogies to the metamorphoses of nature, in which an organism is transformed by its own internal forces, as when a germinating seed bursts its integument or a caterpillar turns itself into a butterfly.[50] In the same way a capitalist economy does not destroy itself as an economy, but rather generates the internal social pressures which transform it into a socialist economy.

Marx was repeatedly and unequivocally clear that he regarded crises in cyclical, not secular, terms. Crises were "transient" and "momentary"[51] phenomena. He said: "There are no permanent crises."[52]

SAY'S LAW

To Marx, J. B. Say was variously "inane,"[53] "miserable,"[54] "thoughtless,"[55] "dull,"[56] "comical,"[57] and a

[49] *Theories of Surplus Value,* p. 377, and, for example, Chapter IV of Vol. I ("Contradictions in the Formula for Capital") and Chapter XV of Vol. III ("Unravelling the Internal Contradictions of the Law" of the falling rate of profit) of *Capital.*

[50] Marx, *Capital,* I, 837; Engels, *Herr Eugen Duhring's Revolution in Science,* p. 117; Marx, "Wage Labour and Capital," Marx and Engels, *Selected Works,* I, 83; Marx, *Theories of Surplus Value,* p. 186; Marx and Engels, *Selected Correspondence,* p. 485; F. Engels, *Engels on Capital,* ed. and trans. L. E. Mins (New York: International Publishers, 1937), p. 60.

[51] Marx, *Capital,* III, 292, 568.

[52] Marx, *Theories of Surplus Value,* p. 373n.

[53] *Ibid.,* pp. 203, 369.   [54] *Ibid.,* p. 369.

[55] Marx, *Capital,* III, 979n.

[56] Marx, *Critique of Political Economy,* p. 232.

[57] *Ibid.,* p. 123n.

"humbug."[58] The doctrine he represented was "preposterous,"[59] "a paltry evasion,"[60] "childish babble"[61] and "pitiful claptrap."[62] However, Marx's general visceral reactions must be separated from his specific objections. On some of the central issues, Marx's substantive arguments against Say's Law differed little from John Stuart Mill's arguments in favor of it.[63] Each denied that overproduction of aggregate real output was possible, and each affirmed that credit contraction could cause temporarily deficient money demand. Both conceived of causation in a sequential sense, Marx tracing the origin of crises to disproportionalities in the real sector and Mill to loss of "confidence" in the monetary sector. Marx's opposition to Say's Law took the form of attacks on specific auxiliary doctrines, rather than on the essential principle:

1. Marx denied that production was a function of the desire to consume, thereby denying the *ex ante* equality of aggregate supply and demand postulated by James Mill and John Stuart Mill. He pointed out that there was no way to equate, *ex ante,* the quantity of a given good produced and the quantity of another good desired, since this would involve a prediction of relative prices.[64]

2. Marx labeled the *ex post* equality of supply and demand in James Mill an "identity" and denounced the "tautological phrases" of his exposition of Say's Law.[65] Marx thus rejected the necessary equality of

[58] Marx, *Theories of Surplus Value,* p. 370.
[59] *Ibid.,* p. 396. [60] *Ibid.,* p. 392.
[61] *Ibid.,* p. 379. [62] *Ibid.,* p. 371.
[63] See Bela A. Balassa, "Karl Marx and John Stuart Mill," *Weltwirtschaftliches Archiv,* 83, 2, 1959, pp. 154–58.
[64] Marx, *Theorien über den Mehrwert,* dritter teil, p. 97.
[65] *Ibid.,* p. 96. See also Karl Marx, *Critique of Political Economy,* pp. 123–24.

181

supply and demand in one sense as untrue and in the
other sense as irrelevant. He never rejected the *possible*
equality of supply and demand, and in fact demonstrated the conditions necessary for equilibrium in his
reproduction schemes in the second volume of *Capital;*
this acceptance, however, of Say's Equality as an equilibrium condition was no concession on the issues
raised in the classical controversies over Say's Law.

3. Marx dismissed the classical comparative-statics
argument that no one would "continue" to produce
without an adequate return as irrelevant to the issues
actually raised: "There can be no doubt that nobody
'will continually produce a commodity for which there
is no demand,' but no one is talking about such an
absurd hypothesis. Also, it has nothing whatever to
do with the matter."[66]

4. The "corresponding deficiency" or "undersupply
of complements" arguments were denied in the sequential causation sense that increased production in
one sector or country—not reduced production in another sector or country—initiated the downturn.[67]

5. The doctrine that sales proceeds are necessarily
immediately respent during the same period was denied by Marx, as by J. S. Mill in his later writings.[68]

6. The accidental nature of crises was denied, since
the basic conditions of capitalist production create the
need for *ex post* sectoral adjustments.[69] The reproduction schemes in the second volume of *Capital* showed
the intricacy of the adjustments required even for
"simple reproduction," and still more so with expand-

[66] Marx, *Theories of Surplus Value*, pp. 380–81.
[67] *Ibid.*, p. 410.
[68] *Ibid.*, p. 380.
[69] *Ibid.*, pp. 408–09.

ing output, so that it is equilibrium which is an accident "under the crude conditions of this production."[70]

Summary and Conclusions

Marxian "value" must be distinguished from classical value theory. Marx criticized the whole approach of classical economics with respect to value, from his earliest writings of the 1840's:

Mill makes the mistake—generally like Ricardo's school—of giving the *abstract law* without the variation and continuous suspension by which it comes into being. If it is an *independent* law, for example, that the costs of production ultimately—or rather with the periodic and accidental coincidence of supply and demand—determine price (value), it is equally an *independent* law that this relationship does not hold and that value and production costs have no necessary relationship. Indeed, supply and demand coincide only momentarily because of previous fluctuations of supply and demand, because of the discrepancy of costs and exchange value, just as this fluctuation and discrepancy in turn succeed the momentary coincidence of supply and demand. This *actual* process, in which this law is only an abstract, accidental, and one-sided factor, becomes something accidental, something unessential with the modern economists. Why? Since they reduce the economic order to precise and exact formulas, the basic formula, abstractly expressed, would have to be: In the economic order lawfulness is determined by its opposite, lawlessness. The real law of the economic order is *contingency* from which

[70] Marx, *Capital,* II, 362.

183

we scientists arbitrarily stabilize some aspects in the form of laws.[71]

Although Marx's position did not, in substance, contradict the classical theory, his emphasis was on the *process* of price determination, not on its hypothetical end results in terms of relative prices. Throughout his career, and that of Engels, the potentialities of the price-fluctuation process for producing crises was a central concern. The relevance of this for invidious comparisons between capitalism and the socialist alternative in the near background was obvious: ". . . the total production of society is regulated, not by a collectively thought-out plan, but by blind laws, which operate with elemental force, in the last resort in the storms of periodical commercial crises."[72] For Marx, equilibrium values imply equilibrium resource allocation: "The postulate that the individual value of a commodity should correspond to its social value has then the significance that the total quantity of commodities contains the quantity of social labor necessary for its production."[73]

But though aggregate equilibrium was a necessary condition for Marxian values to equal empirical prices, it was not a sufficient condition: "It is not the values of the commodities but their prices [costs] of production about which competition causes the market prices in the various branches of production to rotate."[74] It was not a question of temporary "accidental deviations of market prices from prices of production" which were the long-

[71] Karl Marx, *Writings of the Young Marx on Philosophy and Society,* ed. L. D. Easton and K. H. Guddat (New York: Doubleday & Co., Inc., 1967), pp. 265–66.

[72] F. Engels, "The Housing Question," Marx and Engels, *Selected Works,* II, 323.

[73] Marx, *Capital,* III, 215.

[74] Marx, *Theories of Surplus Value,* p. 256.

run equilibrium prices, but rather "the constant deviation of market prices, insofar as these correspond to prices of production, from the real values of commodities."[75] In short, even in equilibrium, prices do not correspond to Marxian values, due to different capital-labor ratios in the production processes of various industries and the need for profit-equalization among firms and industries with different capital-intensities. This key point in Bohm-Bawerk's criticism of Marx had also been a key point in Marx's criticism of Ricardo.[76] Nor was this an inconsistent after-thought or a "change of mind" between volumes I and III of *Capital,* as sometimes suggested. Marx's correspondence outlined his planned "transformation" of values into prices in 1862, five years before publication of the first volume of *Capital,*[77] and the first volume itself repudiated the classical value theory: ". . . average prices do not directly coincide with the values of commodities, as Adam Smith, Ricardo, and others believe."[78]

Marx was quite clear that his "values" would not coincide with prices in disequilibrium and need not coincide with prices even in long-run equilibrium. When there was optimal allocation, "then the products of the various groups are sold at their values . . . or at prices which are modifications of their values or prices of production due to general laws,"[79] i.e., profit equalization. Marxian value was thus a construct rather than a theory.

---

[75] *Ibid.*

[76] *Ibid.,* pp. 212, 214, 221, 224, 231, 232, 249, 250, 282; Marx and Engels, *Selected Correspondence,* p. 243. Cf. Eugen von Böhm-Bawerk, *Karl Marx and the Close of His System* (New York: MacMillan Co., 1898), p. 61 and Chapter III, passim.

[77] Marx and Engels, *Selected Correspondence,* pp. 129–31.

[78] Marx, *Capital,* I, 185n.   [79] *Ibid.,* III, 745.

Marx himself referred to "Value as defined" in the first volume of *Capital*,[80] and this was no isolated verbal slip. Marx's letters to Engels refer to the "definition of value" which he used in his *Critique of Political Economy*,[81] and later in *Capital*,[82] and a letter to another friend referred to the "concept of value" in *Capital* and to the "nonsense" from critics "about the necessity of proving" this concept.[83] Marx's disavowal of any attempt to "prove" his definition of value was in sharp contrast to much of the later critical literature which claims that he had vainly attempted a "dialectical" proof in the opening chapter of *Capital*.[84] To a contemporary critic who had argued along similar lines, Engels replied that his "total lack of understanding as to the nature of dialectics is shown by the very fact that he regards it as a mere instrument through which things can be proved."[85]

Much of the confusion over Marxian value comes from the fact that (1) Marx's *Capital* proceeds by successive approximations, (2) the final approximation appeared (posthumously) twenty-seven years after the first, allowing time for Marx's disciples and critics (notably the rising marginal utility school) to harden their posi-

---

[80] *Ibid.*, I, 45.

[81] Marx and Engels, *Selected Correspondence*, p. 106.

[82] *Ibid.*, p. 232. [83] *Ibid.*, p. 246.

[84] ". . . for his system he needed a formal proof . . . . So he turned to dialectical speculation." Böhm-Bawerk, *Karl Marx and the Close of His System*, pp. 151–52. Böhm-Bawerk made the claim, often echoed since, that Marx had attempted "a stringent syllogistic conclusion allowing of no exception" (*ibid.*, 63), that Marx was making "a logical proof, a dialectical deduction" (*ibid.*, 131). This "proof" continues in some unspecified way to be linked to dialectics or Hegelianism. Cf. Donald F. Gordon, "What Was the Labor Theory of Value?" *American Economic Review* (May 1959), 471.

[85] Engels, *Herr Eugen Duhring's Revolution in Science*, p. 147.

186

tions on a labor theory of value which did not exist, and
(3) the ideas of the so-called "Ricardian socialists" on
value and distribution are often erroneously attributed
to Marx. Marx's writings and correspondence repeatedly
indicated that he was proceeding by successive approximation in *Capital*.[86] He had defended this method earlier
in his *Critique of Political Economy*,[87] and the first volume of *Capital* itself contained numerous references to
problems to be resolved in the Third Book.[88] Engels' objection that the discussion of value and surplus value
in Volume I of *Capital* was likely to be misunderstood
by people who were "not accustomed to this sort of abstract thought"[89] was dismissed by Marx:

> . . . the *conversion of surplus value into profit* . . .
> presupposes a previous account of the *process of
> circulation of capital* since the turnover of capital,
> etc., plays a part here. Hence this matter can be
> set forth only in the third book. . . . Here it will
> be shown whence the *way of thinking* of the philistine
> and the vulgar economist derives, namely, from the
> fact that only the immediate form in which relation-
> ships appear is always reflected in their brain, and not
> their *inner connections*. If the latter were the case,
> moreover, what would be the need for a *science* at
> all?
>
> If I were to *silence* all such objections in advance,
> I should ruin the whole dialectical method of develop-
> ment. On the contrary, this method has the *advantage*
> of continually *setting traps* for these fellows which pro-

[86] Sowell, "Marx's *Capital* After One Hundred Years," *op. cit.*,
pp. 56, 58, 66–67, 73.
[87] Marx, *Critique of Political Economy*, pp. 292–94.
[88] Marx, *Capital*, I, 238, 239n, 357, 574, 618–19.
[89] Marx and Engels, *Selected Correspondence*, p. 220.

voke them to untimely demonstrations of their asininity.[90]

Although Marx's economic theories were presented in terms of labor "value," they could be restated in other terms without distorting their meaning, just as the Keynesian "labour unit" (which has the same meaning) is not essential to that system. Marx declared that "even if there were no chapter on value" in *Capital,* the relationships he demonstrated would stand anyway.[91] While Marx's actual conclusions stand or fall independently of his value concept, this has been obscured by the tendency to attribute to Marx the views of the Ricardian socialists. For example, the idea that workers should receive the full "value" of their product was scorned by Marx as "the utopian interpretation of Ricardo's theory,"[92] and Engels pointed out that Marx "never based his communist demands upon this," which was "simply an application of morality to economics."[93] Similarly, those who wanted labor values to determine prices under socialism were told by Marx that they would have to "prove that the *time* needed to create a commodity indicates exactly the degree of its utility and marks its proportional rela-

[90] *Engels on Capital,* pp. 126–27.
[91] Marx and Engels, *Selected Correspondence,* p. 246.
[92] Marx and Engels, *Selected Correspondence,* p. 172; see also *Critique of Political Economy,* pp. 71n–72n; *The Poverty of Philosophy,* p. 49. "In no conceivable state of society can the worker receive for consumption the entire value of his product." Engels, "Preface," *ibid.,* p. 21. ". . . deductions from the 'undiminished proceeds of labour' are an economic necessity and their magnitude is . . . in no way calculable by equity." Karl Marx, "Critique of the Gotha Programme," *Selected Works,* II, 22.
[93] Engels, "Preface," Karl Marx, *The Poverty of Philosophy,* p. 11.

tion to the demand."[94] Marxian "socially necessary labour" could logically have been translated into the language of the marginal utility theory had Marx had the flexibility, the time, and the energy to do so.

Even Marxian "exploitation" does not depend on the labor value definition, although obviously its exposition is facilitated and its plausibility enhanced by this phraseology. However, since "surplus value" is simply the difference between wages and the worker's average product, it would remain unchanged under a marginal productivity theory of wages in a perfectly competitive market.[95] The crucial assumption on which Marx's results depend is that capital is itself a product of labor rather than an independent source of output or a contribution

[94] Karl Marx, *The Poverty of Philosophy,* pp. 60–61.

[95] The Marxian "rate of exploitation" or rate of surplus value is $S/V = AP - MP/MP$, where $S = surplus\ value$, $V = $ variable capital (the wage bill), $AP = $ the average product of labor, and $MP = $ the marginal product of labor. This is shown on the diagram below, where $W_0 = $ the wage rate and $L_0 = $ the amount of labor hired:

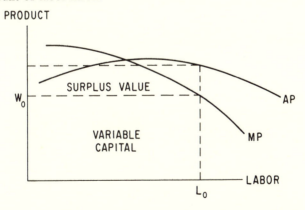

Thus, there is surplus value even though workers are paid their marginal product, with no "exploitation" in Pigou's sense.

189

of its legal owner.[96] Since Marx regarded economics as a study of the relations among men rather than the relations among things, the point was that the Marxian capitalist was left in a *personally* functionless role similar to that of the Ricardian landlord who grew richer in his sleep. It was no more necessary for Marx to argue that capital as such was unproductive than it was for Ricardo to argue that land was unproductive. Indeed, it would have been a complete contradiction for Marx to have argued that the capitalistic means of production were worthless and then that the key to social reconstruction lay precisely in the collective ownership of these means of production.

[96] Karl Marx, *Capital,* I, 637–38; *Theories of Surplus Value,* p. 360; *Economic and Philosophic Manuscripts of 1844,* pp. 23–24.

CHAPTER 7

The Neoclassical Period

D ISCUSSION of Say's Law practically disappeared from the writings of the leading economists during the neoclassical period. The marginalist revolution in microeconomics and general equilibrium theory did not call forth any similar questioning of this pillar of classical economics. Even Jevons, who made the most sweeping condemnations of John Stuart Mill and of the Ricardians generally,[1] left Say's Law unchallenged. Marshall was content to quote or paraphrase Mill. There was, in effect, a "thoroughgoing intellectual boycott"[2] and an "almost total obliteration"[3] of the dissenting doctrines. At the same time, the more systematic development of the quantity theory of money, in keeping with the new technical emphasis of the profession, inadvertently set the stage for the raising of basic questions about the meaning and validity of Say's Law. In the professionally unrecognized "underworld" of economics, challenges continued to be hurled at the orthodox, most notably and persistently by J. A. Hobson. The development of business cycle theories, pioneered by Clement Juglar in 1860, proceeded through the neoclassical

[1] W. Stanley Jevons, *The Theory of Political Economy* (New York: Kelley & Millman, 1957), pp. 275–77.
[2] T. W. Hutchison, *A Review of Economic Doctrines* (Oxford: Oxford University Press, 1966), p. 359.
[3] John Maynard Keynes, *Essays in Biography,* ed. Geoffrey Keynes (New York: Horizon Press, Inc., 1951), p. 117.

period with the work of Tugan-Baronowsky, Spiethoff, Schumpeter, and others, obliquely raising issues related to Say's Law, but not confronting it head-on.

THE PRICING DICHOTOMY[4]

Classical and neoclassical economics typically treated the determination of the relative prices of goods separately from the determination of the absolute or money prices of goods. Relative prices were considered to be structured—whether according to labor cost, marginal utility, etc.—in a money economy in the same pattern that would have emerged in a barter economy. The money supply determined the general price level or the specific money amounts on the respective price tags of the goods. The quantity theory of money, whether viewed as an identical relationship $(MV \equiv PT)$ or as a behavioral theory about the independence of the money supply, the stability of velocity and the passive response of the price level,[5] was an essentially static theory of money price determination which did not formally explain the dynamic process by which individual money prices are determined. At some point in such a process, there must exist a possibility of idle money balances, beyond what is desired, so that there can develop excess demand for goods at the existing price level, thereby raising that level and, alternatively, the possibility of an ex-

---

[4] The discussion in this section draws on an unpublished doctoral dissertation by Charles W. Baird, "The Dichotomy Between Monetary and Value Theory in Classical and Neoclassical Economics" (University of California at Berkeley, 1968). My conclusions differ somewhat from those of Professor Baird, who of course bears no responsibility for my errors or shortcomings.

[5] Irving Fisher, *The Purchasing Power of Money* (New York: Augustus M. Kelley, 1963), pp. 156–57, 159, 172.

cess *supply* of goods, at the existing price level, or an excess demand for money, so as to lower the price level. Moreover, for a determinate equilibrium of money prices, there must be some given marginal rate of substitution of goods for real money balances—some demand for money for *other* than immediate transactions during the current period. If money is literally desired only for transactions during the period under consideration, any sum of money will be consistent with any level of prices, since velocity (or its reciprocal, average cash balances) can vary in such a way as to make them consistent. In short, if there can be no excess demand (or supply) for money, there can be no determinate relationship between the money supply and the price level. In turn, this means that the classical argument that there is only a transaction demand for money (Say's Identity) is incompatible with the quantity theory of money, in which the price level is related (by either a constant or by a stable function) to the money supply.

A distinction must be made between separate treatment of microeconomic pricing and of monetary theory as a pedagogical or expository device, on the one hand, and a substantive belief that the two kinds of price determination were in fact independently derivable in a mutually consistent manner. If they are believed to be independently derivable, then the individual demand functions for the respective goods are *not* dependent on the real value of money balances. If the two kinds of prices are seen to be simultaneously determined as an analytical necessity, as well as in empirical fact, then the demand function for any good must depend upon desired versus actual money wealth. There is an important third consideration: that this problem of an invalid pricing dichotomy (the inconsistency between Say's Identity and

193

the quantity theory of money) was simply not seen by many of the classical and neoclassical economists.

One of the great mysteries of the Marshallian demand curve is just what specifically was supposed to be impounded in *caetiris paribus.*[6] Obviously there would be no need to impound things which do not affect individual demand curves anyway. One of the things Marshall explicitly impounded was "the amount of money or general purchasing power at a person's disposal at any time."[7] This could mean his current real income and/or the real value of his money balances. By extended exegesis, it might be possible to construct some balance of probabilities as to which is more in keeping with the rest of Marshall's writings. However, the very fact that Marshall left the ambiguity standing through a lifetime of work in both micro and macroeconomics seems to be a stronger indication of a lack of confrontation of the issue than any balance of probabilities would be as to his supposed position if he had confronted it.

By contrast, Knut Wicksell (1851–1926) was repeatedly and explicitly conscious of the problems created by the attempt to dichotomize the pricing process. For example:

> . . . in modern reasoning on general commodity prices, money is not infrequently regarded as a kind of amorphous, infinitely elastic, or plastic mass which adapts itself without any pressure to any price level and is therefore entirely passive in relation to the

[6] Cf. Milton Friedman, "The Marshallian Demand Curve," *Journal of Political Economy* (December 1949), 463–95; Martin Bailey, "The Marshallian Demand Curve," *Journal of Political Economy* (June 1954), 255–61.

[7] Alfred Marshall, *Principles of Economics,* 8th edn. (London: Macmillan Co., 1920), p. 838.

194

pricing mechanism, whilst the latter is regulated only by circumstances concerning the commodities themselves.[8]

Although Wicksell's *Lectures on Political Economy* began with a traditional presentation of microeconomic pricing theory, he immediately pointed out the inadequacy of this where money is wanted for more than its transactions role, where it plays an active role in the economy as a store of value rather than a purely formal role as a unit of account:

. . . by the method we have followed, we can only arrive at the relative exchange values of the goods or their relative prices—not at their actual money prices, which must remain quite undertermined; this is obvious so long as we regard the functions of money as purely formal . . . In every market, there are persons for whom money is something more than this; who exchange goods for money or money for goods in order to obtain at a later date new goods for the money they have acquired. To them, clearly, the exchange value of money—and especially its fluctuations—are by no means unimportant; and the function of money in any particular market transaction becomes, in actuality, not merely formal but also real. In other words, money prices, as such, have their laws and their conditions of equilibrium.[9]

The relationship between the pricing dichotomy and Say's Law was also seen by Wicksell:

Every rise or fall in the price of a particular commodity presupposes a disturbance of the equilibrium

[8] Knut Wicksell, *Lectures on Political Economy* (London: Routledge & Kegan Paul, Ltd., 1961), II, 154.
[9] *Ibid.*, I, 67–68.

between the supply of and the demand for that commodity, whether the disturbance has actually taken place or is merely prospective. What is true *in this respect* of each commodity separately must doubtless be true of all commodities collectively. A general rise in prices is therefore only conceivable on the supposition that the general demand has for some reason become, or is expected to become, greater than the supply. This may sound paradoxical, because we have accustomed ourselves, with J. B. Say, to regard goods themselves as reciprocally constituting and limiting the demand for each other. And indeed *ultimately* they do so; here, however, we are concerned with precisely what occurs, *in the first place,* with the middle link in the final exchange of one good against another, which is formed by the demand of money for goods and the supply of goods against money. Any theory of money worthy of the name must be able to show how and why the monetary or pecuniary demand for goods exceeds or falls short of the supply of goods in given conditions.[10]

Wicksell's *Lectures on Political Economy* did in fact separate the treatment of relative prices (Volume I) from the treatment of money (Volume II), as part of an explicit procedure of making successive approximations, "proceeding successively from the simple to the complex,"[11] because "actual economic life is usually too complex to be examined directly with any chance of success."[12] This means that passages can be selected which might suggest the invalid pricing dichotomy,[13] but it is

[10] *Ibid.,* II, 159–60.   [11] *Ibid.,* I, 35.   [12] *Ibid.,* II, 5.
[13] Cf. Don Patinkin, *Money, Interest, and Prices,* 2nd edn., pp. 173n, 587, 624.

196

clear that these do not represent Wicksell's position as fully elaborated.

Various other neoclassical economists fell somewhere between Wicksell's explicit recognition of the significance of the pricing dichotomy for the quantity theory and Say's Law, on the one hand, and Marshall's apparent unawareness of or disinterest in the problem, on the other. But none of the recognized figures in neoclassical economics was guilty of positively supporting the dichotomy as analytically valid. Irving Fisher and his teacher, Simon Newcomb, related money balances and individual product demand,[14] but in a passing way giving no indication of a full appreciation of the issues involved.

J. A. HOBSON

In *The Physiology of Industry* (1889), which he co-authored with A. F. Mummery, Hobson launched the first of many scattergun attacks on Say's Law, along with attacks on marginalism and the whole methodology, philosophy, and social doctrine of neoclassical economics.[15] He was in some ways a crank—short on intellectual discipline or systematic reasoning and full of sweeping declamations and pretentious claims to novelty—and he was laughed aside rather than refuted. Yet the judgments of a later generation of economists were kinder and more respectful than those of his contemporaries.[16]

John Stuart Mill's version of Say's Law was the principal object of attack. The idea that the supply of commodities equaled the demand for commodities *ex ante* was rejected: "Mill, then, has no right to conclude that

[14] Irving Fisher, *The Purchasing Power of Money*, pp. 153–54; Simon Newcomb, *Principles of Political Economy* (New York: Harper & Brothers, 1886), p. 354.

[15] T. W. Hutchison, *op. cit.*, pp. 118–19.

[16] *Ibid.*, p. 119.

the very fact of a thing being produced is a proof that the power to consume it will be exercised. The desire to save and store up purchasing power is as genuine a motive to production in the individual as the desire of immediate consumption."[17]

Hobson did not deny Say's Equality or the economy's abstract capacity to absorb any given level of output. He said in *Imperialism:* "We are not here concerned with any theoretic question as to the possibility of producing by modern machine methods more goods than can find a market."[18] He recognized that factor incomes added up to the value of output.[19] There was no *inherent* need for foreign outlets: "There is no necessity to open up new foreign markets; the home markets are capable of indefinite expansion."[20] But while there was no reason in principle why this could not happen, it would not happen in practice because of artificial constrictions and rigidities which Hobson saw as recent developments in the evolution of capitalism from a competitive into a monopolistic economic system.

According to Hobson, the "concentration of industry in 'trusts,' 'combines,' etc., at once limits the quantity of capital which can be effectively employed and increases the share of profit out of which fresh savings and fresh capital will spring."[21] The "prime motive force" of imperialism were these excess investment funds seeking outlets,[22] the result of "automatic savings"[23] rather than

---

[17] A. F. Mummery and J. A. Hobson, *The Physiology of Industry* (New York: Kelley & Millman, Inc., 1956), p. 105.

[18] J. A. Hobson, *Imperialism* (Ann Arbor: University of Michigan Press, 1965), p. 76.

[19] *Ibid.,* p. 81.   [20] *Ibid.,* p. 88.

[21] *Ibid.,* pp. 75–76.   [22] *Ibid.,* p. 106.

[23] *Ibid.,* pp. 74, 84, 97; J. A. Hobson, *The Industrial System* (New York: Charles Scribner's Sons, 1910), pp. 71, 295.

savings geared to a given rate of return. But though accumulated without regard to the rate of return, these funds would somehow tend to remain idle unless the rate of return were sufficient.[24] The equilibrating role of the rate of interest was denied by Hobson: ". . . the inadequacy of changes in the rate of interest as regulator of the amount of saving is very generally admitted by economists."[25]

Hobson did not argue that savings in excess of the available investment outlets would be realized. Rather, he argued in Keynesian fashion that the *attempt* to save would reduce the level of income. "In a word, any attempt at over-saving will be checked when it has gone a certain way, by means of the underproduction and shrinkage of income it inevitably produces."[26]

This "paradox of thrift" in modern terms was also referred to by Hobson as a "paradox" which was explicable by the fact that "the saving of the thrifty reduces all incomes" to the point where the equality of savings and investment can be restored.[27] Although equilibrium could be restored by "retardation of new saving" sooner or later "the chronic impulse toward over-saving due to surplus income again becomes fully operative, preparing a new period of depression."[28] The only remedy was redistribution, "converting surplus incomes, either into wages spent in raising the standard of comfort of the workers, or into public revenue spent in raising the standard of public life."[29]

Hobson rejected theories of crises, such as that of John Stuart Mill, which turned on the monetary contractions

[24] Mummery and Hobson, *The Physiology of Industry*, p. 142.
[25] J. A. Hobson, *The Industrial System*, p. 296.
[26] *Ibid.*, p. 304.   [27] Mummery and Hobson, *op. cit.*, p. 184.
[28] J. A. Hobson, *op. cit.*, p. 306.   [29] *Ibid.*, p. 307.

199

incident to a loss of confidence. For Hobson, the phenomena causing "this lack of confidence" were "not mere psychological phenomena; they have their ground in natural facts relating to the sale of goods."[30] His theory depended upon real variables which would have been at work in a barter economy, though acting through monetary mechanisms in a money economy. His exposition of what is now called the paradox of thrift was made "ignoring for the moment the use of money."[31]

Although Hobson's theory of imperialism provided the analytical skeleton of Lenin's *Imperialism,* the overall socioeconomic political argument of Hobson was completely incompatible with that of Lenin. For Lenin and other neo-Marxists, the theory of imperialism explained the failure of capitalism to experience the severe economic and political crises predicted by Marx. The idea that advanced capitalist nations were now exploiting the less-developed nations and thus relieving the exploitation of their own domestic proletariat in order to forestall revolution was one suggested in Marx's later correspondence[32] and insistently developed in Lenin.[33] Hobson, on the other hand, argued at length that imperalism was a *losing* venture for an imperalist nation as a whole,[34] though fostered by private interests and accepted by public gullibility. Hobsonian imperialism would have provided no way out of the Marxian dilemmas.

[30] *Ibid.,* pp. 298–99.   [31] *Ibid.,* p. 304.
[32] Marx and Engels, *Selected Correspondence,* pp. 115–16.
[33] V. I. Lenin, *Imperialism: The Highest Stage of Capitalism* (New York: International Publishers, 1963), pp. 13–14, 104, 126.
[34] J. A. Hobson, *Imperialism,* pp. 46, 47, 141, 145, 152.

CHAPTER 8

The Keynesian Revolution

THE ATTACK BY KEYNES on Say's Law, like that of Sismondi more than a century earlier, centered on its denial of a unique equilibrium income. The Keynesian equilibrium income determined by "the point of intersection between the aggregate demand function and the aggregate supply function" was contrasted with Say's Law as "a special assumption as to the relationship between these functions."[1] The statement that "Supply creates its own Demand" meant for Keynes that aggregate demand and aggregate supply functions were "equal for *all* values" of income,[2] "for all levels of output and employment."[3] Instead of a "unique equilibrium value" for income, Say's Law postulated "an infinite range of values all equally admissible,"[4] with "neutral equilibrium"[5] anywhere up to the ultimate capacity of the economy. In short, aggregate supply and aggregate demand functions coincided. This had been the classical version of Say's Law as it appeared before the general glut controversy and as it had reappeared in J. S. Mill's *Principles,* which Keynes quoted.[6] Keynes did not claim that later economists continued to explicitly accept this formulation, but he claimed that unwittingly they were "tacitly

[1] John Maynard Keynes, *The General Theory of Employment, Interest and Money* (New York: Harcourt, Brace and Co., 1936), p. 25.
[2] *Ibid.,* p. 26. [3] *Ibid.,* pp. 22, 26.
[4] *Ibid.,* p. 26. [5] *Ibid.,* p. 29. [6] *Ibid.,* p. 18.

assuming it."[7] He said: "Contemporary economists, who might hesitate to agree with Mill, do not hesitate to accept conclusions which require Mill's doctrine as their premise."[8]

Keynes became in retrospect a partisan of Malthus against Ricardo and the Ricardians[9] and a promoter of the merits of Mandeville, Hobson, and others who stressed the role of aggregate demand.[10] Like Sismondi, Malthus, and Marx before him, Keynes said that despite classical comparative statics analysis, "it is in the transition that we actually have our being,"[11] a forerunner of his more famous remark that "in the long run we are all dead." Yet despite Keynes' generosity in designating his "forerunners," serious questions have been raised as to whether the analyses of such men as Malthus and Hobson were in fact similar to Keynes' analysis or whether they were just similarly critical of the classical tradition. Further questions have been raised whether others who were not identified as forerunners by Keynes might nevertheless have some claims in this regard (the Swedish school, for example).

A distinction must be made between the Keynesian *apparatus*—the consumption function, the multiplier, the liquidity preference schedule, etc.—and the particular forms and values which they take on the basis of Keynesian *assumptions* and *theories*. Both must be further distinguished from Keynesian *policy* prescriptions.

[7] John Maynard Keynes, "The General Theory (5)," *The New Economics,* ed. Seymour Harris (New York: Alfred A. Knopf, 1952), p. 193.

[8] J. M. Keynes, *The General Theory,* p. 19.

[9] J. M. Keynes, *Essays in Biography,* pp. 102–03, 117–18, 121; "Commemoration of Thomas Robert Malthus," *Economic Journal* (June 1935), 233; *The General Theory,* pp. 362–64.

[10] J. M. Keynes, *The General Theory,* Chapter 23.

[11] *Ibid.,* p. 343n.

Modern economists have generally become Keynesians in terms of making use of his apparatus, as well as that of the modern quantity theory of money. Moreover, the same substantive propositions can be expressed in terms of Keynesian apparatus or that of the quantity theory, although historically people who have called themselves "Keynesians" have usually gone on certain assumptions and policy preferences while people who have identified themselves as "quantity theorists" have usually gone on other assumptions and other policy preferences. For example, Keynes made current consumption expenditures a function of current income, with a slope rising at a decreasing rate,[12] and the function itself remaining relatively stable over time.[13] These assumptions have been challenged empirically,[14] and a new consumption function has been constructed, embodying assumptions of the quantity theorists, with current consumption being a function of asset holdings and the interest rate, among other things.[15]

Another distinction must be made between Keynes' formal model, embodying both Keynesian apparatus and Keynesian assumptions, and Keynes' ad-hoc judgments as to facts and policies. Keynes' formal model was a static short-run model, in which all factor supply elasticities were infinite,[16] output was a function of employment,[17] and tastes, technology, and income distribution were fixed.[18] His judgments and prescriptions repeatedly went well beyond this framework to discuss business cycles, secular stagnation, etc.

[12] *Ibid.*, p. 120.   [13] *Ibid.*, pp. 95, 96.
[14] Arthur F. Burns, *The Frontiers of Economic Knowledge* (Princeton: Princeton University Press, 1965), pp. 16, 152–59.
[15] Milton Friedman, *A Theory of the Consumption Function* (Princeton: Princeton University Press, 1957).
[16] J. M. Keynes, *The General Theory*, p. 27.
[17] *Ibid.*, p. 28.   [18] *Ibid.*, p. 245.

Equilibrium Income

While Keynes transferred supply and demand schedules from the microeconomic level to that of national aggregates, he also warned against the errors involved in transferring them *unchanged* from the micro to the macro level, with all their reciprocal interactions still impounded in *caetiris paribus*. For example, wage cuts could not be assumed to increase employment in a depression, despite a downward sloping demand curve for labor, because such wage reductions could not help affect the demand functions for commodities which were among the "givens" in the derived demand functions for labor.[19] Keynes' theory was one of general equilibrium, or of a simultaneous determination of the respective values of related variables, though sometimes expressed as if it were a theory of unidirectional causation. Aggregate income was included among these variables, rather than being taken as given as in much of the preceding literature. Keynes' theory of equilibrium income, with equilibrium occurring at the *point* of "effective demand" where aggregate supply and aggregate demand functions crossed,[20] implied simultaneous equilibrium in various markets: Savings must equal investment (*ex ante*),[21] which in turn implied that "the rate of interest will be equal to the marginal efficiency of capital"[22] at such a rate as to equate the quantity of money demanded by the public with the quantity supplied by the monetary authorities.[23]

As with any equilibrium theory, the practical significance of Keynesian theory lay precisely in how it dealt with *disequilibrium*. First, what constituted equilibrium

[19] *Ibid.*, pp. 258–59.   [20] *Ibid.*, p. 25.   [21] *Ibid.*, p. 27.
[22] *Ibid.*, p. 184.   [23] *Ibid.*, pp. 167–68.

in terms of income need not simultaneously constitute full employment equilibrium, though output and employment were roughly—but not linearly or uniquely—related.[24] Keynes accepted the traditional view (based on competitive labor markets) that real wages were equal to the marginal product of labor,[25] but not the traditional equality of the marginal disutility of labor with the marginal utility of the wage.[26] The marginal disutility of labor determined the limit of the volume of employment at a given real wage, but did not determine where, within that limit, actual employment would be.[27]

Real wages could be reduced to a market-clearing "full employment" level through inflationary monetary or fiscal policy faster than through direct money wage reductions,[28] which would tend to be resisted,[29] and which could establish destabilizing anticipations of further wage reductions if they were not.[30] However, even complete wage flexibility need not automatically restore full employment in the Keynesian system because the money income redirected from workers to nonworkers, in the wake of a money wage cut, need not be spent as readily (for consumption or investment) as it would have been before, and has a greater chance of at least partially ending as idle balances. This was seen as a denial of Say's Law by Keynes, for whom "Say's Law . . . is equivalent to the proposition that there is no obstacle to full employment."[31] From this point of view, it was sufficient to show that there *was* an obstacle, that full

[24] *Ibid.*, pp. 90, 286.   [25] *Ibid.*, pp. 5, 17.   [26] *Ibid.*, p. 28.
[27] *Ibid.*, pp. 28, 30.   [28] *Ibid.*, pp. 10, 15.
[29] Not irrationally, since a cut in real wages is involved in the former case and *both* a cut in real wages and a decline in relative wages (at any given point in the uncoordinated wage reduction process) in the latter. *Ibid.*, pp. 14, 264, 267.
[30] *Ibid.*, pp. 232, 263.   [31] *Ibid.*, p. 26.

employment was not *automatically* achieved whenever there was equilibrium in aggregate output. Keynes did not show that such unemployment would necessarily persist indefinitely under given conditions. There was not a true "unemployment equilibrium" in a rigorous theoretical sense, but only an unemployment situation of some duration, which is important from a social policy point of view. In the formal model, wage rigidities are necessary for "unemployment equilibrium," and on a policy level, destabilizing anticipations are required, which go beyond the static framework of the formal model.

The other great obstacle to the restoration of full-employment income was the Keynesian "liquidity trap." The demand for money—Keynes' liquidity preference schedule—becomes infinitely elastic at a sufficiently low interest rate, because there is some conventional minimum rate of interest below which the public does not expect interest to remain. When this belief is general, it becomes a self-fulfilling prophecy. The formal possibility was not one which Keynes considered important in practice.[32] However, it did show, on the practical level, how easy it was for a slight *shift* upward in the liquidity preference schedule to counteract the expansionary effects of increased money supply and keep interest rates above an equilibrium level.[33]

Hoarding, as such, was not important in Keynes. It was liquidity preference, which Keynes called the "propensity to hoard"[34]—actual *ex post* hoarding being limited by the money supply—which could rise due to lack of "confidence" (sometimes induced by expansionary monetary or fiscal policy), increasing "the" interest rate[35] to

---

[32] *Ibid.*, p. 207.   [33] *Ibid.*, p. 173.   [34] *Ibid.*, p. 174.
[35] Keynes repeatedly noted that this was simply a convenient way of referring to a whole structure of interest rates. *Ibid.*, pp. 28, 137n, 168.

levels too high for full employment income. Again, Keynes stepped out of his formal model to make a point about policy. The formal shape of the liquidity preference function made wage-price flexibility insufficient to insure full employment income; Keynes' ad-hoc judgments about the shifting of the function made monetary expansion insufficient for policy.

Despite the tendency of "Keynesian" economists to deprecate the role of interest, in Keynes' *General Theory* it was vitally important. Keynes considered the interest rate to be relatively *unresponsive* to "automatic" changes in other parameters postulated in traditional theory, but he did not regard the rest of the economy as unresponsive to interest rate changes. Indeed, the level of aggregate output was itself a function of the interest rate, and the key problem of restoring full employment equilibrium was intractable precisely because the rate of interest "does not automatically fall to the appropriate level."[36] The influence of the rate of interest on the *propensities* to consume and to save was small, but this "does not mean that changes in the rate of interest have only a small effect on the amounts *actually* saved and consumed. Quite the contrary."[37] A "rise in the rate of interest must have the effect of reducing incomes"[38]— hardly a "negligible"[39] effect, as suggested in the literature—to the point where savings equal investment:

> Since incomes will decrease by a greater absolute amount than investment, it is, indeed, true that, when the rate of interest rises, the rate of consumption will decrease. But this does not mean that there will be a wider margin for saving. On the contrary, saving and spending will *both* decrease . . . .

[36] *Ibid.*, p. 31.   [37] *Ibid.*, p. 110.   [38] *Ibid.*
[39] Cf. Lawrence R. Klein, *The Keynesian Revolution* (New York: MacMillan Co., 1954), p. 59; see also pp. 60, 65, 66.

The rise in the rate of interest might induce us to save more, *if* our incomes were unchanged. But if the higher rate of interest retards investment, our incomes will not, and cannot, be unchanged.[40]

As with Marxian value, there is a belief by interpreters that Keynes changed his mind on the role of the interest rate, making it important before and after the *General Theory,* but not in his magnum opus itself.[41] It was true that in the *General Theory*, Keynes had little "confidence in monetary policy designed to influence the interest rate,"[42] but this was because of his lack of faith in the efficacy of monetary policy for changing the interest rate, not a lack of faith in the efficacy of the interest rate for changing the level of income.[43]

Keynes' "marginal efficiency of capital" or investment demand schedule differed from the earlier marginal product of capital schedules in being subjective rather than showing the actual physical or value productivity of capital. It was not merely that the marginal efficiency of capital constituted an approximate estimate of the marginal product of capital, but that is was a highly *volatile* estimate responding to all sorts of actions and expectations which might leave the actual marginal product of capital wholly unaffected.[44] The ability of this function to shift in response to changes in "confidence," like the liquidity preference function, was another factor reducing the automatic self-equilibration of the system in a practical sense, and making it necessary in the formal model to qualify the self-adjustment mechanism by limiting it to the special case where these functions were stable.

[40] J. M. Keynes, *The General Theory*, p. 111.
[41] L. R. Klein, *The Keynesian Revolution*, p. 66.   [42] *Ibid.*
[43] J. M. Keynes, *The General Theory*, pp. 179, 180, 184–85.
[44] *Ibid.*, pp. 141–42, 145, 148–49, 315, 316.

Keynes of course considered these functions very unstable, in contrast to the consumption function.

The shift from the formal static model to dynamic expectations analysis, which occurred with respect to Keynesian wage inflexibility, liquidity preference, and the marginal efficiency of capital, also occurred with respect to the "multiplier." An expansion of the production of investment goods which has been entirely unforeseen by the producers of consumer goods must leave the new income earners in the investment goods sector with no way to increase their real consumption out of current production. They may deplete inventories or postpone consumption (perhaps due to rising prices and/or rising interest rates):

> So far as the balance is restored by a postponement of consumption there is a temporary reduction of the marginal propensity to consume, i.e., of the multiplier itself, and in so far as there is a depletion of stocks, aggregate investment increases for the time being by less than the increment of investment in the capital-goods industries,—i.e., the thing to be multiplied does not increase by the full increment of investment in the capital-goods industries.[45]

Keynes thus distinguished "the logical theory of the multiplier, which holds good continuously, without time-lag, at all moments of time, and the consequences of an expansion in the capital-goods industries which take gradual effect, subject to time-lag and only after an interval."[46] After the initial increment to aggregate output, which is less than that given by the multiplier formula (based on the initial marginal propensity to consume), the subsequent increment is sufficiently greater than that

[45] *Ibid.*, p. 124.   [46] *Ibid.*, pp. 122–23.

given by the formula (because of additional production to restore normal inventory balance and parallel developments in consumer goods prices and the interest rate) to offset this and lead to an increase of output, over the time period required for full adjustment, which is the same as that given by the formula. In short, there is "a temporary departure of the marginal propensity to consume away from its normal value, followed, however, by a gradual return to it."[47]

Keynes' frequent shifts from the formal model to practical "realities" (i.e., assumed empirical relationships) make it difficult to distinguish the two, much less to judge them separately on their own respective terms. A further complication in any attempt to properly place the Keynesian system relative to other theories—Say's Law, the quantity theory of money, etc.—is that Keynes did not always accurately formulate these other approaches, so that his objections to them need not reflect the real points of difference. Say's Law, for example, meant for Keynes not only a coincidence of supply and demand functions but also the automatic maintenance or restoration of full employment. No such doctrine was expressed by the classical economists, though they had no theory of unemployment and probably assumed, separately from Say's Law, that full employment was normal or inevitable. The quantity theory of money meant for Keynes a constant velocity of circulation[48] which it did not mean with the classical or neoclassical economists. The quantity theorists postulated a stability, though not absolute constancy, of velocity over long periods, but recognized short-run changes during various phases of the business cycle.[49] They were in fact more flexible about the stable

[47] *Ibid.*, p. 123.   [48] *Ibid.*, pp. 209, 289, 296.
[49] Henry Thornton, *An Inquiry into the Nature and Effects of the Paper Credit of Great Britain* (New York: August M.

velocity of circulation than the Keynesians were about the stability of the consumption function. Long-run stability meant little for a short-run theory intended to produce policy precisely for unusual situations—as many Keynesians discovered in the forecasting debacle following World War II.

The "classical" economist described in Keynes' *General Theory*[50] was a straw man. Keynes' only major suggestion of an empirical counterpart was Pigou, whose *Theory of Unemployment* was a book which preceded *The General Theory* by only three years, setting forth doctrines which a contemporary described as "quite as strange and novel as the doctrine of Mr. Keynes himself."[51] The nebulous nature of the "classical" tradition is further indicated by Keynes' list of those whom he considered to be his modern heretical predecessors in attacking it—Hawtrey, D. H. Robertson, Wicksell, and even Irving Fisher.[52] While the "classical" economist was an interesting expository device, which undoubtedly sped the acceptance of Keynesian analysis as an intellectually revolutionary doctrine, this short-run success led to a longer-run reaction to which it had made itself vulnerable, which questioned whether Keynes had in fact added *anything* to economics.[53]

Kelley, 1965), [originally published 1802], pp. 96–97, 232–33; David Ricardo, *Works*, III, 90; Alfred Marshall, *Official Papers* (London: MacMillan Co., 1926), pp. 267–68; Irving Fisher, *The Purchasing Power of Money*, pp. 159–60.

[50] J. M. Keynes, *The General Theory*, p. 3n, Chapters 2, 14, passim.

[51] J. R. Hicks, "Mr. Keynes and the Classics," *Econometrica* (April 1937), 147.

[52] J. M. Keynes, "Alternative Theories of the Rate of Interest," *Economic Journal* (June 1937), 242n.

[53] James R. Schlesinger, "After Twenty Years: The General Theory," *Quarterly Journal of Economics* (November 1956), 581–602; R. W. Clower, "The Keynesian Counterrevolution: A

SECULAR STAGNATION

The thesis that declining rates of population growth threatened modern industrial capitalist economies with "secular stagnation" is one which has traditionally been associated with Alvin H. Hansen, as an extension of Keynesianism, but its basic analysis was in fact stated by Keynes himself, in an article with which Hansen was already familiar when he presented his elaboration of this thesis.[54]

Keynes began with an empirical relationship that was presumed to be causal—that demand for capital increases "more or less in proportion to population."[55] An additional empirical assertion was that it was predictable "much more securely than we know almost any other social or economic factor relating to the future" that the "steeply rising level of population which we have experienced for a great number of decades" was to become "in a very short time" a "stationary or a declining" population level.[56] The threat of insufficient investment demand required a drastic change in public thinking to meet the drastically changed conditions,[57] and ultimately governmental policies designed to produce sufficient ag-

Theoretical Appraisal," *The Theory of Interest Rates,* ed. F. H. Hahn and F. P. R. Brechling (New York: St. Martin's Press, 1965), pp. 103–25.

[54] J. M. Keynes, "Some Economic Consequences of a Declining Population," *The Eugenics Review,* XXIX, No. 1 (April 1937), 13–17; Alvin H. Hansen, "Economic Progress and Declining Population Growth," *Readings in Business Cycle Theory,* ed. Gottfried Haberler (Philadelphia: The Blakiston Co., 1951), p. 373n.

[55] J. M. Keynes, "Some Economic Consequences of a Declining Population," *op. cit.,* p. 14.

[56] *Ibid.,* p. 13; cf. A. H. Hansen, *op. cit.,* p. 367.

[57] J. M. Keynes, "Some Economic Consequences of a Declining Population," *op. cit.,* p. 13.

gregate demand to replace that lost from population-related expenditures.[58]

Hansen's distinction between a "widening" of capital (capital growth proportional to output) and a "deepening" of capital (more capital per unit of output) was made by Keynes in very similar terms with similar conclusions: that deepening depended on the kind of investments (notably housing) associated with population growth.[59] With declining growth of population, one of the two kinds of investment demand would be drastically curtailed. Keynes and Hansen both acknowledged the possibility that technical innovations might compensate, by shifting upward the marginal efficiency of capital, for movements downward along it with increasing investment, but both were pessimistic as to its actually happening.[60]

It is all too obvious that none of this happened, and it has a strange ring in an age of continuing inflation and "population explosion." It would not do to try to rescue the stagnation thesis with the kind of reasoning sometimes used in trying to salvage the Malthusian population theory—that unforeseeable favorable circumstances prevented or postponed the eventuality predicted. The theory postulated certain basic behavior patterns which simply did not emerge in circumstances which permitted their emergence if they were indeed present. The Keynes-Hansen stagnation thesis never seems to consider that (1) both sharp contractions and long, drawn-out depressions have been familiar occurrences at various periods of history, neither signalling the final disappear-

[58] *Ibid.*, p. 17.
[59] *Ibid.*, p. 15; A. H. Hansen, *op. cit.*, p. 372.
[60] J. M. Keynes, "Some Economic Consequences of a Declining Population," *op. cit.*, p. 16; A. H. Hansen, *op. cit.*, p. 381.

ance of the other as an historical phenomenon, or that (2) the reduction of one kind of spending (capital-intensive goods) could not be translated into a reduction of aggregate demand by arbitrarily holding other things constant (the reason for a reduction in child-bearing could easily be a desire for a higher standard of living, for example).

The Keynesian clarion call to break free of our old ways of thinking was particularly inappropriate in view of his own blindness to previous stagnation theories spawned by previous depressions.[61] There was nothing new in Hansen's claim that "business cycles" were characteristic of a by-gone era, while the new era was one of "secular stagnation" or "sick recoveries which die in their infancy and depressions which feed on themselves."[62] Engels had long before said that the "acute form" of crisis had now (the last quarter of the nineteenth century) "given way to a more chronic, long drawn . . . undecided depression."[63] Similar statements are found throughout the history of economic thought,[64]—an example of the general tendency to transform current problems into unprecedented changes in the nature of the world.

KEYNES AND HISTORY

The recognition of Keynes' originality and his role in inaugurating a new era in economic thinking does not depend upon the dubious claim that he contradicted a fallacious orthodoxy with an unprecedented theory.

[61] J. A. Schumpeter, *History of Economic Analysis*, p. 1172; J. A. Schumpeter, "Science and Ideology," *American Economic Review* (March 1949), 355.

[62] A. H. Hansen, *op. cit.*, p. 370.

[63] Engels in Marx, *Capital,* III, 574n.

[64] J. A. Schumpeter, *op. cit.*, pp. 570, 571, 740, 964n, 1172.

Keynes' basic concept of an equilibrium income must be separated from the particular shapes and shifts of functions which were part of the overall Keynesian "vision" and which have been aptly characterized as "Keynes' *special theory*."[65] Keynes was as original as any of the great figures in the history of economics, which means that his work, like that of Smith, Ricardo, or Marshall, contains much that had been scattered through the writings of "predecessors," some known and some unknown to the respective authors. Keynes openly acknowledged his debt to R. F. Kahn for the multiplier[66] and to Malthus for highlighting the problem of effective demand.[67] Other features of the Keynesian system can be found in various economists of the classical period. The fundamental conception of an equilibrium income was first developed by Sismondi. An unemployment equilibrium (with downward wage resistance) appeared in Malthus. The idea that an excess supply of goods logically implied an excess demand for money first appeared in G. P. Scrope. The argument that idle resources could be activated by monetary or fiscal means was developed by William Blake in the 1820's. But Keynes' *General Theory* was obviously much more than a compilation or even a judicious mixture of these preexisting elements. It was a whole new vision of the economic process.

While the Keynesian system contained many elements from eariler economists' systems, it was not a lineal descendant of any of them. It contradicted the Sismondi-Malthus analysis in fundamental ways: (1) the independence of saving and investment decisions which characterized the *General Theory* was not part of the general

---

[65] J. R. Hicks, "Mr. Keynes and the Classics," *op. cit.*, p. 152.

[66] J. M. Keynes, *The General Theory*, p. 113.

[67] *Ibid.*, p. 32; J. M. Keynes, *Essays in Biography*, pp. 120–21.

glut model, in which savings were made by investors (though sometimes mistakenly in view of subsequent earnings); (2) the monetary analysis that is central to the *General Theory* was wholly unnecessary for the general glut model, which proceeded on the basis of the same kind of barter examples found in the classical supporters of Say's Law and denounced by Keynes; (3) the glut model was a lagged model in contrast to Keynes' formally static analysis; (4) reflationary monetary policy, such as that proposed by Keynes, was opposed by Sismondi, and public works were opposed by Malthus, whose views on the "euthanasia of the rentier" were also the opposite of Keynes'.[68]

The once fashionable attempt to make Karl Marx a forerunner of Keynes was even more unfounded. The two systems were so different from start to finish that it is difficult to find parallel arguments even for purposes of contrast. Marx's "dialectical" approach involved dynamics and secular trends, and he criticized the opposite static approach—"metaphysics" in Marxian terminology—from his earliest writings through *Capital*.[69] Marx was concerned with a sequential explanation of crises and cycles, not a static explanation of general equilibrium. Marx accepted the fundamental proposition of Say's Law which Keynes (and Sismondi, Malthus, etc.) rejected: there can be, initially, only disproportionate production, not excess real output, though later monetary contraction may lead to deficient monetary demand.

[68] Sismondi, *Nouveaux Principes*, II, 84; T.R. Malthus in P. Sraffa, "Malthus on Public Works," *Economic Journal* (September 1955), 543–44; T. R. Malthus, *Principles of Political Economy*, p. 431; J. M. Keynes, *The General Theory*, p. 376.

[69] Karl Marx, *Writings of the Young Marx*, ed. L. D. Easton and K. H. Guddat, pp. 265–66; Marx and Engels, *Selected Writings*, I, 87; Marx and Engels, *Basic Writings*, ed. L. S. Feuer, pp. 84–87; Marx, *Theories of Surplus Value*, pp. 368, 399, 408.

Marx and Engels were unsparing in their denunciations of underconsumptionists.

Marx's similarities to Keynes were on the most general level. Both saw inherent difficulties of maintaining equilibrium and full employment under laissez-faire capitalism, though completely different analyses lay behind this conclusion. Both saw excess demand for money as a key feature in cyclical phenomena, a point which had become commonplace in the classical traditional decades before Marx's *Capital*. Keynes' liquidity trap would be similar to a Marxian underconsumptionist "breakdown" theory, if Marx had had any such theory. The Great Depression of the 1930's could of course be viewed as a confirmation of either or both theories, especially if the facts were not examined too closely. Yet despite the almost total absence of specific evidence, Marx has been repeatedly depicted as a forerunner of Keynes.[70] Ironically, one important point of similarity between Marx and Keynes has been neglected: their measurement of output aggregates in units of labor inputs. The tradition of calling this a "labor theory of value" in Marx persists, despite Marx's repeated statements that he had a labor *definition* of value. Marxian value is essentially the same as the Keynesian "labour-unit"[71] and plays the same role as a convenient building block in the system.

Keynes' role as an inspiration for growth models, econometric analysis, and other variations on his central themes has clearly been great. Perhaps the role that best reflected his own concerns was that of policy advocate. Here the record is by no means unequivocal. Despite early attempts to depict Keynes as the intellectual god-

[70] L. R. Klein, *The Keynesian Revolution,* pp. 130–34; Joan Robinson, *An Essay on Marxian Economics* (London: MacMillan Co., Ltd., 1957), pp. 66–67, 71–72.

[71] See J. M. Keynes, *The General Theory,* pp. 41–42.

father of the New Deal deficit finance policies, it is difficult to see a Keynesian pattern in the economic improvisations of the New Deal. The apparent rationale of the National Industrial Recovery Act was that prices could be forced back up individually rather than by expansionary monetary policy—a view of which neither Keynes nor traditional economics could be held responsible. The actual monetary policies followed included doubling the reserve requirements in the middle of the depression, which again reflected neither "Keynesian" nor "classical" analysis. The Roosevelt administration ran deficits, but so had the Hoover administration, and its lone balanced budget came in 1937, the year after the publication of Keynes' *General Theory*.

In the postwar period, despite the dire warnings of impending depression, the Truman administration ran a large budgetary surplus, with no drastic effects. In recent years Keynesian *talk* has become increasingly common in official circles and various policies (or inaction) are rationalized on Keynesian grounds. But the pervasiveness of Keynesian terminology is not the same as a concrete difference of behavior in a Keynesian direction, as compared to past policies. It is difficult in the nature of things to develop convincing evidence either way, whatever Keynes real influence may have been. The long, unbroken postwar prosperity has sometimes been cited as evidence of Keynesian policy at work. However, large war-related expenditures and inflationary finance have promoted full employment in the past; what is unusual today is the duration of wartime expenditure patterns. Perhaps a similar period of normal peacetime expenditure patterns will likewise see full employment as a result of Keynesian policies, but at this juncture this must remain a speculation.

218

CHAPTER 9

General Implications

BOTH Say's Law and the theory of equilibrium income—its intellectual complement and historical
rival—can be traced back to a common origin in the
Physiocrats and are reunited in post-Keynesian macroeconomics. The basic notion of a circular flow of equal
output and purchasing power, moving in opposite directions, had appeared in *L'Ordre Naturel* by Mercier
de la Rivière in 1767, along with discussions of short-
run expansions and contractions of this flow in response
to changing spending habits.[1] The nearly two hundred
years which elapsed before these related ideas were reunited were not wasted, for the various concepts involved developed richer content and more rigorously
elaborated implications. Yet the questions remain: Why
this long period before these ideas could be reconciled?
Why did two of the biggest controversies in the history of
economics rage between those who supported one-half of
this basic truth and those who supported the other
half? Why did one side win such an overwhelming victory
in the nineteenth century and the other side an almost
equally overwhelming victory in the twentieth century?

More fundamental questions are also raised relating
to intellectual history generally:

1. What are the sources of new ideas and conceptions? Do they come from the accepted leaders of a

[1] Mercier de la Rivière, *L'Ordre Naturel*, II, 138–40, 250.

219

field or from peripheral heretics? What determines why a given challenge to orthodoxy will succeed or fail: why was there a Keynesian revolution but no Sismondian revolution? Why did the Ricardians "win" and Sismondi and Malthus "lose?"

2. What is the effect of ideology on analysis? Do given policy conclusions, including abolition of the existing economy and/or society, logically depend upon given analytical results? Conversely, does a given chain of economic reasoning, or belief in a given collection of analytical or empirical propositions, generally lead to a given policy position, logically or even historically?

3. How is methodology related to ideology and/or analysis? How much of a pattern is there within a given school of economists at a given time? Over time? Are such intellectual considerations as methodology merely expressions of preferences for certain analytical or policy conclusions?

Sources and Success of New Conceptions

One of the striking similarities among the major pre-Keynesian critics of Say's Law is that most of them were *not* primarily economists. Sismondi achieved fame as an historian, Lauderdale was a politician, Malthus a population theorist, Chalmers a moral and social philosopher, and Marx a revolutionary and theorist of history; Hobson could better be described as a crank whose prolific writings often dealt with economics than as an economist with unorthodox views. By contrast, Say, Ricardo, and McCulloch were primarily and almost exclusively economists, as were of course all the leading figures in the neoclassical tradition.

220

The nineteenth century challengers of Say's Law appeared as *outsiders* attacking one of the carefully erected pillars of classical economics. In the early period, it was all too apparent that Sismondi, Lauderdale, and Malthus were no match intellectually for Ricardo, and their work bore many signs of disorganization and even amateurism as compared to the more systematic and tightly reasoned writings of James Mill, McCulloch, or John Stuart Mill. Yet it would be a mistake to say that the theory of equilibrium income simply lost because the defenders of Say's Law were intellectually the better men. The analytical superiority of the Ricardians was not itself directly responsible for their victory in the general glut controversy, since they seldom came to grips with their opponents' real arguments. Rather, they tended repeatedly to interpret their opponents' words in Ricardian senses and then to refute the new meanings which had been created in this manner. Their analytical superiority was important, however, in (1) convincing them that Sismondi, Malthus, etc., could be dismissed as shoddy thinkers,[2] and in (2) establishing enough of a commanding intellectual reputation for themselves to cause the educated public to accept their judgment in this matter. Moreover, the general glut theorists were not sufficiently lucid in their own expositions to present a clear alternative to the Ricardian interpretations of their words. All the elements

[2] McCulloch dismissed Sismondi as "too much of a sentimentalist to make a good political economist" (Ricardo, *Works*, VIII, p. 25), and Ricardo saw in his book only "a very poor performance" (*ibid.*, p. 57). Malthus was considered by McCulloch to be "very much overrated" as an economist (*ibid.*, p. 139) and to have " more of art than ingenuousness" in his work (*ibid.*, p. 189). Ricardo said that Malthus not only failed to understand him but even to understand himself (*ibid.*, IX, 13).

of a coherent system—definitions, arguments, examples, etc.—were scattered through their work but seldom so organized as to make the basic logic stand out in bold relief.

In part, the looseness of the general glut theorists may be attributable to a reaction against the excesses of the Ricardians, whose contrived syllogisms so readily degenerated into tautologies. Both Sismondi and Malthus tended to be not only less systematic than the Ricardians, but less systematic than they themselves had been before their controversies with the Ricardians. Sismondi, for example, was far more rigorous in his use of terms in his *Richesse Commerciale* in 1803 (before his polemics with the Ricardian school), in which he defined many of his concepts both mathematically and in a carefully worded glossary,[3] than in his later writings in which he explicitly stated that he would not follow the "scientific" pretensions and definitional technicalities of his opponents.[4] Malthus likewise changed from a defender of theory in his *Essay on Population* to a highly "institutionalist" critic of it in his later *Principles of Political Economy*.[5]

Marx was a much more systematic thinker than the earlier glut theorists, and yet his *Capital* was no more illuminating because of its strange and difficult manner of presentation. Hobson was in the disorganized tradition of Sismondi, Lauderdale, and Malthus.

The contrast is great between these nineteenth century critics of Say's Law and J. M. Keynes in the twentieth century. Keynes had already established himself as one

---

[3] Sismondi, *Richesse Commerciale,* I, 105n–106n, 342–48.

[4] Sismondi, *Études,* II, 143, 227, 228, I, 115.

[5] T. R. Malthus, *An Essay on the Principle of Population,* Everyman edn., II, 245. Cf. T. R. Malthus, *Principles of Political Economy,* pp. 1–19; Ricardo, *Works,* VIII, 286.

of the leading minds in economics even before the *General Theory.* He was as much in the center of the professional stage as most of the others had been shadowy figures in the wings. Dismissing him was out of the question. His mastery of the technical tools and his ability to construct an impressive system with them assured him a hearing, and the flair with which his theories and conclusions were set forth assured followers and controversy. Sismondi's recurrent laments at the futility of trying to reform a dominant orthodoxy never quite reached the crucial point—that it takes a system to beat a system.

It is tempting to view Keynes' massive success, in contrast to the massive failure of his predecessors, as either a merchandising coup or the result of a more favorable confluence of events. There is another consideration, however. In order to successfully introduce a new conception, the innovator must not only be capable of setting up a persuasive system, he must first be converted to the new idea himself. The highly trained professional may sometimes be as handicapped in seeing the new concept that cuts across the system he has learned as he is at an advantage in successfully conveying it to his colleagues once he has done so. Keynes described his great "struggle of escape from habitual modes of thought and expression."[6] Although Sismondi and Malthus were both converts from an early belief in Say's Law,[7] there was no indication of any such struggle for either of them.

But while Keynes may have had more of a struggle

---

[6] J. M. Keynes, *The General Theory,* p. VIII; see also J. M. Keynes, *Essays in Biography,* pp. 120–21.

[7] Sismondi, *Richesse Commerciale,* II, 446–47; T. R. Malthus, *An Essay on the Principle of Population,* 1st edn., Chapter xv, reprinted in T. R. Malthus, *On Population,* ed. Gertrude Himmelfarb (New York: Random House, 1960), pp. 102–03.

to see a new conception through an old framework, he had the great advantage of having had predecessors who had blazed a trail, however imperfectly. From this standpoint, it may not be fruitful to compare Keynes and his predecessors, as if a Keynes might have succeeded in the 1820's where they failed. Rather, the existence of predecessors may have been itself an essential ingredient in opening up the whole line of thought to successors whose training was an obstacle to thinking in that direction. Possibly cranks are necessary to lead the first suicidal attacks on orthodoxy which enable those who come after to establish a beachhead and win the victory. Alfred Marshall's dictum that nature does not make leaps might be amended to say, in the area of intellectual developments, man will not accept leaps. A Cournot may suddenly conceive of a whole new way of analyzing value and production theory, but nearly a century must pass before the profession would incorporate it all—piecemeal—into its thinking. It is at least possible that something similar had to happen with the theory of equilibrium income.

However the phenomenon of intellectual innovation may best be accounted for, it is clear that resistance and blindness are important and ultimately costly features of an intellectual discipline. Sismondi and Malthus *could* have been understood, for all their shortcomings in exposition. They *were* understood, on such key points as demand schedules and equilibrium income, by Samuel Bailey and by J. B. Say, respectively. Only the Ricardian disciples remained absolutely untouchable, but that was enough to extinguish both lines of thought for another half-century. It was, ironically, John Stuart Mill who said, in another context, that there was an "almost irresistible tendency of the human mind to become the slave of its own hypotheses," to "reason, feel, and conceive under certain arbitrary conditions, at length to mistake these conditions for laws of nature." He added: ". . . the greatest powers of reasoning, when connected with a sluggish imagination, are no safeguard against the poorest intellectual slavery—that of subjection to mere accidental habits of thought."[8]

An established intellectual discipline and/or its major conclusions need not be abandoned at the first challenge, but every challenge need not be approached in the spirit of an adversary proceeding, in which an opponent's weaknesses and inconsistencies are exploited to produce "victory." If the search is for truth rather than victory, there is much to be said for "seeing that no scattered particles of important truth are buried and lost in the ruins of exploded error."[9] The precept is no less true or important for having been formulated by John Stuart Mill, who violated it repeatedly in his treatment of the general glut theories.

IDEOLOGY AND ANALYSIS

It is immediately apparent that the early glut theorists shared other characteristics as well: they were all highly unsystematic, highly critical of those who were systematic and syllogistic, and were very policy-oriented in their thinking. In addition, the Lauderdale-Malthus-Chalmers school was almost monolithic in its socioeconomic political creed: its social bias in favor of the landed aristocracy, government pensioners and sinecurists, the estab-

[8] [John Stuart Mill], "On Miss Martineau's Summary of Political Economy," *Monthly Repository,* VII (May 1834), 319–20.

[9] John Stuart Mill, *Essays on Some Unsettled Questions of Political Economy,* p. 50.

lished church, and fundholders in the national debt, its insistence on the need to keep the poor in their place, to uncompromisingly oppose the ideas and forces of the French revolution and Napoleon, to make religion a more pervasive influence in society, to moderate the trend toward industrialism and toward political reform. The existence of a common pattern is clear. The existence of a very different pattern among the Ricardians, who (as Benthamites) were a philosophical and political as well as an economic school, is equally clear. The question is, to what extent were these logically necessary or logically consistent patterns, to what extent chance historical groupings, and what general significance can be attached to them in either role?

Opposition to Say's Law, as such, has had no logical, or even—in the long view—historical connection with a given philosophical or political orientation. The spectrum of its critics extends from Lauderdale and Malthus at one extreme to Marx at the other, with a fairly even continuum in between. Opposition which centered on the concept of an equilibrium income was highly correlated with a given *Weltanschauung* at a given time and place (the England of Lauderdale, Malthus, and Chalmers), but the contemporary presence of a radically different view in Sismondi and again later in Keynes undermines the idea of anything approaching a necessary connection. Indeed, the most analytically similar systems, those of Sismondi and Malthus, were used to support widely differing policy conclusions: Sismondi advocating government aid to the poor and Malthus advocating government aid to the rich. This does not deny that subjectively a given analysis may have been devised or embraced because of the ideological use to which it could be put. It merely denies that a given ideology is linked in a *determinate* relationship (as cause or effect) with a given analysis, since the same analysis can be made consistent with (and appear to lead to) opposing conclusions, and since the same conclusions can be supported with widely differing analyses.

While no correlation can be demonstrated between specific ideology and specific analysis over time, it cannot be denied that there appears to be more than a chance correlation as of any given time. This may suggest that those most susceptible to criticism of the prevailing analysis (whatever its specific content or their specific analysis to the contrary) are those most disaffected with the philosophical and practical conclusions which have historically become associated with it, whether logically entailed by it or not. On this view, the institutionalist doctrine that analytical alignments tend to reflect ideological alignments can be accepted, while rejecting their belief that specific analysis tends by its inherent nature to lead to or derive from specific ideology. The intellectual validity of an idea cannot be undermined or put out of court with the charge of ideological bias because such bias need not determine a specific analytical position, much less its validity. For example, the defense of a national debt because "we owe it to ourselves" was as strongly identified with conservatism when Lauderdale used it as it has become identified with liberalism in the post-Keynesian era. Similarly, "sound money," tied as closely as possible to gold, was as characteristic of the left when Sismondi, Cobbett, etc., argued for it as it was to become a "conservative" doctrine in a later period.

To say that ideological bias is invalid as an intellectual criterion and misleading as a social theory is not to claim that economists (or others) have always (or usually) been disinterested scientists working in an intellectual

227

vacuum. On the contrary, it suggests that there are so many mutually compatible combinations of ideology and analysis that no specific bias in one area implies any specific position in any other.

METHODOLOGY

The methodological similarities of the opponents of Say's Law are perhaps more striking than any of their other similarities. Criticisms of the unreal abstractions of orthodox economics appear, in very similar terms, from Sismondi and Malthus in the early period to Hobson and Keynes in the later. The importance of seeing the institutional framework within which economic forces operate was a recurring note. However, the significant question is to what extent this was simply a polemical blast at an opponent's exposed weakness (many critics unconcerned about Say's Law made similar criticisms) and to what extent this represented a real difference associated with the other differences between the two sides. There is a further question as to whether these were attacks on abstractions as such or attacks on the particular abstractions of the classical school. There is no reason why, behind the unified chorus of criticism of unreal abstractions, there may not be very great methodological differences among the critics.

Sismondi repeatedly complained of the construction of "a hypothetical world completely different from the real world"[10] and of doctrines which were "abstractly true" but "in a manner inapplicable of political economy."[11] Yet Sismondi's attacks were not attacks on

[10] Sismondi, *Nouveaux Principes,* II, 256.
[11] *Ibid.,* p. 181.

228

abstraction as such. He recognized the need for abstraction, and complained only of its abuse:

> It is a natural habit of the human mind to seek to reduce all its operations to the simplest formula, to generalize all its rules, and to accomplish this uniform procedure whenever it can to avoid more complicated procedures. That habit, which tends to simplify everything, to classify everything, to generalize everything, is no doubt the most essential cause of the progress of various sciences. It is not necessary, however, to abandon onself to it in an unreflecting manner.[12]

Sismondi's methodological views, like his substantive analysis, were soon echoed in Malthus' *Principles* where they were extended further in the direction of modern institutionalism. Malthus argued that economics was more like the study of "morals and politics" than like that of mathematics, because it did not possess the "certainty" which "the stricter sciences" possessed.[13] Moreover, the purpose of any philosophical inquiry must be "to account for things as they are"[14] and to be "practical" and "applicable" to the common business of human life."[15] Malthus also made descriptive realism an important end of theory. His insistence on the importance of money,[16] and his arguments against the actual existence of no-rent land[17] were based on considerations of descriptive realism, not on any attempt to show where analyti-

---

[12] *Ibid.,* p. 115.

[13] T. R. Malthus, *Principles of Political Economy,* p. 434.

[14] *Ibid.,* pp. 8, 329n; Ricardo, *Works,* VII, 122.

[15] T. R. Malthus, *Principles of Political Economy,* p. 9.

[16] *Ibid.,* p. 324n; T. R. Malthus, *Definitions in Political Economy,* pp. 54, 60n.

[17] T. R. Malthus, *Principles of Political Economy,* pp. 181–82.

cally fallacious or empirically untrue results were obtained by deviating from the historically correct assumptions.

Marx was at the opposite pole from Malthus on methodology. Marx regarded abstractions as the essence of science. He had only contempt for those whose "lack of a theoretical bent" led them to "snatch clumsily at the empirical material before them."[18] In Marxian writings "common sense" was a term of opprobrium.[19] Similarly the phrase, "conditions as they are" was used perjoratively in Marx.[20] While it "seems" on the surface to be a valid procedure to begin in this manner, "on closer consideration it proves to be wrong."[21] Those "systems of political economy which start from simple conceptions" are following "manifestly the scientifically correct method."[22] Marx's theory of history did not pretend to explain things as they are, but only to explain the dynamic element leading to change.[23] For example, the family unit might exist for a variety of biological, psychological, etc., reasons, but the question to which the Marxian theory addressed itself was what caused *changes* in the family unit from one era to another. This he regarded—rightly or wrongly is irrelevant here—as the economic changes. This did *not* say, as so many interpreters have assumed, that the economic factor was considered to be in some sense weightier than biological, psychological, etc., factors. The latter might well account

---

[18] Marx, *Theories of Surplus Value,* p. 133.
[19] Marx and Engels, *Basic Writings,* p. 84.
[20] Marx, *Critique of Political Economy,* p. 292.
[21] *Ibid.*   [22] *Ibid.,* p. 293.
[23] See Thomas Sowell, "Karl Marx and the Freedom of the Individual," *Ethics* (January 1963), 121; Thomas Sowell, "The 'Evolutionary' Economics of Thorstein Veblen," *Oxford Economic Papers,* July 1967, pp. 193n–194n.

for things as they are—why families exist at all—better than the economic factor without in any way undermining Marx's theory.

The down-to-earth, things-as-they-are approach has often degenerated into naive reliance on the perception of the economic agents themselves as a substitute for systematic analysis. The businessmen-don't-think-that-way objection to various economic theories has been one by-product of this approach. From the Marxian point of view, it was not merely pointless but misleading to concentrate on the individual's *modus operandi:* "For what each individual wills is obstructed by everyone else, and what emerges is something that no one willed."[24] Since theory is meant to predict "what emerges," it cannot proceed by aggregating or averaging the perceptions or behavior of the individual actors in the drama, but only by seeking to construct the constraining relationships which lead their mutual pulling and tugging to produce one result rather than another.

Hobson and Keynes can only be classified as eclectic. Keynes' casual movements back and forth between a static model and dynamic conclusions are an important feature of the *General Theory.*

Although there is no clearly discernible pattern of methodology in the tradition of dissent from Say's Law, the dissenters were distinguished from the orthodox by their far greater preoccupation with methodological questions. Ricardo said little beyond his assertion that he was using a comparative statics approach, and that his aim was to "elucidate principles" rather than to be as "practical" as Malthus.[25] John Stuart Mill provided the only sustained discussion of methodology in the classical

---

[24] Marx and Engels, *Selected Correspondence,* p. 476.
[25] Ricardo, *Works,* VIII, 184; see also p. 130.

tradition,[26] though it received somewhat more attention in the neoclassical period, notably at the hands of Alfred Marshall and John Neville Keynes.[27]

The Ricardians were repeatedly criticized, in discussion having nothing to do with Say's Law, for moving directly from their abstract models to policy conclusions about the real world.[28] Schumpeter was later to dub this practice "the Ricardian Vice."[29] The relevant question here, however, is whether this vice was linked, either as cause or effect, to the ideology or analysis of classical economics. Perhaps the quickest answer is to point out that the modern economist most subject to the same accusation was John Maynard Keynes.[30] In methodology, as in analysis proper, agreement with the most diverse individual conclusions was possible for those on opposite sides of Say's Law.

How well these generalizations from the history of the controversies over Say's Law apply to the history of economic thought generally is another and larger question. It should be noted, however, that those who took part in these controversies constituted a substantial portion of the major figures in the history of economics.

[26] John Stuart Mill, *Essays on Some Unsettled Questions of Political Economy,* pp. 120–64; *A System of Logic* (London: Longmans, Green and Co., Ltd., 1959), pp. 571–606.

[27] Alfred Marshall, *Memorials of Alfred Marshall,* ed. A. C. Pigou (New York: Kelley & Millman, Inc., 1956), pp. 152–74, 295–311; John Neville Keynes, *Scope and Method of Political Economy.*

[28] For example, William Whewell, "Prefatory Notice," Richard Jones, *Literary Remains* (London: John Murray, 1859), p. xiii.

[29] J. A. Schumpeter, *History of Economic Analysis,* pp. 472–73.

[30] *Ibid.,* p. 473n; A. F. Burns, *The Frontiers of Economic Knowledge,* pp. 7–8.

ANNOTATED BIBLIOGRAPHY AND INDEX

ANNOTATED BIBLIOGRAPHY

PRIMARY LITERATURE

[Samuel Bailey]. *An Inquiry into those Principles Respecting the Nature of Demand and the Necessity of Consumption lately advocated by Mr. Malthus* (London: R. Hunter, 1821). One of the most closely reasoned analyses, during the classical period, of the weaknesses of both sides in the general glut controversy.

Thomas Chalmers. *On Political Economy* (Glasgow: William Collins, 1832), Chapters I, II, III, IV, V. This is the clearest, systematic presentation of the Malthusian theory of gluts, by a disciple of Malthus in this and other areas.

James Maitland, 8th Earl of Lauderdale. *An Inquiry into the Nature and Origin of Public Wealth* (New York: August M. Kelley, 1962 [originally published in 1804]), Chapter IV. This is the best statement of the essence of Lauderdale's theory of an equilibrium limit to sustainable investment.

————. *Three Letters to the Duke of Wellington* (London: John Murray, 1829), Letters II and III. A somewhat discursive explanation of Lauderdale's theories and their practical application.

Thomas Robert Malthus. *Definitions in Political Economy* (London: John Murray, 1827), Chapter VI. Mal-

235

thus' most careful and systematic criticism of Say's Law. Note also some key definitions (which apply in other Malthusian writings) in his glossary on pp. 244–47.

————. *Principles of Political Economy,* second edition (New York: Augustus M. Kelley, Inc., 1951 [originally published in 1832]), Book II, Chapter I. This is the classic and most extensive statement of the Malthusian glut theory, though not the most careful (see above and Thomas Chalmers). The first edition of this work contains an analytical appendix with capsule summaries of the arguments in the text that are useful aids in interpretation. An even better aid in interpreting this long and somewhat tangled chapter are the letters between Malthus and Ricardo in the latter's *Works and Correspondence,* cited below.

Karl Marx. *Capital,* Volume III (Chicago: Charles H. Kerr & Co., 1909), Chapter XV. An important and often-cited chapter on Marx's theory of crises, though not as significant and revealing as the reading below in his *Theories of Surplus Value.* Chapter XV of the third volume of *Capital* occurs in Part III, dealing with the tendency of the falling rate of profit as a secular phenomenon, and so can be misleading if this is not kept in mind. Crises are treated as short-run offsets to this secular tendency, especially on p. 292.

————. *Theories of Surplus Value* (New York: International Publishers, 1952), pp. 368–414. Here is the largest single piece of Marx's crisis theory and criticism of Say's Law found in any one place.

J. R. McCulloch. *The Principles of Political Economy,* fifth edition (Edinburgh: Adam and Charles Black, 1854), Chapter VII. A clear, standard Ricardian treatment of Say's Law, incorporating much of the material from McCulloch's anonymous article in the *Edinburgh Review* of March 1821.

[Pierre François Joachim Henri Le Mercier de la Rivière]. *L'Ordre Naturel et Essentiel des Sociétés Politiques* (London: Jean Nourse, 1767), Volume II, Chapters XXXII, XXXVI, XXXVII. The Physiocratic versions of ideas later developed as Say's Law and equilibrium income theory.

James Mill. *Commerce Defended* (London: C. and R. Baldwin, 1808), Chapter VI. The classic statement of Mill's version of Say's Law.

————. *Elements of Political Economy,* third edition (London: Henry G. Bohn, 1844), Chapter IV, Sections II, III, IV. A more systematic or "textbookish" development of Mill's version of Say's Law.

John Stuart Mill. *Essays on Some Unsettled Questions of Political Economy* (London: John W. Parker, 1844), Essay II. The most sophisticated classical version of Say's Law.

————. *Principles of Political Economy,* ed. W. J. Ashley (London: Longmans, Green, and Co., 1909), Book I, Chapter V, Section 3; Book III, Chapter XIV. Another vindication of Say's Law and refutation of the general glut theories.

David Ricardo. *The Works and Correspondence of David Ricardo* (Cambridge: Cambridge University Press, 1951–55) Volume II, pp. 302–452; Volume IX, pp. 9–27. Volume II contains Ricardo's painstaking point-by-point criticism of Malthus' *Principles of Political Economy,* the pages cited being his criticism of the Malthusian theory of gluts. The letters between

Ricardo and Malthus in Volume IX focus on the central issues between them on gluts and Say's Law, and here they come as close to a meeting of the minds as they were ever to come.

Jean Baptiste Say. *Traité d'économie politique,* 5th edition (Paris: Chez Rapilly, 1826), Volume I, Chapter XV. This is the classic chapter on Say's Law—as *modified* in 1826 by the addition of several paragraphs at the end expounding a theory of equilibrium income strongly reminiscent of Sismondi. Unfortunately this edition has not been translated into English.

————. *A Treatise on Political Economy* (Philadelphia: Grigg R. Elliott, 1834), Chapter XV. The standard translation of the chapter on Say's Law from the fourth French edition of 1821.

J. C. L. Simonde de Sismondi. *Nouveaux Principes d'économie politique,* second edition (Paris: Delaunay, Libraire, 1827), Volume I, Books One and Four; Volume II, Appendix. The readings in Volume I give Sismondi's theory of equilibrium income and the Appendix to Volume II his replies to his critics.

SECONDARY LITERATURE

Gary S. Becker and William J. Baumol. "The Classical Monetary Theory: The Outcome of the Discussion," *Essays in Economic Thought,* ed. Joseph J. Spengler and William R. Allen (Chicago: Rand, McNally & Co., 1960), pp. 753–71. A careful analysis of modern and classical meanings of Say's Law.

Harry G. Johnson. "The Keynesian Revolution and the Monetarist Counterrevolution," *American Economic Review* (May 1971), 1–12. An historical and analytical, but nontechnical, account of Keynesian economics and its aftermath.

Axel Leijonhufvud. *Keynes and the Classics* (London: The Institute of Economic Affairs, 1969). A critical analytical pamphlet seeking to bring out specifically what was Keynes' substantive contribution to modern economic theory.

Thomas Sowell. "The General Glut Controversy Reconsidered," *Oxford Economic Papers,* November 1963, pp. 193–203. Despite its ambitious title, this article focuses on the Ricardo-Malthus dialogue on general gluts.

Joseph J. Spengler. "The Physiocrats and Say's Law of Markets," *Essays in Economic Thought,* ed. J. J. Spengler and W. R. Allen, pp. 161–214. A solid survey and an invaluable bibliography on the role of the Physiocrats in the early development of macroeconomics.

Oswald St. Clair. *A Key to Ricardo* (New York: Augustus M. Kelley, 1965), Chapter III. A careful, accurate and useful survey of Ricardo's controversy with Malthus on general gluts—one of the very few available in the literature which can be described in this way, despite a number of more theoretically elegant writings on the subject.

Jacob Viner. *Studies in the Theory of International Trade* (New York: Augustus M. Kelley, 1965), Chapters III, IV. An analysis of the monetary history and the macroeconomic thought of the first two decades of the nineteenth century.

INDEX

abstraction, 54, 140, 228–229
agriculture, 7n, 41–42, 85, 87, 113, 123
anonymous writings identified, 8n–9n, 11n–12n, 93n, 131n
Attwood, Thomas, 146

Bailey, Samuel, 54, 131–134, 139, 150, 224, 235
Baird, Charles W., 192n
barter, 8, 15, 147, 216
Baumol, William J., 238
Becker, Gary, 238
Berliner, Joseph S., vii
Black, R. D. C., 101n, 102n, 128n
Blake, William, 134–138, 139, 215
Blaug, Mark, 5n, 108n, 126n–127n
Bohm-Bawerk, Eugen von, 185
Bronfenbrenner, Martin, 172n
Brougham, Henry, 115n
Burns, Arthur F., 12n, 232n
business cycles, 177–180, 191, 203, 214

Cannan, Edwin, 108n
capital, 22, 31, 47, 80, 88, 100, 104, 109–112, 122, 124, 145, 150–154, 212–214; export of, 84, 87, 98, 152; fixed, 41, 63, 118; human, 41; idle, 47, 125–127, 135–136, 139; marginal efficiency, 133, 150–151, 208
Capital by Karl Marx, 169, 177, 179, 180, 186, 187, 216, 222, 236
Carlyle, Thomas, 164
causation, sequential, 98, 113, 138, 139, 146, 181, 182, 216; simultaneous, 204
Chalmers, Thomas, 7, 8, 13, 34, 59, 61, 76, 81, 87, 96, 109–114,

123, 142–143, 150, 151, 220, 225, 235
chance vs. necessity, 172, 173–174, 183
changes of mind, 18, 77, 133–134, 139–140, 143–146, 148, 185, 208, 223–224
Chipman, John S., 12n
"Chrematistics," 65–66
clearing the market, 25, 46, 55, 71, 83, 90n, 102, 118–119, 125, 138, 152
Clower, Robert W., 211n–212n
Coleridge, Samuel Taylor, 164
comparative statics, 32, 38, 46, 53–54, 75, 137, 182, 231
Comte, Auguste, 164
consumption, 102, 116, 118, 207; equals production, 102; governs reproduction, 24; productive, *see* investment; unproductive, *see* unproductive consumption
consumption function, 202, 203, 209
controversies, 3, 5, 14, 15, 18, 38, 50–51, 76–77, 78n, 79, 115–141, 191, 202–203, 219
corresponding deficiency, 20, 22, 55, 137, 182
Corry, B. A., 86n, 89n, 128n
cost-covering prices, 63, 75, 121, 158
costs, 122, 130
credit, 145, 148
Cournot, Antoine Augustin, 224

demand, aggregate, 33, 59, 60, 74, 103, 116, 117, 129, 134, 145–146, 173, 214; effective (effectual), 75, 91, 95, 129, 158, 204; quantity, 75, 83, 91, 156, 158; schedule, 75, 90, 91, 155. *See also* utility, purchasing power, underconsumption